On *The Confessions* as *Confessio*

READING AUGUSTINE

Series Editor: Miles Hollingworth
In collaboration with the Wessel-Hollingworth Foundation

Reading Augustine presents books that offer personal, nuanced and oftentimes literary readings of Saint Augustine of Hippo. Each time, the idea is to treat Augustine as a spiritual and intellectual icon of the Western tradition, and to read through him to some or other pressing concern of our current day, or to some enduring issue or theme. In this way, the writers follow the model of Augustine himself, who produced his famous output of words and ideas in active tussle with the world in which he lived. When the series launched, this approach could raise eyebrows, but now that technology and pandemics have brought us into the world and society like never before, and when scholarship is expected to live the same way and responsibly, the series is well-set and thriving.

Volumes in the series

On Music, Sense, Affect, and Voice, Carol Harrison
On Solitude, Conscience, Love and Our Inner and Outer Lives, Ron Haflidson
On Creation, Science, Disenchantment, and the Contours of Being and Knowing, Matthew W. Knotts
On Agamben, Arendt, Christianity, and the Dark Arts of Civilization, Peter Iver Kaufman
On Self-Harm, Narcissism, Atonement, and the Vulnerable Christ, David Vincent Meconi
On Faith, Works, Eternity, and the Creatures We Are, André Barbera
On Time, Change, History, and Conversion, Sean Hannan
On Compassion, Healing, Suffering, and the Purpose of the Emotional Life, Susan Wessel
On Consumer Culture, Identity, the Church and the Rhetorics of Delight, Mark Clavier
On Creativity, Liberty, Love and the Beauty of the Law, Todd Breyfogle
On Education, Formation, Citizenship and the Lost Purpose of Learning, Joseph Clair
On Ethics, Politics and Psychology in the Twenty-First Century, John Rist
On God, the Soul, Evil and the Rise of Christianity, John Peter Kenney
On Love, Confession, Surrender and the Moral Self, Ian Clausen
On Memory, Marriage, Tears, and Meditation, Margaret R. Miles
On Mystery, Ineffability, Silence, and Musical Symbolism, Laurence Wuidar

On *The Confessions* as *Confessio*

A Reader's Guide

Barry A. David

BLOOMSBURY ACADEMIC
LONDON • NEW YORK • OXFORD • NEW DELHI • SYDNEY

BLOOMSBURY ACADEMIC
Bloomsbury Publishing Plc
50 Bedford Square, London, WC1B 3DP, UK
1385 Broadway, New York, NY 10018, USA
29 Earlsfort Terrace, Dublin 2, Ireland

BLOOMSBURY, BLOOMSBURY ACADEMIC and the Diana logo are trademarks of Bloomsbury Publishing Plc

First published in Great Britain 2022

Copyright © Barry A. David, 2022

Barry A. David has asserted his right under the Copyright, Designs and Patents Act, 1988, to be identified as Author of this work.

For legal purposes the Acknowledgments on p. x constitute an extension of this copyright page.

Cover image: Young boy reading in a ruined bookshop in London devastated by an air raid, 1940. Stock imagery / Alamy Stock Photo.

All rights reserved. No part of this publication may be reproduced or transmitted in any form or by any means, electronic or mechanical, including photocopying, recording, or any information storage or retrieval system, without prior permission in writing from the publishers.

Bloomsbury Publishing Inc does not have any control over, or responsibility for, any third-party websites referred to or in this book. All internet addresses given in this book were correct at the time of going to press. The author and publisher regret any inconvenience caused if addresses have changed or sites have ceased to exist, but can accept no responsibility for any such changes.

A catalogue record for this book is available from the British Library.

A catalog record for this book is available from the Library of Congress.

ISBN: HB: 978-1-3502-0325-9
PB: 978-1-3502-0324-2
ePDF: 978-1-3502-0327-3
ePUB: 978-1-3502-0326-6

Series: Reading Augustine

Typeset by Deanta Global Publishing Services, Chennai, India

To find out more about our authors and books visit www.bloomsbury.com and sign up for our newsletters.

All Christian vigilance is bent upon the pious and thoughtful understanding of the Trinity, and that understanding is the goal of all of one's progress

(ON FREE CHOICE OF THE WILL 3.21.206)

Grant me Lord to know and understand (Ps. 118: 34, 73, 144) which comes first—to call upon you or to praise you, and whether knowing you precedes calling upon you. But who calls upon you when he does not know you? . . . . Lord, I would seek you, calling upon you—and calling upon you is an act of believing in you. You have been preached to us. My faith, Lord, calls upon you. It is your gift to me. You breathed it into me by the humanity of your Son, by the ministry of your preacher.

(CONFESSIONS 1.1.1)

I make my prayer, through our Lord Jesus Christ your Son . . . mediator between yourself and us. . . . you sought us that we should seek you, your Word by whom you made all things, including myself, your only Son by whom you have called to adoption the people who believe (Gal. 4:5). . . . I make my prayer to you through him "who sits at your right hand and intercedes . . . for us" (Rom. 8:34). "In him are hidden all the treasures of wisdom and knowledge (Col. 2:3)." For those treasures I search in your books.

(CONFESSIONS 11.2.4)

Our knowledge (scientia), therefore, is Christ and our wisdom (sapientia) is also the same Christ. He implants faith in us through temporal things and He exhibits the truth to us about eternal things. Through Him we are led to Him, we move through knowledge to wisdom; we never depart from the one and the same Christ in whom is hidden all the treasures of wisdom and knowledge (Col. 2:3)

(THE TRINITY 13.19.24)

CONTENTS

Preface viii
Acknowledgments x
List of Abbreviations xi

Introduction: Augustine's Purpose—*Confessio* 1

1. *Confessions* 1–4, Departing from and Returning toward *Confessio* 11
2. *Confessions* 5–7, Discovering *Confessio* is Reasonable 43
3. *Confessions* 8–10, Living *Confessio* 63
4. *Confessions* 11–13, *Confessio*'s Ultimate Ground is the Godhead 87
5. Conclusion: *Confessions* is about *Confessio*—and *Confessio* Imitates Divine Incarnation 115

Notes 139
Bibliography 197
Index 209

PREFACE

I am glad to be invited to say a few words about Augustine's *Confessions* and about this book by Barry David which determines to put Augustine's *Confessions* with purpose before a new generation of readers.

Augustine's most famous book has kept on for over 1,600 years now and never gone out of print. In that time, it has been stretched out and dissected by many experts. Yet its beating heart must be found elsewhere, in the lives of the untold hundreds of millions who have read it and been touched by it. To all these it has been something: to each something different and unique, even though the book itself gives no more than the private testimony of a single man—Augustine—who lived moreover in an age that is long gone.

How can this be? Three reasons, I think. The first is that Augustine was an acclaimed intellectual before he converted to Christianity. He was one of the Roman Empire's famous clever men and a rubber-stamped genius. When someone like that converts to Christianity at the relatively late age that Augustine did, it makes a great statement and compels others to think again and follow suit. The second is that when such a person as this is prepared to be so candid about their own life as Augustine is in his *Confessions*, and so generous and unstinting in the documenting of their failings, it comforts the reader. For it is quite a thing to learn that someone like Augustine has felt what you have felt, and feared what you have feared, and wondered what you have wondered, and done what you have done. Many also have been grateful simply to have had Augustine articulate and put into words what they could not—whether for lack of the skill or the daring. The third reason is made up out of these two and comes home a little later, after they have sunk in: it is that only Christianity offers a God Who will take a personal interest in the byways and contingencies of each human life.

Those who mock Augustine's *Confessions* or who study it only to detract from it mock this very feature of it. To them, it somehow is wrong—it is ethically wrong—that an individual life should become so original and so forsaken that only the Christian God could intervene to save it with words chosen specially for the event. This promise of Christianity—that if you will call out to its God and mean it, He will answer it—is the enemy, then, and has always been the enemy, then, of religions and philosophies that will save instead the "general you" in the "general case."

Barry David takes Augustine at face value in this. Moreover, his schematic and cumulative approach turns it into a brand new thesis for the Augustine specialist even as it carefully brings the novice reader through the book as it was meant to be read: as *confessio*. This is an important achievement and the fruit of decades of learning and teaching, and we are lucky to have it here. Thanks to Barry David, we get to see that Augustine's most popular book is written through with consistencies and developments that make it the theological equal of any of his others.

Miles Hollingworth, Series Editor

ACKNOWLEDGMENTS

With gratitude to mentors, family, Miles, and colleagues.

ABBREVIATIONS

Augustine's works

Civ. Dei	*De civitate Dei (The City of God)*
Conf.	*Confessiones (The Confessions)*
Doc. Chr.	*De doctrina christiana (On Christian Doctrine)*
F. et symb.	*De fide et symbolo (On Faith and the Creed)*
Lib. Arb.	*De libero arbitrio voluntatis (On Free Choice of the Will)*
Retr.	*Retractationes (The Retractations)*
Simpl.	*Ad Simplicianum (To Simplicianus)*
Trin.	*De Trinitate (On the Trinity)*

Other

CC	On *The Confessions* as *Confessio*

Introduction

Augustine's Purpose—*Confessio*

Why did Augustine of Hippo (354–430 AD) write *Confessions* (*conf.*) (397–401 AD)?[1] Obviously, there are historical matters pertaining to his time, place, ecclesial position, and specific intellectual and spiritual concerns. However, Augustine's essential purpose, as his title attests, consists in *confessing*. What does that mean? My provisional definition[2] is "witnessing, before God and man, to the presence of God's goodness (*bonitas*—13.1.1–2.2) in the human heart (1.1.1) by recognition and praise so each can cultivate God's presence (11.1.1) and ultimately achieve immutable enjoyment thereof (1.5.5–6) within an afterlife (9.10.23–6; 10.27.38; 10.42.67–43.69)."

This definition of *confessio*, however, is only partly accurate because it is not grounded in Augustine's notion of God incarnate. Focusing on Him has threefold importance. It is not only (i) that *confessio* is for the goal of participating immutably in God, and (ii) confessing is a divinely established means toward that end, but also (iii) that the confessor's awareness of the above properly motivates him toward unlimited praising of God. Hence, Augustine implies that Christ is *confessio*'s end and means—for, as immutable God *and* mutable man immutably united, He is both why and how Augustine confesses. Stated in terms of the personal (books 1–10) and exegetical (books 11–13) matters *conf.* discloses Augustine's medium, viz. his *confessio* mode of presentation, guides his message, and makes it congruent therewith. Since God's goodness in Christ is responsible for the good in Augustine's life, confessing His goodness both shows gratitude for good received and prepares for greater future good. Augustine's fundamental point, a common refrain in this chapter, is that God in Christ is better (i.e., more good) and, therefore, man owes Him more praise than commonly claimed.

Toward Understanding *Confessio*

Confessio has an obvious universal dimension. At *conf.*'s outset, Augustine speaks so concerning God and man—including man's need to praise God:

> "You are great, Lord, and highly to be praised (Ps. 47: 2)." ... Man, a little piece of your creation, desires to praise you. ... You stir man to take pleasure in praising you, because you have made us for yourself, and our heart is restless until it rests in you.[3]

Augustine clarifies *confessio*'s universal dimension in book 10 by arguing that man's core activity consists in pursuing happiness: "The happy life is joy based on the truth. This is joy grounded in you, O God, who are the truth. ... This happy life everyone desires; joy in the truth everyone wants."[4]

Hence, it is easily surmised that Augustine's principal motive, as many contemporary readers of *conf.* recognize, is claiming that man's quest for happiness (1.1.1; cf. 10.20.29–27.38)[5] is attained by praising God. Accordingly, Augustine's confessing his personal circumstances and developments throughout *conf.* exemplify man's quest for happiness. The "Augustine" narrated by Confessor Augustine is "everyman."

Thus far, we have noticed *confessio*'s (i) universal dimension, (ii) concern with happiness, and (iii) the related claim that happiness is attained by praising God. These matters are helpful but do not exhaust Augustine's notion. Why not? To start, *confessio* claims happiness is achieved by praising a certain God. Who does Augustine mean by God? Through the end of 1.1.1, Augustine speaks of God incarnate, claiming it is through Him he confesses:

> "Grant me Lord to know and understand" (Ps. 118: 34, 73, 144) which comes first—to call upon you or to praise you, and whether knowing you precedes calling upon you. But who calls upon you when he does not know you? ... Yet "how shall they

call upon him in whom they have not believed? and how shall they believe without a preacher?" (Rom. 10: 14). "They will praise the Lord who seek for him" (Ps. 21: 27).

In seeking him, they find him, and in finding they will praise him. Lord, I would seek you, calling upon you—and calling upon you is an act of believing in you. You have been preached to us. My faith, Lord, calls upon you. It is your gift to me. You breathed it into me by the humanity of your Son, by the ministry of your preacher.[6]

Therefore, comprehending *confessio* entails understanding Augustine's notion of God incarnate since, for Augustine, He is both the object of praise (the one named "Lord") and the medium through Whom he praises. *Confessio* is incarnational.

Consequently, distinguishing *confessio*'s formality requires more study. To see, though, how *confessio* is grounded in Augustine's notion of God incarnate and shapes *conf.*'s content, our analysis commences by considering *confessio*'s proximate causes. While some of these are extrinsic to his "restless heart," others are intrinsic and dovetail with the former. First, as a Catholic priest (391 AD) and bishop (395 AD) in volatile Roman North Africa (397 AD), Augustine fields queries about his identity and, especially, his sincerity. Since it was well known he was a Manichean and obtained the highest rank of *rhetor* in the Western Roman Empire through his Manichean connections,[7] some wondered if Augustine was actually a crypto-Manichean?[8] *Conf.* answers this question by showing acquaintance with Manichean doctrine and its relationship with Catholic teaching.[9] Likewise, some were suspicious of Augustine's conversion, aided by Platonist[10] philosophy, to the Catholic religion in Milan.[11] Did he convert to Catholicism or to Platonism?[12] Hence, *conf.* explains Augustine's familiarity with Platonism[13] and the latter's relationship with the Catholic religion.[14] Furthermore, in 395 AD Bishop Alypius of Thagaste, Augustine's close friend, was asked by Paulinus (*c*. 355–431 AD), a wealthy Gallic aristocrat who later became Italy's bishop of Nola (*c*. 404–15 AD), to recount how (i) he became baptized and ordained, and (ii) embraced the ascetic life.[15] Hence, *conf.*, as liberal mention of Alypius's development shows,[16] also takes impetus from Paulinus's request to Alypius that the latter had relayed to Augustine.[17] And that query explains, in part,[18] Monnica's profound presence, including Augustine's *vita* of her (9.8.17–9.22), in *conf.* Additionally, it is asserted that Bishop Augustine—though he never once names the topic in *conf.*[19]—responds to the specter of North Africa's dominant Donatist church,[20] whose leading members hold that Christianity, especially her priests, is only for the morally pure.[21] Augustine, then, has significant motive to explain why he is Catholic rather than Donatist and evinces, in *conf.* 10.28.30–43.70, that he is neither an avid sinner nor without sin but oriented toward God—and therefore, even though imperfect, away from sinning.[22]

Then there are the particular intellectual causes, dovetailing with some of the earlier ones, contributing to Augustine's writing *conf.* First, Augustine claims to have recently achieved insight, in his letter *Ad Simplicianum* (*Simpl.*) 1.2 (*c.* 395–6 AD),[23] concerning the dynamic of divine grace and human responsibility. While responding to Simplicianus, Ambrose's former mentor and imminent bishop of Milan,[24] regarding certain passages in Rom. 9.10-29, Augustine, as he later remarks in *retr.*, maintains he finally understood the relationship between grace and responsibility. Reviewing his epistle to Simplicianus, Augustine writes: "I . . . tried hard to maintain the free choice of the human will, but the grace of God prevailed. Not otherwise could I reach the understanding that the apostle spoke with absolute truth when he said, '. . . What hast thou that thou didst not receive?'"[25] Whereas previously Augustine had implied everyone possessed "free choice of will," understood as the ability to choose between good and evil,[26] he now believed he had overstated the matter. Rather, free choice of will is something people only have by Christ's grace.[27] Since God, Augustine then thought, needs to be present to the will and chosen for will to be free,[28] what people have before enjoying Christ's grace is "choice of will" instead.[29] The latter includes responsibility, since one can know how one should act. However, conforming to God, i.e., embracing positively His way of life, stands beyond "choice of will's" power. That will, Augustine claimed, can choose between greater and lesser evils, and to want to do good and avoid evil but, without Christ's grace, it cannot do the good it ought.[30] So, will is only "free" when it cooperates with Christ.

Consequently, Augustine's position stands between two extremes. First, he does not think man's will[31] before receiving grace is totally depraved, i.e., only capable of thinking and doing evil.[32] Second, contrary to Pelagius' (360–420 AD) opinion,[33] which Augustine attempts to rebut in the future (*c.* 411–12 AD),[34] he does not judge that man, before receiving grace, has free choice of will, i.e., the ability to *both think and do* good. Rather, Augustine's view in *Simpl.* 1.2, subsequently presented in *conf.* 8,[35] is somewhere between those extremes. In fact, *conf.* explains Augustine's, Alypius's, and Monnica's identities as Catholics through the prism of *Simpl.* 1.2.[36]

Additionally, Augustine's intellectual preoccupations coincided with questions about his identity. First, he was pondering the relationship between the Catholic and Manichean religions—recently, it seems, concerning the nature of human responsibility.[37] Second, Augustine had long considered the connection between Catholic and Platonist philosophical theology (to which his assessment of Manichean doctrine was intimately connected), and this concern was heightened by being forced, in a way, into becoming a priest in 391 AD.[38] Simply stated, Augustine wondered how the aforementioned theologies might be "properly" reconciled. In fact, just after joining the priesthood, Augustine (*Epistula* 21) requested opportunity to study assiduously the Catholic scriptures[39] since, although he revered these documents from the time just before his baptism,[40] he was more familiar with philosophical texts and did not know how to harmonize his diverse inheritances.[41] From 391 AD onward, Augustine strives to integrate his inheritances, including especially by considering how man is *imago Dei*.[42] This desire[43] permeates several of Augustine's finished and unfinished[44] books during that period. For example, his anti-Manichean *On Free Choice of the Will* (*De libero arbitrio voluntatis* [*lib. arb.*], *c.* 387–95 AD) makes clear the desire to reconcile his inheritances by commonly asserting that "right" philosophical understanding, identified with Platonism, of the relationship between responsibility and moral evil accords with Christian doctrines of divine incarnation and Trinity.[45] Along that line, Augustine begins *De doctrina christiana* (*doc. Chr.*), which speaks liberally about the benefit of pagan learning (e.g., 2.39.58–42.63), in 396 AD but puts the book aside to write *conf.* and finishes *doc. Chr.* much later (*c.* 426–7 AD). As books 11–13 highlight, *conf.* also represents Augustine's attempt to harmonize his biblical and philosophical inheritances.

Nevertheless, since *conf.* is a single prayer, the most important material cause is Augustine's devotion to David's Psalms. Augustine is decisively influenced by the Psalms, beginning with the time of his preparation for baptism,[46] since finding in them "songs of faith, utterances of devotion which allow no pride of spirit to enter in!"[47]

Augustine's love for the Psalms grows as he immerses himself in scripture after becoming a priest,[48] and he emulates the Psalmist's approach to God and man. As Brown writes, David's Psalms

> provided Augustine with a model portrait of the inner world of the true servant of God. . . . And for King David, to confess also meant to praise: to praise God for His being; to praise Him for his mighty acts of mercy and deliverance; to lay before him a whole life, not only personal sins, but also those agonizing, unsolved problems that showed the extent of human ignorance and the ease with which the human mind could be misled by false solutions.[49]

In this respect, confessing displays an *exitus-reditus* ("departure from and return to Origin"), and therefore universal and progressive, structure since the confessor dialogues with God, praising His goodness while reflecting on matters—like God's goodness and human behaviors—in light of and to cultivate divine presence. The confessor's activity begins while enjoying divine presence; departs from this, in a way, by considering some matter (mentioned earlier) within the context of divine goodness; and returns to enjoying and augments divine presence by assessing that matter in terms of authentic relationship with and/or doctrine of God. Therefore, since the confessor's goal is to recognize, cultivate, and augment God's presence, confessing has an *exitus-reditus* structure containing universal and progressive elements. Prior to writing *conf.*, Augustine had sometimes presented his deepest thoughts in a manner imitating David's *confessio*.[50]

Stated earlier, then, are commonly cited extrinsic and intrinsic causes motivating Augustine to write *conf.* Hence, as O'Donnell remarks, "It is impossible to take the *Confessions* in a vacuum."[51] However, these only constitute *conf.*'s material cause; its formal cause is something else. *Conf.* results from Augustine's choice since it is his work of art. Writing *conf.* is best deemed "fitting," since it results from Augustine's response to the aforementioned influences. *Conf.* did not inexorably result from the aforementioned influences—as if the presence of flour, baking powder, sugar, cooking oil, and chocolate compels a baker to make chocolate muffins. Augustine's heart produces *conf.*; it did not have to happen, but it did; and we now analyze its formality.[52]

This requires reconsidering Augustine's principal material cause. Following David's influence, Augustine centers *confessio* in praising God's goodness[53] for His salutary response to human behavior.[54] Therefore, as its name shows,[55] *Confessions* evinces that Augustine selects *confessio* as the appropriate manner to unify the aforementioned extrinsic and intrinsic causes.

In his *retr*.[56] Augustine states his book is about praising God:

> The thirteen books of my *Confessions* praise [*laudant*] the just and good God concerning both my evil acts and my good acts, and they excite the understanding and affection of men towards Him. That, in any event, pertains to me—when they were written they had that effect upon me and they bring about [the same effect upon me] when they are read. What others think about them, they themselves shall determine; nevertheless, I know that they give pleasure to many [Christian] brothers and that they greatly pleased them.[57]

By this, Augustine means to encourage both his own and his readers' understanding and affectivity toward God by praising God's goodness and justice for governing his good and evil acts.[58] In short, Augustine's principal theme in *conf.* consists in distinguishing and inspiring man's proper disposition toward God.

Augustine also remarks that *conf.* includes two major parts, viz. (i) a biographical component in books 1–10 and (ii) an exegetical component in books 11–13.[59] He writes: "The first ten books were written about myself; the final three [were written] about the holy scriptures from this passage, 'In the beginning God created heaven and earth,' all the way to the sabbath rest."[60] This, then, is the principal content through which Augustine advances his doctrine of *confessio*.

But questions arise concerning exactly how Augustine's effort to encourage praising God encompasses the two topics he places in *conf.* What connects the biographical content in books 1–10 with that shown in books 11–13, focusing on "the holy scriptures" to account for God's creation from its beginning unto its Sabbath rest? How does the entirety belong to Augustine's teaching on praising God?

Although many studies of *conf.* have tried to explain this,[61] none has taken adequate account of Augustine's claim that *conf.*

is governed by praising an incarnate God. Indeed, it is one thing to assert that *conf.* praises God for His goodness,[62] but something more to explain that Augustine praises *God incarnate* for His goodness *and* how that structures Augustine's praising.[63]

The important point here, which centers CC, is that Augustine reforms David's notion of *confessio*, and therefore the purpose for praising God, by his concept of divine incarnation. Augustine augments David's notion of God with the concept of a God Who, understood as God *and* man—as God *having united to Himself* a human nature ("the Word made flesh")—is both Augustine's goal and the way thereto. In other words, Christ is the One to Whom confession is made, as well as confession's medium and exemplar.

What is meant, practically speaking, by Augustine's confessing God incarnate? Since Augustine and David each embrace God as exemplar, medium, and goal, what does Augustine's confessing add to David's?[64] In general, Augustine's notion of God incarnate enhances the entirety, giving more security and, therefore, more reason for gratitude. In particular, Augustine's notion of *confessio* shares an *exitus-reditus* structure with David's but (because he understands God in Christ is somehow implanted within his soul) he explicitly anchors that structure, and therefore its universal and progressive components, in divine immutability. This makes Augustine's *confessio explicitly* teleological since the confessor *knows* his confessing is from a mutable-immutable God for attaining immutable union with Him. Accordingly, confessing's mutable aspect, i.e., all confessing prior to immutably enjoying God, is recognized as teleological since it is from God incarnate so humans can attain immutable union. Like David, Confessor Augustine piously dialogues with God to augment His presence. For Augustine, however, it is known, through piety toward God incarnate, that confessing (though mutable) is essentially for attaining immutable participation. As such, the progressive element of confessing, consisting in praising God's goodness, is mutable because it leads, through *God's joining Himself with human mutability*, to immutable participation in God.

Therefore, just as God incarnate is mutable *and* immutable whereby participating in His mutability is both through and for the sake of participating in His immutability, so Augustine's *confessio* embraces mutable divine presence to enjoy God immutably. Additionally, Augustine's notion of *confessio* augments the reason for gratitude, and therefore for praising divine goodness, since the confessor's awareness of Christ, and therefore of *confessio*'s above components, gives unlimited reason for praising God. In this regard, the confessor, by Christ's grace, recognizes His presence and securely embraces Him as origin, guide, and *telos*. Put differently, God's omnipresence is not only because He is man's source and governor but also since He is man's *telos*. Consequently, since the confessor sees that God incarnate offers man everything possible, his reason for praising Him is, in principle, unlimited!

In every respect, then, Augustine's *confessio*, moving to Christ through Christ, heightens awareness of the nature, purpose, and attainment of divine presence. By contrast, David's *confessio* certainly implies much of this but is not explicitly governed as such. Augustine's fundamental point is that God is better (i.e., more good) toward man than the Psalmist thought; and, consequently, that man should be more thankful toward God and praise Him more intensely. Augustine's incarnational notion of *confessio* is akin to "new wine in new skins"—for which reason *conf.* represents a kind of Christian Psalm.

Conclusion

CC claims, therefore, that *conf.* is rooted in Augustine's intention to progressively encourage himself and his readers to praise an incarnate God's omnipresent goodness (*bonitas*) and ultimately achieve immutable enjoyment thereof in an afterlife. This brings three obvious and interrelated implications. First, our original definition of *confessio*, stated at the outset, points in the right direction but its account of God's goodness, and therefore of *confessio*, is understated. For Augustine, God's goodness, manifested in Christ, is greater than embraced by the Psalmist and by adherents to the Manichean religion and Platonist philosophy. Man owes greater love to God than conceived by David, the Manicheans, or the Platonists. Second, Augustine's teaching on praising God is richer than originally claimed. Augustine's notion of God incarnate mandates He be praised not only for His active presence but also because He can be known and embraced as man's origin, guide, and *telos*. Third, as CC's "Conclusion" considers, recognizing Augustine's notion of *confessio* enables comprehension of *conf.*'s unity.

Consequently, after commencing *conf.* by highlighting that *confessio*'s *exitus-reditus* structure and universal and progressive aspects are grounded in praising Christ (1.1.1–5.6), Augustine recounts the stages whereby, through Christ, his heart embraced *confessio* as the truth of thought and action (books 1–10). Furthermore, as Christ—*confessio*'s goal, medium, and exemplar—contains "the treasures of wisdom and knowledge (11.2.4)," Augustine's purpose also includes showing *confessio*'s ultimate cause. Hence, books 1–10 prepare the ground for his confession in books 11–13 that details, on theological[65] and eschatological levels, *confessio*'s ground in an incarnate Godhead. From beginning to end, Augustine confesses Christ through Christ.

To aid comprehension, I divide study of *conf.* into five parts. First, I distinguish Confessor Augustine's first major division, books 1–10, into three portions (viz. 1–4, 5–7, and 8–10) while leaving as is his other major division, books 11–13. I make these divisions since they demarcate distinct stages in Confessor Augustine's doctrine of *confessio*, viz. (books 1–4) "Departing from and Returning Toward *Confessio*"; (books 5–7) "Discovering *Confessio* Is Reasonable"; (books 8–10) "Living *Confessio*"; and (books 11–13) "Discovering *Confessio*'s Ultimate Ground Is the Godhead." Finally, I present *CC*'s "Conclusion" (*CC* 5) wherein I draw together and develop the insights offered in CC 1–4.

1

Confessions 1–4, Departing from and Returning toward *Confessio*

Introduction

In these books, Augustine introduces his reader to *confessio* (1.1.1–5.6) and begins to explain, by his *confessio*-centered spiritual biography, how one embraces it. Augustine's account contains universal and progressive elements governed by his doctrine and practice of *confessio*. Therefore, after 1.1.1–5.6, the remaining portion of books 1–4 is divided into two parts, viz. (i) 1.6.7–3.3.6, where young Augustine's journey away from *confessio* is distinguished, and (ii) 3.4.7–4.16.31, explaining his first steps toward *confessio*.

CC 1 commences with Augustine's account of *confessio* in 1.1.1–5.6 and proceeds, in that light, to analyze young Augustine's progressive disintegration in the course of his infancy and early school years, and its nadir in his pear-theft as a sixteen-year-old.[1] By the latter study, Confessor Augustine shows the essential intellectual and moral dimensions of *praesumptio*, i.e., of a mindset determining truth and falsity, good and evil, and reward and punishment. Following this, we meet young Augustine's profound encounter with Wisdom while reading Cicero's *Hortensius* (3.4.7–8), his reasons for joining the Manicheans, and aspects of his dissatisfying mindset as a Manichean. All told, books 1–4 explain the dimensions of rejecting *confessio* and certain of the cognitive and practical elements needed for progress toward *confessio*.

Confessions 1.1.1–5.6: What is *Confessio*?

In these chapters, Augustine introduces his reader to *conf.*[2] and, therefore, to *confessio* by focusing on three things. These are (i) the natures of the (a) implicit (or natural) and (b) explicit (or supernatural) relationship between God and man, (ii) the means whereby man can achieve an explicit relationship,[3] and (iii) the nature of the divine presence enjoyed by those having explicit relationship—including its key components and limitation.

Augustine begins *conf.* with these famous words:

> "You are great (*magnus*), Lord, and highly to be praised (*laudabilis valde*) (Ps 47.2) great (*magna*) is your power (*virtus*) and your wisdom (*sapientiae tuae*) is immeasurable" (Ps 146.5). Man, a little piece of your creation, desires to praise you (*laudare te vult*), a human being "bearing his mortality with him" (2 Cor 4:10), carrying with him (*circumferens*) the witness of his sin (*testimonium peccati sui*) and the witness that you "resist the proud" (1 Pet 5:5). Nevertheless, to praise you (*laudare te*) is the desire of man, a little piece of your creation. You stir man (*tu excitas*) to take pleasure in praising you (*ut laudere te delectet*), because you have made us for yourself (*quia fecisti nos ad te*), and our heart is restless (*et inquietum est cor nostrum*) until it rests in you (*donec requiescat in te*).[4]

These words have fourfold importance. First, Augustine underscores that his narrative publicly confesses to God. Augustine speaks in the first person before God and, through Him, to neighbor, to praise God so each will love Him. What shall Augustine confess? Looking ahead in *conf.*, that is especially his present relationship with God, how it has been attained and, through that, how others can attain explicit relationship with Him. *Conf.*, then, is a work that praises God, and Augustine hopes that each will be motivated to conform to God's goodness (11.1.1) since it is by His goodness that God created man and draws him toward Himself (13.1.1–2.2). This is evinced not only by God's creating man with the desire to praise Him but also, and more important, by His strengthening that desire through His grace. God's activity on man is entirely for his benefit.

Second, since Augustine confesses the possibility of enjoying an explicit relationship with God, he signals that *conf.* will have universal and progressive elements. In the former regard, Augustine will talk not only about God, broadly conceived, but also about man and the explicit and ultimately complete relationship he can have with God (e.g., 10.27.38). In the latter regard, Augustine will use his life to show how spiritual progress is available.

Third, as *conf.*'s opening words suggest, Augustine will ultimately specify (i) God in terms of the Godhead, i.e., as Trinity (13.5.6), and (ii) mind, soul, or heart[5] as essentially analogous to Him, i.e., trinitarian (13.11.12), since fashioned so by Him.[6] Hence, the opening paragraph in 1.1.1 hints about the spiritual relationship between God and man so that the relations constituting the Godhead structure man—a profound matter *conf.* points out and (CC's "Conclusion" argues) derives from divine incarnation. Augustine implies in 1.20.31 and 10.22.32–27.38 but openly states in 13.11.12 that his long-term project includes distinguishing how God is present to the heart. In 1.1.1 Augustine speaks of God's power, wisdom, and goodness, which, as *conf.*'s later considerations show, are loosely affiliated with God the Father, Word, and Holy Spirit. Augustine cultivates this spiritual union throughout *conf.*, occasionally mentions it (e.g., 10.20.29–27.38), and finally explains it in 13.11.12. But, since God as Trinity and man as trinitarian are not specified until book 13, we see that Augustine's primary focus is not on the Trinity but, as a subsequent portion in 1.1.1 suggests (see later), on divine incarnation. This is because he thinks man is established in God through the incarnation (e.g., 7.9.13–21.27) and travels from there toward embracing God as Trinity.[7]

Fourth, Augustine signifies the problem of sinning regarding both Original and personal sin.[8] Due to man's proud response to God's goodness in Adam, Augustine thinks man's present condition is less than his original created nature. This has three related implications. First, man, as God's creature, owes Him praise. Second, God's goodness is undeterred by human sinfulness; He employs His grace to lead man toward Him. Third, God's goodness refashions man so that in the face of Original and personal sin, his *telos* can be clear and enjoyed. No matter what, God is "on man's side."

After his opening words, Augustine considers in universal form the conditions by which man can enjoy an explicit with God. Augustine explains how man's relationship with God can be by the mode of *confessio* rather than by "natural" humility (which Augustine thinks is man's proper attitude, apart from Christ's grace, toward God[9]) or presumption (which contradicts man's proper disposition toward God). How does this occur? According to Augustine, it happens by Christ's mediation through His church. By Christ's humanity, as represented in His church's priests/preachers, God's Word and sacraments are dispensed so people can receive His gift of faith, be established in His church and, consequently, in explicit relationship with God.[10] Augustine writes:

> "Grant me Lord to know and understand" (Ps. 118: 34, 73, 144) which comes first—to call upon you or to praise you, and whether knowing you precedes calling upon you. But who calls upon you when he does not know you?.... Lord, I would seek you, calling upon you—and calling upon you is an act of believing in you. You have been preached to us. My faith, Lord, calls upon you. It is your gift to me. You breathed it into me by the humanity of your Son, by the ministry of your preacher.[11]

This passage is important for two closely related reasons. First, since it claims Augustine has faith in and praises God incarnate because of Him, it denotes Augustine's notion of God incarnate. What does Augustine mean? First, it is that God in Christ takes to Himself a human nature (hence Augustine speaks of God the Son's humanity) so wayward humanity can embrace His infinite goodness (e.g., *conf.* 4.12.19). According to Augustine, divine incarnation means that the immutable God (e.g., 7.10.16) unites to Himself a human, and therefore mutable, nature (7.9.13; 7.21.27) so man can know and embrace His infinite goodness. Therefore, the God Who transcends Augustine as goal is present as medium so he can attain Him. Augustine does not teach that God's mutability, i.e., humanity, is one thing and His immutability, i.e., divinity, another—it is not that one nature is simply medium while the other is simply goal. Nor is it that the two natures are mixed into one. Rather, it is that God's humanity is medium because it is ineffably united with His divinity (e.g., 10.41.67–9), and the latter is man's goal precisely because it is ineffably united with His humanity (e.g., 7.19.25). Christ is medium because He is goal and goal because He is medium. His divine and human natures are distinct and unequal yet spiritually united through His divinity. Christ, therefore, is *both* what man should want to be like, viz. a human being completely united with God, and how to become like him. Hence, for Augustine, the One he names "Lord" (in 1.1.1) is God the Father, considered in terms of the Persons constituting the Godhead, but in terms of the divine nature, "Lord" is God incarnate—through Whom Augustine addresses God the Father.[12] This is an important distinction showing how Confessor Augustine's notion of God depends on his notion of God incarnate (cf. 11.2.4).

Second, since this passage claims the reason Augustine has faith in and praises God is because He has gifted him with faith through His preachers, it speaks of the contingent character of divine incarnation and God's application thereof to humanity. God takes to Himself a specific human nature (i.e., belonging to a specific time and place) and applies His incarnation to particular humans through means He deems fitting. The assumption of *this* human nature (i.e., of this son of Joseph and Mary) stands beyond human reasoning.[13] Moreover, it is evident that God incarnate bestows His gift of faith by implanting faith in His elect community (i.e., His church) through His elect community. Hence, Augustine maintains his faith has been implanted in him by Christ's humanity through the preaching of His ministers.[14] Man's ordination to immutable participation in God is accomplished by Him, and by human cooperation thereto, through mutable means, viz. by Christ's humanity and, consequently, by His church and gift of faith. Therefore, while God incarnate is first cause, humans are at once His effect and secondary cause. It follows that man neither has nor can procure faith in Christ by nature, though God creates man to seek it. Rather, God bestows faith upon certain persons—presumably, according to His wisdom (1.1.1)—and Confessor Augustine has the good fortune of being a recipient.

In 1.2.2–5.6, Augustine focuses on the relationship between God incarnate and man to detail what lies at the core of *explicit* relationship with God, viz. the divine presence whereby man seeks and has a foretaste of beatitude. To encourage cultivation of God's presence, Augustine considers its marvelous mode, i.e., how God, the Creator of all (of "heaven and earth"), is united with man and what that means. Since Augustine cites Christ as his starting point, his analysis intentionally moves beyond his Manichean, pagan Platonist,[15] and (as *CC*'s "Introduction" argued) ancient Hebrew biblical inheritances.

In 1.2.2 Augustine begins considering the proximate conditions whereby he is capable of "calling on . . . [God] . . . to come into . . . [him]."[16] Augustine wonders about the kind of "place" that "God can enter into."[17] He inquires whether it is physical or spiritual but does not mention that distinction as such. Augustine also wonders how "this place" is related to awareness of God's presence. These are difficult matters to consider since, as God is creator of "heaven and earth,"[18] He already contains all things, including Augustine. How, then, does this occur? According to Augustine, it is because God, as creator, causes to exist all things caused to exist: "Without you, whatever exists would not exist."[19] This means, then, that God is present in Augustine since he is contained in God: "I would not have any existence, unless you were in me."[20]

But, Augustine wonders how he is "in" God. What, Augustine asks, does it mean to "call on you to come if I am already in you? Or where can you come from so as to be in me?"[21] Augustine is contained in God since he exists, but God's containing him allows him to be conscious of God and ask Him to be more present. It belongs to man's being caused to exist by God to both know that and seek greater divine presence. Does this consciousness of God mean, Augustine wonders, that he is somehow able to "move outside of heaven and earth so that my God may come to me from there?"[22] Simply put, if God contains all things, does being aware of one's dependence on God and asking Him to be more present entail that one somehow exists *outside* of the created order? But, thinking about God's presence to awareness in that way implies making man into God and God into a creature. How so? Because if God contains man insofar as he exists, man belongs to "heaven and earth." To hold otherwise, i.e., that man is uncreated, implies man is divine.

It is inferred, then, that the place in man where God is present must be created but since man's awareness of God allows him to transcend the created order, he has ontological kinship with God. This entails that in some marvelous manner, God is both transcendent of the cosmos and immanent within.[23] Augustine can be sure, then, that God is both transcendent of and immanent within man—so He is always "whole and intact" *and* somehow present to man. On the human side, Augustine knows man is contained by and able to call on God since God has constituted him so, i.e., to be contained by and contain God. However, this poses a problem:

for that God contains and is present in Augustine (who is mutable) implies God is somehow mutable.

This motivates Augustine to consider more precisely (1.3.3) how God contains "heaven and earth" (and, consequently, man). At first, as Augustine's terminology "fill them and overflow them" and "vessels" suggests,[24] he thinks of the matter as Manicheans might,[25] i.e., corporeally. But he shows that is wrong. For if God contains things corporeally, i.e., if God is body, and those united with Him are likewise, then if these are broken, He too is spilt: "We cannot think you are given coherence by vessels full of you, because even if they were to be broken, you would not be spilt. . . . You are not scattered but reassemble us. In filling all things, you fill them all with the whole of yourself."[26] Moreover, to view God corporeally (cf. 7.1.1) would invite other absurdities. For example, creatures would contain some part of God; and each would contain some different part of Him: larger things containing larger parts, smaller ones containing smaller parts—meaning God has larger and smaller parts: "Does that imply that there is some part of you which is greater, another part smaller?"[27] But none of this is compatible with the claim that "the whole of . . . [God is] . . . everywhere, yet without anything that contains . . . [God] . . . entire."[28] Hence, a materialist theology contradicts the claim that God, whether transcendent or immanent, is always "whole and entire."

By the end of this chapter, then, Augustine has made it evident that God contains all things; He is present to human consciousness (in which respect He deigns to be mutable since His presence can increase); and, therefore, man contains God non-corporeally. Augustine now implies that God, Who is always "whole and entire," is present in human creatures whereby He remains "whole and entire" and therefore, that humans, being conscious of God, have something enabling them to contain Him to the extent He deigns to be present. Hence, the mutable mode whereby God is present to man and, correspondingly, the mutable mode whereby man is present to God are not corporeal.

Augustine does not use here the terminology "corporeal" and "non-corporeal." But he implies that (i) God is supreme "non-corporeal" or spiritual substance; (ii) man contains some kind of created, and therefore non-supreme, spiritual substance able to contain and seek to be more contained by God; and (iii) God is present in a manner upholding His integrity. Augustine suggests, therefore, that God is able to be present in man according to the mode of human mutability because He is spiritual rather than corporeal and, consequently, the union between Him and man is spiritual. In the following passages, Augustine marvels at how God embraces mutability and thereby encourages man to cultivate His presence so he can participate immutably in God.

In 1.4.4, Augustine focuses on God as self-sufficient and non-corporeal, i.e., as immutable spirit,[29] and yet causal of and present to creatures. Augustine exclaims: "Who then are you, my God? What, I ask, but God who is Lord?. . . . Most high, utterly good (*summe*), utterly powerful, most omnipotent, most merciful and most just, deeply hidden yet most intimately present."[30] To underscore God's goodness, Augustine rattles off a series of apparently contradictory claims concerning God's nature and actions. He says, for example, that God is "immutable yet changing all things . . . always active, always in repose."[31] What does this mean? First, it asserts that God's nature is non-corporeal[32] and, therefore, that His presence is also non-corporeal, i.e., spiritual. For if God's presence were corporeal it would mean He is divisible and in all things as a part belongs to a body. But this, of course, contradicts the claim that God is always "whole and entire" and cannot explain His goodness, i.e., His presence to things in general and to man in particular. That the self-sufficient God causes man's existing and is present to him entirely for his benefit, so he can become what God has created him to become—in which sense God is "Lord"—is marveled at. Why so? Because the transcendent, and therefore immutable, God makes Himself immanent, so He can lead man, His mutable creature, to share immutably in His immutability!

In 1.5.5–6, Augustine (moving well beyond his pagan Platonist inheritance)[33] instructs that his, and therefore man's, proper response to this mystery is to cultivate God's presence to achieve "rest" in God. Man properly views God as "Lord." Augustine begins 1.5.5 with these words: "Who will enable me to find rest (*adquiescere*) in you? Who will grant me that you come into my heart and intoxicate it, so that I forget my evils and embrace my one and only good (*unam bonum*), yourself?"[34] God, Augustine remarks, deigns to be present in man for his benefit.

Moreover, Augustine's claim that God is present so men can find "rest" in Him both returns us to *conf.*'s opening words and connects us with the biography (books 1–10) and exegesis (books 11–13) that soon follows. Concerning *conf.*'s opening words, it underscores the power, wisdom, and goodness that Augustine had there ascribed to God. How so? Corresponding with His goodness, God deigns to create and be present to man entirely for his welfare; concerning His wisdom, this is God's plan; and, regarding His power, His plan will be accomplished. What does it signify about man? That he should embrace God as "Lord," since that is his proper response to God and, if he does, he shall enjoy in this life a taste of the complete happiness belonging to the afterlife. Accordingly, throughout 1.5.5–6, Augustine implores God to increase His presence so that, by restoring and augmenting him, he can achieve the divine rest for which he is created.

Conclusion: What, then, does Confessor Augustine disclose about the nature of God's presence in 1.1.1–5.6? First, we see that Augustine's foremost notion of God, in this context, is He is incarnate immutable spirit. God's spiritual presence to man is incarnational in the sense that, as manifest in "the Word made flesh," it is entirely gratuitous and offered according to the mode of man, i.e., by mutable means, so he can participate immutably in God. The latter is underscored by the claim that faith in the incarnation comes to man through God's church. Therefore, as divine incarnation shows, God gives His presence to man entirely for his benefit.

The latter does not make God mutable but means He makes Himself present by the mode of human mutability. In this respect, God in Christ, as immutable-mutable, presents Himself to man gradually so he can ultimately participate immutably in Him. According to Augustine, this is only possible because since God is incorporeal, His union with man is spiritual. Therefore, whereas God, being "whole and entire," is immutably incorporeal, the place in man He inhabits must be mutably incorporeal. If God were corporeal and His presence corporeal, that would entail He is not "whole and entire," thereby denying divine immutability. Therefore, although the nature of God's presence demands some "amalgam," as it were, of God in Himself and man in himself, the content thereof neither diminishes nor augments God (for Whom it is subaltern) but augments man since his incorporeal soul is mutable. It does not mean, then, that divine substance and human soul are mixed together into one "middle" or distinct substance.

Rather, insofar as that unity is *spiritual*, God, who is "whole and entire," shares His presence to make man "whole and entire." Each party remains itself, but man is augmented through becoming more united with God. Hence, God's special spiritual presence, which is both stated and offered in Christ, develops soul for the better so man can become more himself.

According to Augustine, divine incarnation—proclaimed by the Church as "The Word made flesh" (meaning, ontologically, that God in Christ is immutable-mutable)—teaches man that God, gratuitously, offers him the spiritual reality of immutable participation in His goodness and employs Christ's humanity to bring that about. Accordingly, Augustine's *confessio* teaches that, in this life, there are two kinds of (mutable) divine presence in man's soul. First, there is an implicit presence, i.e., spiritual union with God remaining after Original (and personal) sin and is somewhat hidden by Original and personal sin. Second, and more important to Augustine, since he focuses on it here and throughout *conf*., is an explicit presence that the implicit presence is for, which man cooperates with, and that Augustine presently enjoys and encourages his audience to embrace. Therefore, while both forms consist in the spiritual union of God with man, explicit presence, dependent on Christ's mediation through His church, properly augments implicit presence. Explicit presence is what Augustine now enjoys, encourages his audience toward, and is consummated in the Sabbath rest (*conf*. 13.35.50–38.53).

Looking ahead some, 1.1.1–5.6 also instructs concerning Augustine's handling of his Manichean and pagan Platonist inheritances in *conf*. In this regard, Augustine asserts that the Catholic doctrine of God and Church, generally identified with Nicene Christianity,[35] is decisive. This is visible, in principle, in 1.1.1's vague signification of the Trinity but is made clear in 1.1.1's subsequent accounts of divine incarnation, Church, and Catholic priesthood (which office Augustine holds while writing *conf*.). It is helpful to consider 1.1.1–5.6 in light of Confessor Augustine's subsequent disclosures in *conf*. for while he thinks that Manichean philosophical theology and psychology, since corporeal,[36] is subordinate to pagan Platonist philosophical theology and psychology since that is grounded in recognizing the primacy of incorporeal substance,[37] he also thinks that pagan Platonist insight is limited. In terms of *conf*.'s early passages, Augustine's discussion of divine presence in 1.2.2–3.3 (aiming to show the deficiency of a corporeal, Manichean-like approach thereto) is subordinate to his account of divine presence in 1.3.3–4.4 claiming the relative superiority of an incorporeal, and hence pagan Platonist-like, account of divine presence. 1.5.5–6, however, asserts the superiority of Catholic teaching on divine presence since it includes the pagan Platonist doctrine that divine presence is incorporeal but, unlike the latter, has a complete sharing in divine goodness as its origin, guide, and *telos*. In this respect, Augustine thinks that Catholic doctrine, by its teaching on divine incarnation (returning us to 1.1.1),[38] exceeds his pagan Platonist inheritance.

Nevertheless, Augustine also implies that each of the previous approaches has some kind of merit. How so? While the Manicheans have a doctrine of divine presence, it is primitive because corporeal; and while the pagan Platonists have a relatively superior doctrine because it claims God is incorporeal, it is incomplete because it unduly limits God's sharing immutability with humans. Augustine thinks, then, that Manichean and pagan Platonist teachings are, in various ways, propaedeutic.[39] Each is on the right track, but while the one misinterprets divine immanence, the other misinterprets divine transcendence. By contrast, the Catholic approach, grounded in divine incarnation, emphasizes divine immanence and transcendence in the right ways and shows, therefore, that God is better (i.e., more good) than the Manicheans and pagan Platonists think since He shares His transcendence with man via immanent or mutable means. *Conf.* claims that Catholic doctrine includes the best parts of Augustine's intellectual inheritance.

Moreover, as the previous discussion shows, 1.1.1–5.6 is developmental, by the mode of *exitus-reditus*, in two related ways. First, and primarily, it develops the account of divine presence articulated at the outset. Augustine explains the conditions, grounded in divine incarnation, whereby God is present to man so he can ultimately become immutably present to God. Hence, we note a transition, on the human side of things, from implicit to explicit union with God. Second, in a related vein, Augustine develops his account of divine immutability so his reader understands that God is incorporeal and immutable rather than either corporeal and divisible *or* incorporeal and mutable. Hence, Augustine's confession in 1.1.1–5.6 has some kind of *exitus-reditus* structure since it begins (i.e., *exitus*) with the claim that happiness is found by resting in God and finishes by explaining how that can occur, thereby returning the reader (*reditus*) to the passage's original claim.

Finally, we also detect a loosely presented trinitarian pattern to 1.1.1–5.6. Since Augustine maintains it is through divine incarnation that one knows and embraces God as Trinity (e.g., 11.2.4), and implies therefore that the Godhead, through Christ, is incarnate, emphasis on the incarnational nature of spiritual union in 1.1.1–5.6 necessarily points toward the Trinity, understood as first cause, medium, and goal of the created order. This is hinted at in the opening paragraph's distinction between God's power, wisdom, and goodness, and in the account of spiritual presence in 1.1.1–5.6. The aforementioned distinction is later translated, albeit analogically, into the Persons constituting the Godhead (e.g., *conf.* 11–13). Moreover, Augustine's account of divine presence in 1.1.1–5.6 arguably proceeds from God the Father (recognized as creator—1.2.2–4.4) to God the incarnate Word (recognized as communicator to man of God's purpose and how that is accomplished—1.3.3–4.4) to God the Holy Spirit (1.5.5–6), the divine Person through Whom man's immutable participation in God is accomplished.

Conf. 1.6.7–2.10.18: Descent toward Anti-*Confessio*

Confessor Augustine now details young Augustine's rejection of God (i.e., rebuffing God's natural presence) and therefore of the humble attitude toward truth properly belonging to *confessio*. This descent begins at infancy, continues through childhood, and reaches its nadir in a pear-theft committed as a teenager. As Confessor Augustine recounts this descent, he shows that young Augustine was its primary cause. Although the means to practice *confessio* (or, at minimum, the humility leading thereto) were especially available to him through his Catholic mother, Augustine chose otherwise and his parents, friends, and teachers influenced him accordingly.

At one point in childhood, young Augustine, at mother Monnica's behest, asked for and was being prepared for baptism and, at another, he received counsel from her concerning sexual activity. However, his mindset turned more and more away from God due (i) principally to personal sin and (ii) secondarily to deficient social influence—including mother Monnica (in a way), father

Patricius, friends, and teachers. Finally, to gain his peer-group's praise, Augustine steals pears from a neighbor's vineyard. Since he intended to supplant God's truth and law with his own desires and wants, Confessor Augustine counts that mindset as his worst ever for he had become "a region of destitution (*regio egestatis*)."[40]

Conf. 1.6.7–1.20.31

(i) **Infancy** (*conf.* **1.6.7–7.12**): While highlighting the universal aspect of *confessio*, Augustine describes his infancy (from the Latin word *infans*, meaning "unable to speak") as typical.[41] Like all persons, he has no memory of ultimate and proximate origins[42] but is born into a ready-made order (note Augustine's emphasis on the incarnational-like structure of mutable reality) wherein the community provides him with the nourishment and education needed for self-preservation.[43] The newborn signifies its needs by crying, i.e., apart from knowledge, and its surrounding community knows what the infant needs and consciously supplies it. Therefore, while the infant has inchoate awareness of its dependence, the adult members of community have knowledge of the infant's dependence and aim to supply it with what lacks. This shows not only that the infant has awareness of dependence on community, and that community has awareness of its role in providing for the infant's welfare, but also that community depends on some higher order. Accordingly, Augustine maintains that community, in a way, is divinely structured. God is first cause, and the infant and its community are, entirely for their benefit, His secondary causes. In the latter respect, each member of community properly acts for its welfare.

Yet Confessor Augustine also recognizes, by observation, that the infant exhibits a self-destructive attitude, coupled with some hostility or arrogance toward its surrounding community.[44] In short, the infant aims to subordinate community. What evidence does Augustine provide? First, he maintains infants want things that would destroy them—hence the need for adult supervision.[45] Second, Augustine claims infants are filled with jealousy toward others to the extent that after having their own appetite satisfied, they want another to not have his/her appetite satisfied since they want the nourisher to be exclusively their source.[46] In this regard, the infant, albeit inchoately, aims to subordinate others. This is not only the welfare of its fellow infant, by keeping the latter from receiving sustenance, but also the nourisher, by contradicting its role to nourish. What does this mean? The infant requires guidance from its community since, left to its own, it would destroy itself and others. Therefore, the infant needs help to eradicate its disordered, destructive desire.

What originates the infant's destructive desire? Looked at in one way it is neither the infant's nor the community's responsibility—for it appears innate. The infant seems to have this unruliness, brings it to community, and, in a way, forces the latter to respond thereto. Is it God the creator's fault? It cannot be if He, as defined in 1.1.1–5.6, is self-sufficient. Therefore, if God cannot create defective beings, the fault is traced to creatures, since these are capable of defecting. If the fault, then, is caused neither by the infant nor by the community into which it is born, it must be inherited from some previous human disobedience as part of the human condition.[47]

Can this disorder be fixed? Since it belongs to the human condition, it cannot be repaired by man (for if he is beset by that condition he cannot rid himself of it). Rather, as Augustine implied (e.g., 1.1.1 wayward man needs Christ's mediation), it can only be fixed by God in conjunction with human cooperation. Community can attempt to mitigate this disorder within itself and in its newest members, but the ultimate cure must come from God *in conjunction with* human community and that is engendered, Augustine claims, by practicing *confessio*.

Unfortunately, as *conf.* recalls, neither the infant Augustine nor his peers were interested in diagnosing and fixing his disordered desire. While Augustine's peers acknowledged his disorder,[48] they were interested in harnessing it for arrogant purposes. Although recognizing that the infant needs education, their standard of education is not divine union (and thereby toward eradicating disordered desire). Rather, it consists in an "order" (really a disorder) governed by the same kind of arrogance found in the infant. This order, premised on dominating and subjugating others, is hostile not only toward the divine order but also toward itself. As Confessor Augustine will show, this "society" is riddled by contradiction for by encouraging its members to pursue domination it seeks to destroy the same "society" it upholds. Consequently, young Augustine guides himself and is guided toward *presumption* instead of *confession*.

(ii) *Childhood* (*conf.* 1.8.13–20.31): Confessor Augustine recounts how young Augustine passes from infancy into childhood, i.e., *ab infantia . . . in puertiam*,[49] since he becomes capable of speech.[50] The latter shows that human nature is essentially rational (for words derive from concepts whereby reality is represented according to the mode of intelligibility).[51] Moreover, humans invent words to signify things, wants, and values; and, as Confessor Augustine understands scripture (e.g., *conf.* 11.2.2), words are employed by God to signify divine and salvific realities so humans can seek eternal beatitude. Henceforth, Augustine's relationship with community, i.e., with the human order, and with divine community, i.e., the Church, will be mediated by words.

However, the mode whereby Augustine's human order uses words engulfs everything else, including Augustine's assimilation of divinely ordained words. The problem, as *conf.* recounts, is that following the bad influence of his family, friends, schoolmates, and schoolmasters,[52] Augustine then used words and things for presumptuous instead of humble purposes.[53] Concerning his family, mother Monnica and father Patricius wanted him to become educated for secular success.[54] Regarding his schooling, Augustine's education is oriented toward using words for essentially sophistical purposes. Students were taught a wide vocabulary and appropriate forms of grammar via studying the classics[55] under the auspices of harsh discipline.[56] But the goal was to use words, in the form of rhetoric, to get what one desires rather than what, as a human being, one should want.[57] While Augustine's teachers uphold the rules of grammar, i.e., the "tongue arts," they subordinate moral law so that those succeeding at the former use speech to seek honor, fame, power, and wealth by exploiting the less successful.[58] Note, then, the contradiction: students are taught the "tongue arts," but these are not used for sharing truth, i.e., for what is objective and therefore beneficial to each. Rather, these arts are taught so students can exploit their fellows, including those teaching them and those with whom they study!

Yet Augustine engaged, albeit at some distance, the Catholic religion mother Monnica was raising him in for two reasons. First, he was taken aback by the beatings he received at school and sought relief by praying to the God he learned about through Monnica and/ or at Church.[59] Second, he suffered a severe illness and, by Monnica's aid, sought the sacrament of baptism.[60] Hence, the divine order, and therefore the disposition of *confessio*, was made present to Augustine. But he succumbed to the ridicule he received for praying to God to relieve his beatings[61] and, upon recovering from his illness, neither he nor Monnica continued to pursue his baptism.[62] As such, Augustine subordinated divinity to a disordered human order.

Moreover, Augustine grew accomplished at learning both words and the art of persuasion—he was considered a good student[63] and, in a related vein, successfully attained the glory and power he wanted, especially while playing games with his schoolmates, where the victory he sought was often achieved through lies, deceit, and temper tantrums.[64] All told, Augustine embraced a presumptuous attitude, avidly subordinating divinity and, thereby, the possibility of *confessio*, to a self-contradictory human order encouraging the use of rhetoric and immoral behavior to gain from others power, honor, fame, and wealth. Young Augustine was pursuing finite goods through exploiting his fellows. Therefore, although his primary, divinely bestowed, powers of memory and understanding were developing (Confessor Augustine both notes this and thanks God for it—1.20.31; cf. 1.7.12), these were employed for sordid purposes.[65]

In sum, Augustine's childhood is colored by the same disorder found in infancy, viz. the desire to subordinate all things to his finite, and therefore irrational, wants. He is moving away from humility and, consequently, from *confessio*.[66]

Conf. 2: Early Adolescence

Unfortunately, Augustine's disorder becomes worse in early adolescence[67] as he encounters the developments of his natural powers in puberty and, more significantly, of his rational powers.[68] Consequently, *conf.* maintains that young Augustine reaches the nadir of presumption, and therefore of an essentially anti-*confessio* mindset, at this time in his life. He became a *"regio egestatis"*—what T. S. Eliot famously translates as "a wasteland" in his namesake poem.

(i) ***Conf.* 2.1.1–3.8:** *Conf.* explains this by stating and then detailing young Augustine's mindset. *Conf.* analyzes first Augustine's sexual lust embodied in using women for sexual pleasure and his peer-group for praise, and second, his spiritual lust (his mindset's root) instantiated in a theft of pears committed at the behest of and in league with his peer-group.⁶⁹ Confessor Augustine wants to instruct that young Augustine subordinates both the human and, more important, divine order⁷⁰ to the satisfaction of his own irrational desire. Young Augustine claims that his thought and action is the *Summum Bonum*.

How so? First, Augustine is aware of God's truth and law⁷¹ concerning sexual maturity. Through his mother's general influence,⁷² he has some awareness that right response to sexual maturity consists in pursuing chastity within the settled states of consecrated life or marriage.⁷³ However, Augustine's parents, peer-group, and actions fancy otherwise. Patricius, Augustine's father, encourages his son to have children so that he (i.e., Patricius) can soon have grandchildren.⁷⁴ Monnica, who Confessor Augustine views as "living," at that time, "on the outskirts of Babylon"⁷⁵ (presumably, Patricius lives at Babylon's center) counsels young Augustine concerning Church teaching but urges him "above all to refrain from fornication."⁷⁶ Confessor Augustine claims his parents were more interested in his secular success via a fine oratorical education than he become properly human.⁷⁷ (In fact, Augustine was not enrolled in school so his father could amass sufficient funds to send him to a "fine" school in Carthage.)⁷⁸ So Augustine's parents, albeit to varying degrees, subordinate the divine and human orders to their own satisfaction.

Young Augustine's peer-group is likewise oriented. Based on what Confessor Augustine reports in these pages, they encourage sexual exploits not only for the pleasure of sex but also for pleasure in praise gained from reporting to them sex acts (whether real or imagined).⁷⁹ Augustine was an eager participant in these matters since he longed not simply for sensual pleasure⁸⁰ but even more so for the group's praise.⁸¹ In fact, Confessor Augustine remarks how young Augustine used to lie about committing sex acts to procure the group's praise.⁸² Hence, vice was employed in the service of vice. At bottom, Augustine's parents and his peer-group, along with Augustine himself, subordinate the divine and human orders to subjective satisfaction. Each exploits others to enjoy some finite end.

(ii) *Conf.* 2.4.9–10.18: Confessor Augustine describes his mindset at that time by analyzing a pear-theft⁸³ he committed in league with his peer-group.⁸⁴ Why did he steal? First, he wanted the group's praise.⁸⁵ However, the besought praise differs from that presented in his account of sexual lust. In this instance, Augustine's motive for sinning⁸⁶ had nothing to do with enjoying the pears or sharing them with others.[87] Nor was it simply concerned with enjoying the group's praise for arrogating persons (which was an object of his sexual lust).[88] Rather, it concerned enjoying a different kind of praise. Augustine wanted the group's praise based on sharing its orientation to claiming divine status, i.e., to determine good and evil, right and wrong, reward and punishment.[89] In sum, Augustine stole the pears to gain the group's praise for joining them in arrogating divine status. He belonged to the group because it subordinated the divine order along with the human order properly participating therein:

> "What fruit had I," wretched boy . . . above all in that theft in which I loved nothing but the theft itself? The theft itself was a nothing, and for that reason I was the more miserable. Yet had I been alone I would not have done it. . . . Therefore my love in that act was to be associated with the gang in whose company I did it. . . . my pleasure was not in the pears; it was in the crime itself, done in association with a sinful group.[90]

However, there is a further twist. Since Augustine's relationship with the group from whom he sought praise was motivated by utility (rather than by virtue),[91] his ultimate arbiter is himself alone; he implies that he is God.[92] On this basis, Confessor Augustine claims that young Augustine embraces an outlook that is radically presumptuous and, therefore, anti-*confessio*.[93]

Books 3–4: Young Augustine's Ascent toward *Confessio* Begins

Conf. 3: Conversion to Wisdom and to the Manichean Religion[94]

But, *conf.* explains that Augustine, now studying in Carthage,[95] is dissatisfied with his pear-theft mentality and seeks to overcome it.[96] In a way, he is conscience-stricken. We see this by his disassociating from the "Wreckers."[97] However, Augustine's new pursuits elicit pleasure and pain. In particular, his principal desire "to love and be loved," i.e., to enjoy women's bodies and loyalties,[98] brings pangs of conscience he seeks to assuage. These disturbances are visible in his captivation "by theatrical shows,"[99] "sacrilegious quest for knowledge,"[100] and study to become a lawyer—in which respect he distanced himself from his iconoclastic schoolmates.[101] Augustine engages in these activities to feel better about himself, to become less disturbed by feelings of jealousy, envy, and anger resulting from his desire "to love and be loved." He attends the theatre to think his emotions are rightly ordered (when in reality they are not)[102] and worships demons, presumably so he can control his future through having foreknowledge (therefore, he will not be upset over things he cannot control)—including to pursue sexual activity during Catholic worship.[103] Moreover, Augustine studies rhetoric—he is at the top of his class—to enjoy both present and future social success (and, therefore, be a constant object of desire).[104]

There is no doubt that Augustine is vain; his motive for becoming a lawyer shows this. But he obviously intends to minimize his pain by seeking catharsis at theatrical shows and engaging in activities whose outcomes he knows are favorable to his social and sexual ambitions.

Nevertheless, as his subsequent affinity for Wisdom manifests,[105] Augustine's conscience remained troubled not only about his feelings of jealousy, envy, and lust[106] but also, it seems, about their principal cause, viz. personal vanity. Hence, he is attracted, while reading Cicero's *Hortensius*,[107] to Wisdom, i.e., to a lifestyle promising peace by behaving in a "proper" way.[108] Reading Cicero's exhortation to study philosophy gave Augustine

> *different values and priorities*. Suddenly every vain hope became empty . . . and I longed for the immortality of wisdom with an incredible ardor in my heart. I began to rise up to return to you [i.e., to God] . . . the one thing that delighted me in Cicero's exhortation was the advice "not to study one particular sect but to love and seek and pursue and hold fast and strongly embrace wisdom itself, wherever found."[109]

Put differently, Augustine wants to subordinate himself to divinity. However, he ultimately embraces as Wisdom an account thereof that promotes his arrogant desire for honor and praise. So he still subordinates the divine and human orders to secular ambition.[110] Although we detect improvement, Augustine pursues presumption rather than *confessio*.

How does this happen? First, Augustine is disappointed that Cicero makes no mention of Christ since he had heard from infancy, through his mother, that Christ is Wisdom.[111] Accordingly, Augustine began reading the Catholic Church's "holy scriptures."[112] But, finding the Bible formally and materially uncouth—scripture's doctrine seemed irrational and its diction paled beside the ornate prose of Cicero[113]—he turned instead to the Manichean religion which also identified Wisdom with Christ. Well-spoken adherents, who both delivered and promised to Augustine what he then conceived of as an intelligible account of reality, introduced him to Manichean teachings and practices.[114]

What did young Augustine imbibe?[115] *Conf.* claims he was attracted to the Manicheans because they asserted that Christ is Wisdom in a way intelligible to his "inflated conceit" (*tumor enim meus*) and "pride" (*turgidus fastu*).[116] What doctrine of Christ attracted Augustine? It is hard to say[117] since he immediately speaks about the falsity of Manichean doctrine rather than about their Christology. This is probably because as the orthodox account of Christ as "Word made flesh" depends on understanding immutable and mutable substance, Augustine intends to show how the Manicheans lacked the right doctrine of Christ since lacking philosophical understanding.

According to *conf.*, Augustine imbibed an essentially upside-down account of reality, wherein physical reality was perceived as imaginary while mental images of bodies were perceived as reality. Confessor Augustine writes: "The dishes they placed before me contained splendid hallucinations. Indeed one would do better to love this visible sun, which at least is truly evident to the eyes, than those false mythologies which use the eyes to deceive the mind."[118] Instead of acknowledging (i) the dependence of images on bodies and (ii) the intellectual judgment that mutable realities depend on the immutable and supreme reality who is God,[119] the Manicheans held much the opposite. Supreme divinity is some kind of immutable yet corporeal and divisible reality (an obvious contradiction in terms). Moreover, since "God" is attacked by some evil principle and particles of God are consequently entrapped in evil material,[120] non-divine being is composed of good and bad components[121]— including, in human being, a good soul and a bad soul.[122] Due to intellectual immaturity, Augustine was particularly enamored with Manichean criticisms of aspects of the Catholic Old Testament concerning (i) man being in the image of God,[123] (ii) polygamy,[124] and (iii) the apparent changes happening to the divine law.[125]

Conf. recounts that young Augustine had difficulty comprehending these matters since he viewed God as immutable and corporeal. Rather than understanding how an immutable (and therefore incorporeal) God has fashioned each human in His likeness (regarding soul's structure), Augustine thinks this claim means what is contrary to the Manichean doctrine of God, viz. that God is a composite of good and evil matter.[126] Likewise, rather than recognizing how the unchanging God discloses the nature of marriage and divine law to humans in accord with their mutability,[127] he holds that changes in the nature of marriage and/or divine law entail divine mutability. Augustine is right that God is immutable but wrongly conceives of Him as corporeal.

Augustine was also foolishly attracted to Manichean religious practice. *Conf.* claims the latter is rife with imagination for the Manicheans maintained, among other things, that humans were not responsible for evil actions (this was caused naturally, as it were, by man's evil component).[128] Additionally, they also held their elect's digestive powers would, by burping after eating figs, release divine particles from captivity[129] so these particles would return to supreme divinity.[130] However, Augustine found therein a way to assuage his itchy conscience. How so? On Augustine's reading, the Manichean religion claimed that his itchy conscience was essentially an aberration, something "natural," resulting from some evil principle's capturing and enclosing parts of a divine principle.[131] Therefore, since Augustine thinks he is composed of good material and evil material, the evil he commits is not his fault, and his misgivings are not decisive since, by following Manichean rites, all this can be removed. As a result, Augustine has found both a justification and expiation for his vain ambition.[132]

At book 3's conclusion, Confessor Augustine shows young Augustine's immersion in imagination[133] by contrasting that mindset with mother Monnica's.[134] When she recounted a dream stating that Augustine would eventually become a Catholic, standing "on the rule" where she now stood, he denies her dream by claiming it means exactly the opposite, viz. that she will become a Manichean.[135] Hence, Augustine's loyalty to imagination causes him to claim truth to be falsity.

All told, it is good that Augustine wants to subordinate himself to Wisdom, i.e., to an objective standard of thought and action. This is certainly an advance upon the pear-theft, described in book 2, where he upholds his judgment as *Summum Bonum*. However, since Augustine conceives of Wisdom in his own image and likeness, he embraces a counterfeit Wisdom as a tool in his quest for sensual pleasure, power, honor, fame, and wealth. Although his mindset is improved by the desire to conform to Wisdom, a major portion of the presumption found in infancy, childhood, and early adolescence remains. Young Augustine is far from humility and, therefore, from *confessio*, but he is moving in the right direction.

Conf. 4: Augustine's Manichean Lifestyle[136]

Conf. shows that young Augustine's embracing the Manichean religion brought a measure of intellectual and practical progress, but his lifestyle was nevertheless woefully contradictory and deficient. Where do we find progress? In Augustine's becoming a teacher, taking a concubine, pursuing public praise, mourning the death of his best friend, writing a book, viz. *On the Beautiful and the Fitting*, and studying the liberal arts in general and Aristotle's *Categories* in particular. Why is this progress? Because in each instance Augustine explicitly subordinates himself to some order. However, the very same matters enumerated earlier also show that his lifestyle remains contradictory and deficient. This is because it continues to pursue temporal reality as *Summum Bonum*. Augustine's improvement, therefore, is palpable but only by degree.

By teaching rhetoric so students can achieve victory at court, Augustine pursues money and power; yet he prefers virtuous students who employ their rhetorical skills to, at least sometimes, benefit the innocent.[137] Augustine procured a concubine to whom he was faithful and through whom he learned, albeit reluctantly, to love children.[138] While participating in a poetry contest, Augustine refused to consult a soothsayer who promised him victory via animal sacrifice (to propitiate certain spirits)[139]—though he continued to consult astrologers for that purpose (while nevertheless listening to someone explain the futility of astrology).[140] In each instance, then, Augustine seeks secular success. But, unlike before (e.g., 3.1.1–3.6), he *explicitly* subordinates his desire to some common good, whether that be for the welfare of other persons and animals or, as the example with astrology shows, to benefit close friends. We see, then, how Augustine's quest for praise, glory, and fame is limited by adhering to some external good.[141] In one way, he moves toward *confessio*; but, in another and more significant way, he remains far away.

All this, together with judgment upon the Manichean religion, is included in Augustine's subsequent treatment of his response to the death of his dearest companion.[142] Augustine describes the profound bond he shared with his friend who was also from Thagaste, with whom he was a student, whom he had persuaded to join the Manichean sect, and whose close friendship he had enjoyed for a year.[143] Since Augustine has a best friend, we see how, to some degree,[144] he subordinates himself to some common good, viz. to another's welfare. However, Augustine's friend takes fever, returns to the Catholic religion on his deathbed, shows anger at Augustine for ridiculing his baptism, and subsequently passes away.[145] Augustine, therefore, is desolate mostly because he lost his best friend but probably also—and in a related vein—because his friend's return to Catholicism showed to Augustine the finitude of his rhetorical skill[146] and the Manichean religion.[147] Augustine is shattered by his friend's death: "My eyes looked for him everywhere, and he was not there. I hated everything because they did not have him."[148] In retrospect, Augustine claims he loved his friend in a disordered manner,[149] as if he were God: "So at that period of my life I used to love people on the basis of human judgement, not your judgement, my God, in whom no one is deceived."[150]

However, *Conf.* points out this was possible because, ontologically speaking, that friend (i.e., this concrete soul-body composite) was more real than the fictitious, imaginary account of God (and of human identity) he embraced as a Manichean.[151] Accordingly, Augustine ultimately found consolation neither in the Manichean God nor in a Manichean doctrine of the afterlife[152] but in the company of Manichean friends.[153] Most important, the friend's death likely had the effect of loosening both Augustine's (i) bond with the Manichean religion and (ii) pursuit of glory through rhetoric. Why so? First, Augustine noticed that the Manichean God was less real than humans and, therefore, than the realities appearing to his senses. Second, Augustine recognized that rhetoric is limited—people can refuse persuasion, and rhetoric is powerless before death.

Augustine considers two more related matters before concluding book 4.[154] First, he wrote a book, soon lost, named *On the Beaut-*

iful and the Fitting[155] dedicating it to a famous orator at Rome named Hierius.[156] Second, he becomes an avid student of the liberal arts, studying various topics on his own, including Porphyry's translation[157] of Aristotle's *Categories*.[158] *Conf.* likely includes these matters to show that young Augustine's intellectual activity was oriented toward knowing the truth of things, viz. concerning the nature of beauty[159] and the fitting, and regarding the nature of substance in general and of God in particular. Moreover, dedicating his book to Hierius shows both Augustine's truculence and appreciation for oratorical excellence.

All told, young Augustine's pursuit of knowledge and practical skill have a positive aspect since, in each instance, he acknowledges some objective reality to which mind conforms. However, Augustine subordinated these things to temporal success. While his book, as its dedication to Hierius at Rome shows, was written to achieve renown and considered beauty and fittingness corporeal realities, his study of Aristotle's *Categories*, accomplished apart from any formal instruction, was undertaken to know all substance, including God, as corporeal.[160] Obviously, Augustine's learning was, in certain respects, contrary to his core Manichean belief about God for whereas he believed God was both immutable *and* divisible (an obvious contradiction) his conceptual understanding of God was that He was divisible. Therefore, just as Augustine desired to enjoy the mutable realities of power, honor, fame, and wealth so he conceived of reality as mutable. This is probably because, as 4.1.1 claims, he wanted to use knowledge of mutable reality as means to attain that reality.

But *conf.* points out more contradiction. The problem is not only that young Augustine's motive in each instance is colored by personal vanity but also that his affinity for Wisdom causes him to recognize his vanity. Although Augustine's conscience is troubled, his adherence to Manichean religion tells him the latter is not his fault and he can repeatedly purge himself of guilt by religious practice (4.1.1). So young Augustine is knowingly vain and, according to Manichean religion, has no way to escape vanity in this life. By practicing Manichean rites he can be "forgiven" for his inexorable vanity and prepare for death wherein the divine element by which he is composed will be formally liberated from captivity by the evil element. At death, however, Augustine, this composite (as the Manicheans claim) of good elements and evil elements, will cease to be. So, if vanity is inevitable in this life, and the afterlife brings extinction, why bother fighting vanity? Augustine has no significant motive for intellectual and moral progress.

Book 4 instructs, then, how young Augustine's Manichean mindset is intellectually and practically contradictory, and that, as the death of his friend and failure to procure Hierius's sponsorship show, he has some awareness of contradiction. Therefore, because of Augustine's overarching pursuit of Wisdom (3.4.7–8), including his desire to escape vanity, something has to give. Either the Manichean religion includes truths Augustine has not yet apprehended or else it is false and he will either need to forsake his quest for Wisdom or look for it elsewhere.

Conclusion

Juxtaposing Confessor Augustine's incarnational account of *confessio* in 1.1.1–5.6 with his analyses of infancy, childhood, young adolescence, and Manichean lifestyle in 1.6–4.16.31 shows that Augustine's confession is essentially universal, progressive, and fashioned according to the manner of *exitus-reditus*. It is important to note, however, that the universal element does not cause the progressive and *exitus-reditus* elements. The generally accepted claim that all men seek happiness (1.1.1) does not produce Augustine's account of how he thinks happiness is attained. Rather, it is other way around. For, as *conf.* 1.1.1 opening lines show, Augustine displays his account of happiness in the context of explaining how it is gained. Hence, it is through *confessio* that Augustine distinguishes his doctrine of happiness and, consequently, the (progressive) stages whereby it is attained. This means not only that *conf.*'s universal and progressive elements depend on its *exitus-reditus* structure but also that Augustine's medium, viz. his confessing, is congruent with his message.

How, then, is Augustine's confession *universal*? His understanding of happiness makes it universal in a twofold manner, viz. (i) principally or directly *and* (ii) indirectly or by sub-alternation. While *conf.*'s principal audience consists in those having an explicit relationship with God, its indirect audience numbers those having an implicit bond with God.[161] At *conf.*'s outset, Augustine maintains his confession is universal and distinguishes primary and secondary audiences. In general, Augustine evinces his confessing is addressed to God, self, and neighbor since he judges that God is present to each—whether they know it or not (e.g., 10.27.38). The self-sufficient creator of "heaven and earth" (1.2.2—cf. 13.1.1) is spiritually present so each can achieve immutable union with Him (1.5.6) in His Sabbath rest (13.35.50–38.53).

However, due to man's earlier rebellion against God (1.1.1), humans have either implicit or explicit divine presence. Although God's presence is for man's benefit, implicit presence (which Augustine suggests is the mode of divine presence remaining in man after Adam's disobedience) is for explicit presence since the latter is concretely linked to attaining the Sabbath rest. Augustine thinks that achieving immutable participation in God requires increasing divine presence, and explicit presence, wherein one actively cooperates by and with His goodness in Christ, is the mode of divine presence proximate to immutable divine presence. Therefore, whereas implicit presence has the disposition of natural humility (7.18.24; 8.1.2)—i.e., recognizing that God is good and worshipping Him as *terminus ad quem*, the *terminus ad quem* of explicit presence is the disposition of *confessio*—i.e., worshipping God in Christ (9.1.1) for attaining immutable participation in His Sabbath rest.

How does one transition from implicit to explicit relationship? In the last portion of 1.1.1 Augustine claims it is by receiving Christ. Through the mutable realities, given through His church, of hearing His Word preached and receiving His sacraments, man receives Christ and is established and nurtured in the lifestyle of *confessio*. Augustine instructs it is like and through the mutable-immutable Christ that one transitions from implicit relationship, and by receiving and persevering in His mutable realities one journeys to immutable participation in God. Hence, Christ is both man's goal and medium thereto.

Augustine writes *conf.*, therefore, by practicing incarnational *confessio* to explain the nature of God's explicit presence so his audience can grow therein toward enjoying immutable divine presence in the Sabbath rest. For this reason, Augustine distinguishes the stages by which he enjoys explicit presence and how the latter points toward complete participation in God.

Therefore, after describing *confessio*'s nature in 1.1.1–5.6 by (i) focusing on a universal God, universal Church, and the human soul as such, and (ii) showing that, in and through His Christ, God employs special mutable means whereby humans can ultimately participate immutably in Him, Augustine begins *conf.*'s biographical component to disclose how his present relationship with God has been attained. Nevertheless, although Augustine's account of infancy is only based on data taken from his observation of infants, both that teaching[162] and the accounts of childhood and early adolescence which follow can appear specific since they speak of matters particular to Augustine—whether that is his view of human nature or personal behavior. For example, not everyone is born in Thagaste in 354 AD, has a Catholic-leaning mother and pagan father, goes to school in Thagaste, deceives for the sake of victory, lusts for sexual pleasure, steals pears with his friends, arrogates supreme divinity, is intellectually alert, has a vision of divine Wisdom while reading Cicero's *Hortensius*, joins the Manicheans, engages in immoral behavior, has a concubine, practices astrology, loses a dear friend to death during their teenage years, writes a book, *On the Beautiful and the Fitting*, and dedicates it to a certain Hierius at Rome, studies Aristotle's *Categories* (by themselves), and masters the liberal arts.

How, then, is Augustine's account "universal"? It is typical that persons have parents, friends, and schoolmasters. But it is not typical that people consider their past by the mode of *confessio*. However, as mentioned earlier, *confessio* includes the claim that each seeks happiness. It is typical that people seek happiness (i) according to understanding, for which reason their account of happiness might be true or false, and (ii) by engaging in behavior they think allows them to pursue what they uphold as happiness (10.23.33–4). People seek happiness, then, by thought and action—which, on Augustine's terms, is by making truth claims and embracing accordant behaviors.

Confessor Augustine's concern, then, is with spiritual biography. He does not consider everything that occurred during certain periods in his life but only those matters through which he can display his transition to explicit relationship. Consequently, Augustine encourages his proper (and implicitly encourages his subaltern) audience to conform to divine goodness; it should praise God for His infinite goodness and blame itself for spurning Him. Furthermore, as Augustine confesses how he has attained his present disposition of *confessio*, his direct audience should join him in praising God for His salutary presence in Augustine's past and present life, and feel holy remorse for those times when he spurned God.

How is Confessor Augustine's teaching "progressive"? Because it shows the stages whereby he transitioned toward an authentic happy life. However, since Confessor Augustine explains this within his objective account of happiness, we recognize that the progressive element is ultimately fashioned by the manner of *exitus-reditus*. What does this mean? First, Augustine imitates God incarnate by encouraging his audience to embrace *confessio*. Therefore, Augustine understands his present relationship with God as a positive development with more development, God-willing, to come. Most important, Confessor Augustine's recounting his past through his present (cf. 11.28.38) is characterized by praising God, so that confessing his past (through the prism of praising divine goodness) returns himself and his audience to their present for the purpose of augmenting divine praise. Hence, Augustine's *exitus* into his past, from his present, is for the sake of *reditus* to the present, i.e., to promote *confessio*.

Consequently, after explaining key aspects of *confessio* in 1.1.1, Augustine considers how his mindset developed in infancy, childhood, and early adolescence. Our analysis has shown, however, that Augustine's teaching depicts how he rejected God (*exitus*) and began to return to Him (*reditus*). In this respect, books 1–4 are generally rather than strictly progressive. However, since the principal matter Augustine considers consists in showing the dynamic of right relationship—through Christ—between divine goodness and human response, the decline away from God he describes in books 1–2 is subordinate to the partial return to God depicted in books 3–4. Moreover, just as Augustine's account of the decline is "progressive" since his mindset goes from bad to worse, so his doctrine of conforming to God, described in books 3–4, is progressive since his mindset is improving.

What constitutes Augustine's confessing these earlier stages in his life? Using aspects of *conf*.'s account of infancy, we see that young Augustine, to ever-greater degrees, subordinates the divine to the human order and the entirety to his desire for praise through domination. As *Conf.* explains it, this negative development culminates in Augustine's pear-theft since he then subordinates the whole of external reality to self-praise. Why is this theft so bad? Not because of the pears as such but because of claiming divine status for oneself and the gang. In one way, Augustine's mindset is consistent with his earlier presumptuous mindsets in infancy and childhood. But this mindset is worse since it intentionally subordinates the divine to a counterfeit order that Augustine and his friends have invented—perhaps even to some counterfeit order belonging to Augustine alone. Young Augustine behaved as if he were God.

By contrast, books 3–4 depict positive development because Confessor Augustine presents a younger self who, while presumptuous, moves *toward* natural humility and, therefore, *toward confessio.* Riddled with guilt by his exploitation of others in service of self-divinization, young Augustine is open to embracing a rule of life allowing him to live what he then conceives as proper. As such, he is motivated, while reading Cicero's *Hortensius,* to pursue Wisdom. But what Augustine then embraces as Wisdom, viz. Manichean religion, only moderates rather than eradicates his egoism. While Manichean religion offers Augustine a way to salve his conscience, it nevertheless countenances a lifestyle encouraging vanity since it understands vanity to be natural rather than voluntary. Hence, the religion's practical import, which includes feeding select foods to the so-called elect, is absurd. Moreover, as Confessor Augustine both directly claims (e.g., 3.6.10–10.18) and shows by recounting his younger self's response to the death of his then best friend (4.4.7–12.19), the Manichean account of reality is absurd since it substitutes constructs of the imagination for mutable and immutable reality knowable via reflection on sense experience and intelligence.

However, Confessor Augustine shows his younger self progressed morally and intellectually during these years. At the beginning of book 3 (3.1.1–3.6), Augustine—in pursuing women, knowledge, and enjoyment of theatrical spectacles—is both vain and thereby discomforted. However, at the outset of book 4 (4.1.1–3.6), we find that Augustine, though principally motivated by vanity, readily subordinates himself to aspects of the human order and, more important, to intellectual reality. Although his pursuits and notions of God and everything else remain contradictory, we notice (as his determination to pursue Wisdom shows) a *greater* willingness to subordinate mind and will to things objective. In this respect, Augustine is progressing toward Wisdom.

All told, Confessor Augustine's universal and progressive confession within books 1–4 maintains his younger self implicitly rejected and began to journey toward *confessio*. While negative development is found in books 1–2 and positive development in books 3–4, Augustine's confessional standpoint entails that the entirety is set within a universal and progressive framework. According to Augustine, each human is structured to pursue happiness (1.1.1; 10.20.29). But whether persons are intermittently and ultimately happy or miserable depends on whether each embraces true happiness, manifest in practicing *confessio*. Because Confessor Augustine wants people to be both intermittently and ultimately happy, he confesses the key developments in his early life toward achieving "joy in God" (10.23.33).

Most important, as Augustine's confessing his past is always for returning himself and his audience to *confessio*, the universal and progressive elements we distinguished occur within, and are therefore caused by, the *exitus-reditus* structure of confessing. Those elements are presented through the prism of Confessor Augustine's praising God for His infinite goodness in Christ. Hence, Augustine begins both generally (e.g., 1.1.1–5.6) and particularly (e.g., 2.1.1; 3.1.1; 4.1.1) by praising God in Christ. Next, through the prism of praising God for His infinite goodness, Augustine considers how His presence in the past, even though it was unrecognized, has led him to Himself (in general, 1.6.7–4.16.30; in particular, 2.1.1; 3.1.1; 4.1.1). Finally, Augustine concludes by praising God, in principle more than before, since he now recognizes how God's goodness has led him to Himself (e.g., 1.20.31; 2.10.18; 4.16.31).

But, Augustine's notion of *confessio* is more extensive; therefore, as *conf.* teaches us more about *confessio*, we will supplement our account.

Further Study

Book 1: What does Confessor Augustine mean by *confessio*?
Who is Augustine's direct audience?
Who is Augustine's indirect audience?
How does Augustine think humility is related to *confessio*?
How does Augustine think persons can embrace *confessio*?
How does Augustine's doctrine of *confessio* handle its Nicene, pagan Platonist, and Manichean inheritances?

By what structure does Confessor Augustine judge young Augustine's infancy?

How does Confessor Augustine characterize young Augustine's relationship to *confessio* in childhood?

Book 2: What is young Augustine's relationship toward *confessio* as he falls into sexual lust?

Why does young Augustine steal pears, and why does Confessor Augustine think that entailed an explicitly anti-*confessio* mindset?

Book 3: Why is young Augustine inspired to pursue Wisdom?

How does Confessor Augustine characterize young Augustine's mindset as a Manichean?

Book 4: What does Confessor Augustine mean to teach by young Augustine's response to the death of his best friend?

How does young Augustine's mindset develop for the better while he is a Manichean?

Articles

Breyfogle, 35–52
Cavadini, 25–34
Crosson (1989), 84–97
David (2018), 8–32
MacDonald (2003), 393–414
Mann (2006), 1–16
Mathewes, 7–23
Wetzel (2003), 53–69

Books

BeDuhn (2010), 21–105, 303–29
David (2019), 17–66
McMahon (1989), 42–74
O'Donnell, 2@3–280
O'Meara (1965), 69–86
Starnes (1990), 1–112
Vaught (2003), 22–114
Wills (2001), 88–123; (2011), 17–38

2

Confessions 5–7, Discovering *Confessio* is Reasonable

Introduction

Confessor Augustine now instructs that *confessio* is man's proper disposition toward Wisdom in three parts. First, he explains why young Augustine's (i) study of the liberal arts, especially his analyses of the natural philosophers and the skeptical doctrines of the Academics, and (ii) listening to Bishop Ambrose's sermons helped him leave the Manicheans and reenroll as a Catholic catechumen. Second, Confessor Augustine describes catechumen Augustine's miserable lifestyle. While pursuing an indubitable knowledge of Wisdom (he wants to know Wisdom [6.4.6] with the same certitude as 7+3 = 10) he sought, as his *Summum Bonum*, sexual pleasure, money, honor, and fame. As such, *conf.* teaches it is better to "believe to understand" than "to pursue understanding to believe." Although Augustine's pursuing certitude allows him to recognize, more than before, the futility of his secular pursuits, it is misplaced because, as a catechumen, he would have been better off if he had believed the Catholic religion. Then, like Monnica (6.1.1–2.2), he would have embraced a reasonable lifestyle disposing him to discovering Wisdom's cognitive aspects.

Finally, in book 7, Confessor Augustine details how catechumen Augustine's philosophical analyses of materialist and then of pagan Platonist philosophical theologies and cosmologies helped him see that the Catholic religion's account of Wisdom, and, consequently, the disposition of *confessio*, is reasonable. Based on catechumen

Augustine's indubitable experience of Wisdom (7.10.16), and subsequent recognition that Catholic teaching of "the Word made flesh" persuasively articulates Wisdom, Confessor Augustine instructs that man's proper disposition toward God entails union with Christ.

Conf. 5: Leaving the Manicheans to Reenroll as a Catholic Catechumen

Conf. 5[1] begins by juxtaposing young Augustine's learning regarding Nature with his growing dissatisfaction, on that basis, with Manichean doctrine. Significantly, he understands that the natures and movements of the celestial bodies are accessible to human intelligence. Concerning their essence, these bodies, taken individually, are naturally organized units (i.e., substances—cf. 4.16.28–9) rather than, as Manichean cosmology implies, unnatural unities resulting from "evil" material's taking captive "good," i.e., divine, material. This is because these bodies' movements, viewed both individually and as parts of a collective, are essentially rational since intellectual study, including sense observation and mathematical calculation,[2] shows they are predictable and law-like.[3] By contrast, the Manichean account of these bodies' movements, as young Augustine then understood the matter, could not be verified by analysis. While the Manicheans claimed these movements were intelligible they could not show how.

Augustine was bothered by the discrepancy between the natural philosophers and Manicheans, but he was told that Bishop Faustus would eventually explain Manichean doctrine. Augustine, "probably" because of his piety, was willing to wait for Faustus's arrival and explanation.[4] I say "probably" since, although Augustine might have been dissatisfied with Manichean piety on other grounds (e.g., because of what he had learned from his friend's death [*conf.* 4]), it recognized and sought to expiate vanity. On this score, the Manichean religion at once indicted young Augustine's vain pursuits yet, since viewing these as unavoidable, gave him license to pursue them, offering some means, however bizarre, for the divine elements constituting him to be released, after death, from captivity to the evil elements also constituting him. In short, Augustine likely believed the Manicheans were right about the evil of vanity and probably enjoyed that their doctrine supported his vain ambitions. When Faustus finally arrived, however, he was unable to explain Manichean doctrine. Although Augustine was pleased by Faustus's intellectual humility[5] and manner of speaking,[6] and even deigned to teach him certain liberal arts,[7] he was disappointed by Faustus's ignorance of Manichean cosmology.[8] Consequently, Augustine lost his ardor to progress in the Manichean sect.[9] His viewpoint was that he would remain a Manichean until he could find a more reasonable account of Wisdom: "My position was that I had not found anything more satisfactory than that into which I had somehow fallen. I decided to be content for the time being unless perhaps something preferable should come to light."[10] Augustine probably judged that Manichean Wisdom, which set together science and piety,[11] was doubtful about science but appealing regarding vanity. While he may have had reservations about the Manichean religion as a whole, at least a portion was to his liking. Hence, he would remain a Manichean until finding a more credible account of Wisdom—i.e., an account that not only identified Wisdom with Christ but also had a more reasonable view of science and an at least equal attitude toward vanity.

In conjunction with his dissatisfaction, yet continued affiliation with the Manicheans, the ambitious Augustine resolves to move from Carthage to Rome to procure a better teaching position. Confessor Augustine claims his decision was based principally on news that the students at Rome were more virtuous than the ones at Carthage since they "went quietly about their studies and were kept in order by a stricter imposition of discipline"[12]—note Augustine's desire for honest students. Encouraged by his Manichean friends,[13] and while lying to his mother (note the contradiction concerning honesty) about his intention to cross the Mediterranean,[14] Augustine departs for Rome.[15] When he arrives, however, he is seriously ill.[16] Once he recovers, though, and while remaining within the circle of and receiving sociopolitical favors from highly influential Manicheans, Augustine finds something in the skeptical doctrine of the Academics[17] that appears, in a threefold manner, to give impetus to his quest for Wisdom.

First, the skeptical doctrine underscores Augustine's dissatisfaction with the Manicheans—for their total position was incoherent. While he probably agreed with their indictment of vanity, he was unsure of their natural science. However, since they joined religious understanding and practice with scientific claims about physical reality, doubt about the latter naturally raised doubts about the former. So, Augustine found in skepticism something congenial to his view of Manichean Wisdom. His secular ambitions could remain. Second, Augustine probably noticed that although the natural philosophers had knowledge concerning the celestial bodies' movements, their knowledge was incomplete. For, as Nature does not always agree with human discovery, Nature's law must ultimately transcend the natural philosophers' calculations.[18] Put differently, the scientist's conclusions depend on, rather than cause, the celestial bodies' movements. Moreover, the natural philosophers lacked an account for the presence and expiation of vanity. Hence, Augustine's acquaintance with skeptical doctrine probably helped him notice the natural philosophers' (i) relatively superior but still limited intellectual insights and (ii) disinterest in the claim that Christ is Wisdom—and all this likely motivated him to search for Wisdom. Third, it is evident that Augustine's skepticism opened his mind to the Catholic religion. Since he was skeptical about Manichean doctrine but continued to think carnally concerning Catholicism's teachings about God, evil, Christ, and the Old Testament,[19] he more respected than defended his Manichean hosts' viewpoints.[20]

However, based on his Manichean affiliation, Augustine maintained his ambition and, in a manner laden with irony,[21] this eventually leads him from the Manicheans.[22] This is because the ambitious Augustine's eventual appointment, by the aid of Manichean, Count Symmachus,[23] as chief *rhetor* at the Milanese imperial court brings him into the orbit of Ambrose, the kindly Catholic bishop of Milan,[24] whose oratorical skill is renowned and, for which reason, *rhetor* Augustine attended his sermons. While assessing Ambrose's oratorical skill, which he found impressive,[25] Augustine somewhat reluctantly[26] judged that the Catholic account of Wisdom was, in fact, defensible and "equally valid" to the Manichean account.[27]

Why, therefore, does young Augustine eventually leave the Manicheans and reenroll as a Catholic catechumen?[28] Confessor Augustine claims that choice was eminently *reasonable*. How so? Following from young Augustine's (i) preeminent desire to identify Wisdom with Christ (3.4.7–8) and (ii) the Academic's doctrine to doubt all things, he appears to have considered the three possibilities concerning Wisdom standing before him, viz. (i) the Manichean religion, (ii) the natural philosophers, and (iii) the Catholic religion. Since he preferred the philosophers' account of Nature to the Manichean, but the Manicheans connected Wisdom with their teaching on Nature,[29] he discounted their claim to Wisdom. However, since the natural philosophers made no mention of Christ he "altogether refused to entrust . . . [to them] . . . the healing of . . . [his] . . . soul's sickness."[30] The self-consciously vain Augustine preferred the Catholic religion since, like the Manicheans, it identified Wisdom with Christ (and consequently promised to heal vanity) but, unlike the Manicheans, its teachings on Wisdom were not based on ostensible natural science. Therefore, although Augustine did not identify the Catholic religion as Wisdom, he thought it *reasonable* to learn about it. Hence, he "decided for the time being to be a catechumen in the Catholic Church, which the precedent of my parents recommended to me, until some light should come by which I could direct my course."[31]

Confessor Augustine teaches, then, it is reasonable for persons of intelligence and conscience to consider whether the Catholic religion is Wisdom and, consequently, that man's proper disposition is humility. It is important to note *conf.* shows how young Augustine has progressed intellectually (and perhaps morally too). How so? Based on his study of the liberal arts Augustine desires to conform his mind and will, in a greater degree than before, to "objective" reality. What young Augustine recognized about Wisdom in 3.4.7, viz. that it mandates a proper understanding *and* way of life, is becoming stronger in his mind as he aims to know the truth of things rather than impose his judgments thereon. While the earlier Augustine, both before and during his Manichean affiliation, sought to conform physical reality and Wisdom itself to figments of his imagination, book 5's Augustine strives to conform his sense observation and judgments thereon to physical reality itself, and shows the same attitude toward Wisdom. That attitude is less presumptuous than before.

What about conscience? Although book 5 hardly mentions this, a principal reason Augustine vows to explore the Catholic religion is because he knows his pursuits are vain (lying to his mother and taking new jobs at Rome and Milan give evidence for this) and wants to be healed thereof. Hence, Augustine's decision to reenroll as a Catholic catechumen shows recognition of an objective standard and motion toward humility. Augustine's (i) assimilation and application of liberal learning, and (ii) eventual enrolling as a

Catholic catechumen evince intellectual and moral progress since he embraces, to a greater extent than before, the notion that the Wisdom he met, while reading Cicero's *Hortensius*, is objective.

Confessor Augustine instructs, therefore, that pursuing liberal learning, broadly conceived, within the quest for Wisdom is fruitful since it implies openness to subordinating oneself to an objective order. As such, we distinguish movement toward *confessio*. But is the Catholic religion Wisdom? In books 6–7, Confessor Augustine explains why the answer is affirmative and, therefore, that man's proper disposition is *confessio*.

Conf. 6: The Skeptical Catechumen

In *conf.* 6,[32] Confessor Augustine characterizes his mindset as a new catechumen: "I had no confidence and had lost hope that truth could be found."[33] Contrasted with mother Monnica's faith, hope, and love,[34] young Augustine's life was riddled by ignorance, frustration, and despair because of his desire to attain an indubitable knowledge of Wisdom equivalent to the certitude available in mathematics.[35] Confessor Augustine shows how this attitude—that even young Augustine knew to be untenable[36]—prompted painful practical difficulties, by recounting the pursuit of honor, money, and marriage at that time. Yet, we notice a measure of progress since we detect a greater recognition and willingness, than before, to conform to some objective standard and therefore embrace the humility leading to *confessio*.[37] Augustine sees, albeit negatively, not only the need for normativity but also that the latter, like mathematical principles, is properly unchangeable.

Conf. discloses that young Augustine's practical problems proceeded from frustrations concerning knowing whether the Catholic religion represents Wisdom. There are two closely related reasons for this. First, he was filled with self-reproach and embarrassment[38] for he saw, through attending Ambrose's sermons, that the accusations he had formerly levelled against Catholic doctrine were based on opinion rather than knowledge.[39] Second, and more significantly, since Augustine recognized the value of belief or opinion in cognitive matters, and therefore favored the Catholic religion's view of the Bible,[40] he nevertheless refused to embrace the Catholic religion as Wisdom. Why not? Worried about "a precipitate plunge,"[41] he was unwilling to assent apart from certitude:

> I wanted to be as certain about things I could not see as . . . that seven and three are ten. I was not so mad as to think that I could consider even that to be something unknowable. But I desired other things to be as certain as this truth, whether physical objects which were not immediately accessible to my senses or spiritual matters which I knew no way of thinking about except in physical terms.[42]

This mindset accentuated Augustine's misery in several ways since he saw, more than before, his vain lifestyle. First, while preparing to deliver a panegyric on the emperor he encountered a drunken beggar whereupon, comparing the latter's state to his own, he recognized the beggar was relatively better off.[43] Why so? Because the beggar, being drunk, already enjoyed his besought pleasure; and the means to attain that pleasure, viz. alcoholic drink, was honestly obtained by wishing well to others.[44] By contrast, Augustine, racked with anxiety, had not yet achieved the pleasure he wanted, and the means to attain it, viz. the audience's approval of lies, was both dishonest and uncertain.[45] So, although the drunken beggar and Augustine were seeking different kinds of pleasure by different means, the outcome, viz. a kind of transitory mental pleasure,[46] was essentially the same. In that respect, the beggar was in a relatively better state since he already enjoyed pleasure and obtained it by honest means.

Augustine already recognized his vanity, and the problem of vanity had caused him to seek Wisdom in the first place. However, looking at the beggar's plight in light of his own quest for an indubitable knowledge of Wisdom allowed Augustine to recognize more his vanity.[47] Augustine's self-disgust was probably severe because his cognitive state was clearer than ever on the difference between the Wisdom he preferred, as cognitively certain, and the secular honor, being transient and uncertain, he was seeking. Psychological pain is heightened since Augustine has more awareness of the difference between what ought to be and what is.

Augustine's close friends and friendships[48] are likewise vitiated. Based on awareness of Wisdom's stability, Confessor Augustine notices how he and his friends practiced behavior both motivated by and recognized as vanity. Augustine's close friend Alypius,[49] for example, had an affection for Augustine, the young *rhetor*, because Augustine seemed "good and cultured"[50] and had befriended Alypius by appealing to "virtue."[51] Alypius, moreover, has a job as assessor "to the court of the Italian Treasury"[52] wherein he behaves with honesty and integrity.[53] However, Alypius brags about his practical "virtue" (note his desire for glory[54]) and it fails when tested for, succumbing to curiosity (note his vanity), he both contradicts chastity[55] and avidly enjoys the gladiatorial shows at Rome after originally stating he would forsake them.[56] As such, Alypius's "virtue," however laudable, ultimately has fickle human praise, rather than stable Wisdom, as its object. Moreover, although he is little mentioned, another close friend of Augustine living with them at Milan, viz. Nebridius, had a similar character.[57]

Unfortunately, Augustine shares the same mindset. By appealing to "virtue," Augustine persuaded Alypius to join him in seeking Wisdom[58] and seems to have established a household comprised of fellow-seekers after Wisdom.[59] Moreover, he consents, due to his mother's matchmaking and blessing, to pursue a Christian marriage,[60] and considers establishing some kind of commune wherein he, his companions, and their wives and families can continue searching for Wisdom.[61] In addition, Augustine dismisses his longtime concubine (i.e., common-law wife), who he deeply cares for[62] and with whom he has fathered a son, Adeodatus (whom he keeps after that relationship dissolves), for the noble intention to practice chastity in advance of marriage;[63] and he claims that friendship is this life's greatest good.[64]

However, Augustine's "virtue" was inadequate since it was permeated by vanity. His example of sexual lust encourages Alypius to indulge his curiosity for illicit sexual activity.[65] Moreover, Augustine's dismissal of his concubine seems callous;[66] he wants to marry the Christian woman for money and regular future sexual activity rather than from love of Truth or of marriage;[67] and the commune project explodes since he and his companions had not taken counsel concerning that matter from their wives and/or wives to be.[68] Additionally, Augustine refrains from finding out, notably from Bishop Ambrose,[69] if the Catholic religion is Wisdom;[70] and soon after dismissing his concubine, he quickly takes another because he cannot do without regular sexual activity.[71] At bottom, Augustine subordinates his quest for Wisdom to secular ambition—including, it seems, to his satisfaction in human friendship.[72]

Therefore, like Alypius and Nebridius, Augustine's desire for Wisdom is subordinate to transient goods. Moreover, recognizing this contradiction caused him great pain. Although Augustine knows he does not know Wisdom, he knows enough about Wisdom to know his mindset is vain—and this hurts. He has long known his vanity, but recognizing this now is more painful on account of thinking that Wisdom, whatever it is, must be unchanging. How does this contribute to Augustine's misery? This notion of Wisdom allows him to see not only that he seeks transient pleasures but also that he commonly uses dishonest means to attain them.

Hence, *conf.* shows that Augustine has progressed toward Wisdom, and therefore *confessio*, by showing greater awareness of vanity. Although Augustine remains vain, his dissatisfaction with that has increased. While he lacks positive knowledge of Wisdom, the fact that he thinks it is permanent allows him to see, more clearly than before, the essentially transient forms of pleasure he seeks and the sometimes dishonest means he employs to achieve them. Obviously, Confessor Augustine thinks the catechumen has some kind of genuine zeal for Wisdom and wishes us to notice the benefit found therein. However, Confessor Augustine also claims the catechumen would have been better off to have lived, like mother Monnica,[73] on the basis of faith, hope, and love.[74] For, other things being equal, that would have allowed discovery that the Catholic religion possessed the certitude Augustine affiliated with Wisdom, along with a cogent account of those matters concerning Wisdom, viz. sensible particulars, outside of Augustine's immediate experience.[75] Imitating Monnica, then, would have allowed him to behave in accord with what he then knew of Wisdom.

Nevertheless, since Augustine subordinated his quest for Wisdom to transient satisfactions, his vanity closed off that avenue of discovery. Although progressing toward *confessio*, he continues to pursue Wisdom on his own terms.

Conf. 7: Discovering that Confessio is Reasonable

In *conf.* 7[76] Confessor Augustine instructs (i) on the proximate steps whereby he learned the Catholic religion proclaims Wisdom and, consequently, (ii) that man's proper disposition toward Wisdom is *confessio*. Catechumen Augustine ultimately embraces (intellectually) the Catholic religion's claim that Christ, "the Word made flesh," is Wisdom because he finds therein two things he was seeking. These are, *first*, the certitude concerning Wisdom introduced to his pursuit of Wisdom through applying thereto the Academic's skeptical doctrines[77] and, *second*, a prospective cure for the vain lifestyle he was leading both before and after his decision, at eighteen, to pursue Christ as Wisdom.[78]

Confessor Augustine's verification of the Catholic religion's claim concerning Christ can be difficult to recount since it moves on two overlapping levels, viz. (i) intimate, personal experience and (ii) "universalizable" personal experience. As such, Augustine cites his intimate experience of Wisdom (e.g., 7.10.16; 21.23), subsequent quest for verification, and the significant material causes facilitating these.

Augustine maintains the indubitable truth found in his intimate experience of God is available through common means and, *therefore*, the Catholic doctrine of "the Word made flesh" is *cogent*. This is because while one portion of that doctrine can be known with certitude, another portion can be known by a kind of high probability and "fittingness" grounded in certitude. What does that mean? First, Augustine maintains that adhering to Catholic teaching (as a catechumen), certain intellectual principles, and specific study of pagan Platonist philosophy allows one to know, *certissima ratione*, the existence and key attributes of the immutable Word. Augustine teaches that each of (i) Wisdom's goodness, (ii) the existence of objective norms for thought and action, and (iii) that Wisdom provides a way for persons to enjoy Him both in this life and in hereafter can be known with certitude. Second, Augustine implies that the Catholic claim concerning the Word's assumption of a human nature (i.e., of *flesh*) is *cogent* because it includes the above certitudes and, on that basis, fulfills what can be known with certitude about divine mediation.

The Catholic doctrine of divine incarnation, therefore, cannot be known *certissima ratione* but as highly probable or fitting since grounded in the certitude of the Word's being and therefore goodness. Why is that teaching fitting? Since man is mutable, divine mediation needs to employ mutable circumstances. Consequently, that one can verify the doctrine "the Word made flesh" by a combination of (i) certitude and (ii) certitude governed probability means Catholic teaching is cogent. Augustine argues, then, that man's proper disposition consists in *confessio* since each owes to Christ his being, governance, and *telos*. (While *confessio* to God is known with certitude, *confessio* to God incarnate follows by implication.)

Near the beginning of *conf.* 7, catechumen Augustine resolves to assess Catholic doctrine[79] to see whether its claim that Christ is Wisdom can be verified, to some extent,[80] by indubitable knowledge.[81] Since Augustine now recognizes that Wisdom, in its entirety, cannot be verified *certissima ratione* (6.5.7–8), he focuses instead on certain key corollaries. These are that (i) God, the creator of all, is good,[82] (ii) God made all things good,[83] (iii) evil is not created by God,[84] and (iv) humans sin by free choice of will (*liberum voluntatis arbitrium*)[85] rather than by necessity (as the Manicheans had implied). Augustine examines these claims by employing several intellectual principles co-implicate with his desire to achieve indubitable knowledge of Wisdom. These principles are "that what is immutable is better than what is mutable,"[86] "that what is incorruptible is superior to what is corruptible,"[87] and "that what is immune to injury is superior to what can be injured."[88] Although *conf.* does not say so,[89] these principles appear concomitant with catechumen Augustine's quest for an indubitable knowledge of Wisdom since they maintain, similar to mathematical truth, that Wisdom (if capable of being known) must be immutable and unchanging.[90]

Hence, catechumen Augustine examines the Church doctrine by applying the aforementioned principles. To illustrate how this went and what was discovered, Confessor Augustine divides book 7 into three parts. These show (i) the irrationality of materialism (7.1.1–6.10), (ii) the advantage of employing pagan Platonism as a material cause (7.9.13–16.22), and (iii) why the Catholic doctrine that Christ is Wisdom is cogent (7.17.23–21.27).

Augustine initially applies the aforementioned principles to his corporeal notions of God and being, and the result is insight and frustration. First, he sees that such notions contradict a coherent account of God, the origin of evil, and human responsibility—and prove false the Manichean religion. While thinking God is corporeal means He is divisible and corruptible rather than immutable and incorruptible,[91] the notions He creates evil and humans sin by necessity entail the same.[92] Hence, Augustine understood the folly both of astrology[93] and of Manichean cosmology[94] since each is premised on the claim that God is mutable. However, Augustine is frustrated since he lacks knowledge of God.[95] Although he *believes* the Church's claims concerning God, the origin of evil, and human responsibility, he cannot verify them. Confessor Augustine remarks, however, that catechumen Augustine has the good fortune of receiving direction from persons willing to share key texts in Platonist philosophy.[96] This has the happy result that Augustine finally achieves an indubitable knowledge not only concerning the previously mentioned matters but also, and more important, concerning Wisdom's relationship with man. It is vital to note, though, that Confessor Augustine introduces his audience to Platonist philosophy, to the "*quosdam platonicorum libros ex graeca lingua in latinam versos*,"[97] with a great caution and reserve. At the outset, Augustine (i) remarks he received these books from a "man puffed up with monstrous pride *(immanissimo typho turgidum)*"[98] and (ii) uses words found in the Catholic scriptures, specifically from *the Prologue to John's Gospel*, to signify the realities he both found and did not find *(non ibi legi)* in the Platonist books.[99]

Why does Confessor Augustine do this? Three closely connected reasons come to mind. First, he wants his reader to recognize the "Platonist books" are deficient since they encourage an attitude of pride, rather than humility, toward God—engendering knowledge *and* folly[100] rather than knowledge *in the service of* wisdom.[101] Second, Augustine shows that learning found outside Catholic scriptures can help one understand that scripture[102] and, correspondingly, that scripture contains the highest learning.[103] Third, and perhaps more important, Augustine claims that the scriptures, by contrast with pagan Platonist philosophy, employ words in a special manner. How so? It is not simply that divine realities are signified in a noncontradictory manner but (as *conf.* 12 clarifies) words are employed in humility, apart from ostentation, to encourage love of God and neighbor.[104] Taken altogether, Augustine asserts that learning gained from Platonist philosophy is a material cause within Christian wisdom.

How do the Platonist books aid catechumen Augustine discover several related truths?[105] Most important, he sees that God is immutable[106] and therefore incorporeal;[107] and Wisdom is knowable with certitude by intelligence[108] since soul, and therefore its primary powers, is incorporeal and mutable and depends on Wisdom.[109] From those insights follow four important corollaries. First, Wisdom/God provides a way for man to enjoy Him in this life and forever in eternity.[110] Second, God has created all things good.[111] Third, evil is a privation in a substance rather than a substance.[112] Fourth, moral evil results from abusing choice of will by subordinating the Creator to some creature.[113]

To begin, Augustine claims he was more certain of God's existing than of himself: "I would have found it easier to doubt whether I was myself alive than that there is no truth 'understood from the things that are made' (Rom. 1: 20)."[114] Difficulty arises, however, as he tries to verify the Catholic doctrine of Wisdom. The account of God as immutable is fine since it can be substantiated by Platonist philosophy but, as the remainder of *conf.* 7 shows, Augustine wonders about the means God employs to bring about the beatitude He promises. If God is immutable, what is the medium by which He augments mutable man so he can permanently share in divine immutability? How does immutable Wisdom mediate Himself to man since, as Augustine's experience showed and Platonist philosophy implies, that mediation needs to be both immutable (since God is man's *telos*) *and* mutable (since Wisdom mediates to man)? Augustine, moreover, pursues mediation not only because of his ontological separation from God[115] but also because he recognizes his separation is exacerbated by vanity in general and unruly sexual desire in particular.[116] In short, Augustine is motivated to pursue divine mediation by his vision of God and by his long-held desire to embrace a wise lifestyle.

Nevertheless, catechumen Augustine initially rejects the teaching that "the Word made flesh" is mediator, since he thinks it maintains that God becomes human.[117] Since this notion contradicts knowledge that mediation is immutable *and* mutable, he searches the Platonist books. Once again, however, he finds contradiction. How so? Platonist doctrine teaches that mutable reality depends on immutable reality and therefore that man requires greater participation in Wisdom to be united with Him.[118] However, the Platonists maintain that "mediation" is effected by subordinating immutable to mutable reality, i.e., by worshipping creatures and imitating Platonist philosophers.[119] Hence, Augustine maintains that Christ, perhaps like Plotinus, is merely an excellent man showing an exemplary lifestyle. This is problematic because Augustine, by the aid of Platonist philosophy, knows the Word is immutable and, by His intimate experience, that He offers *man* means to completely participate in Him. Hence, catechumen Augustine discovers that pagan Platonists do not actually have a doctrine of mediation.

Motivated by insight and desperation, Augustine reexamines the Catholic scriptures and finds a reasonable account of mediation in scripture's description of Christ as "the Word made flesh."[120] He now understood that "the Word made flesh" does not mean that God became man.[121] Rather, by reading closely the epistles of St. Paul, Augustine learned Catholic doctrine means God takes to Himself a human nature so humans can, by grace, overcome their ontological and moral differences from God and, consequently, lead a divine lifestyle.[122] Catholic doctrine, Augustine discovers, teaches that mediation is immutable *and* mutable since Christ is both God and man.

Hence, Confessor Augustine teaches that the Catholic account of divine mediation is coherent since it fulfills what can be known with certitude about Wisdom. How so? Not in the way of drawing through a certain implication from what can be known about Wisdom—as 8–4 = 4 follows from 4+4 = 8. Rather, verification pertains to drawing through the certain implication that Wisdom offers mutable means of mediation. The claim that Christ is mediator, since pertaining to mutable reality, cannot be verified *certissima ratione*. While one can know from knowing the Word that there is divine mediation employing mutable reality, mediation's concrete character cannot be inferred *certissima ratione* since that is God's prerogative.

However, the Catholic doctrine of "the Word made flesh" is eminently reasonable (and therefore "fitting") since, from a cognitive perspective, it coheres with what can be known *certissima ratione*. It is reasonable because it presents a mutable means cohering with the aforementioned certitude. The "made flesh" aspect of "the Word made flesh" describes both what the Word does for "the flesh," i.e., for wayward humanity, and how He does that, viz. by taking human mutability to His immutability. Hence, Augustine finds Catholic doctrine *cogent* since he has achieved certitude about Wisdom— including His promise of meditation—and has before him, in the Catholic scriptures, an account of mediation grounded therein. Taken altogether, Augustine recognizes as reasonable the Catholic claim that Christ is Wisdom. As such, he is eager to "embrace Him": "I meditated upon your works and trembled (Hab. 3:2)."[123]

Conclusion

In books 5–7, Augustine confesses in a universal and progressive manner that *confessio*, centered in humble worship of God incarnate, is man's proper disposition.

How is Augustine's confession universal? As before, it appeals to a principal audience, viz. those sharing Augustine's account of happiness and, because of happiness' nature, it addresses a subaltern audience that does not share, but has a general orientation toward, Augustine's view of happiness. It is true, then, that Confessor Augustine relates his personal experience. Among other things, young Augustine studied the liberal arts, found intelligible certain teachings of the natural philosophers, met the Manichean bishop Faustus, was disappointed with Faustus's account of Manichean cosmology, left Carthage for Rome and Milan to procure a better job, lied to his mother when departing from Carthage, benefitted from Manichean friends, was appointed chief *rhetor* at the Western imperial court in Milan, embraced the skeptical aspects of the Academic philosophy, listened to and benefitted from Bishop Ambrose's sermons at Milan, reenrolled as a Catholic catechumen, was engaged to be married, dismissed his concubine but quickly replaced her with another, analyzed Catholic teachings according to criteria placing immutable above mutable reality, studied Platonist philosophy, had an intimate experience of Wisdom, measured the Catholic and pagan Platonist accounts of Wisdom by the aforementioned experience, and often behaved immorally. But, as mentioned previously, Augustine selects those events to illustrate his mindset regarding his response to divine goodness at those times.

Since Augustine's primary goal is to explain to those sharing with him an explicit relationship with God how and why *confessio* presently centers his life, he cites and interprets events in his past life. However, as mentioned previously, Augustine also speaks to a subaltern audience, i.e., to those having an implicit relationship with God. Therefore, while many differ from Augustine concerning historical circumstances, he thinks that each reader, *whether implicitly or explicitly*, either conforms to or rejects divine goodness. Since that, Confessor Augustine claims, is universal, he writes about a portion of his experience to encourage praising God.

How is Augustine's confession in books 5–7 progressive? First, his conclusion that *confessio* is reasonable is explained in consecutive stages. It is helpful to remember that Augustine presents us with a younger self who is seeking Wisdom (3.4.7–8), understood as man's proper life. Moreover, that younger self, when he first embraces Wisdom, is at the beginning of a trajectory wherein he will eventually discover, by reflection on doctrine and practical experience,

Wisdom's actual content. Therefore, Confessor Augustine argues that young Augustine embraced the Manichean religion not so much because it claimed that Christ is Wisdom (3.4.8) but, mostly, because he viewed it capable of serving his vanity. Young Augustine sincerely pursued Wisdom in the Manichean religion but did not then see its nature.

Concerning the Manichean religion, Augustine's attraction is twofold. First, he found what he thought was an intelligible philosophical theology and cosmology. Augustine was enamored with Manichean teaching because it, like him, conceived of reality by the mode of imagination and body—and, therefore, could be employed as a tool toward secular success. Second, Augustine also thought he noticed an intelligible philosophical anthropology. He was uncomfortable with his vain lifestyle and found in Manichean religion both recognition of the problem of vanity and some means to mitigate it. While Manichean religion recognized the problem of vanity, it tried to overcome it in a manner that, in the end, hardly interfered with vanity. Hence, Augustine liked the Manichean religion because it claimed loyalty to Christ and served his vain aims.

In book 5, Augustine progresses toward *confessio* in two obvious ways so that by book's end he has left the Manichean religion and reenrolled as a Catholic catechumen. First, he learns, through studying the liberal arts, that knowledge of natural bodies is achieved by conforming judgments to bodies rather than contrariwise. As such, his affinity for the Manicheans was relaxed but he remained in the sect, presumably because of its approach to ethical purification. Second, Augustine applies to his quest for Wisdom certain skeptical doctrines he learned while studying the liberal arts. That, together with his new learning (especially procured through the sermons of Bishop Ambrose) that the Catholic religion was credible, motivated him to reenroll as a catechumen.

Augustine preferred the teaching about the celestial bodies advanced by the natural philosophers. However, he preferred more the Catholic religion's claim to Wisdom since it promulgated a Christ-centered doctrine of Wisdom that (i) did not contradict the natural philosophers' teachings and (ii) teaches an appropriate way of life. Hence, Augustine shows willingness to pursue Wisdom in accord with "objective" reality. By this, Confessor Augustine implies the Catholic religion's account of Wisdom, and therefore of *confessio*, has significant rational underpinning.

In book 6, Confessor Augustine shows progress toward *confessio* by focusing on young Augustine's vitiated lifestyle. Augustine's mindset is contradictory but, due to his attempt to know objective reality, he recognizes his vanity more clearly than before. Because he wanted an indubitable knowledge of Wisdom, catechumen Augustine sees both the vain ends and sometimes vain means he seeks and/or employs. Since he thinks if there is Wisdom it must be objective, he better recognizes that his pursuits of fame, money, and marriage are essentially for transient pleasure. Hence, what bothers Augustine is not only, as before, that he pursues secular goods but also that he is more aware of his vanity; because he is clearer on his irrational behavior, he is more pained by it. Standing in contrast to Augustine's contradictory mindset is mother Monnica, whose mindset is peaceful since she embraces Catholic Wisdom by faith, hope, and charity.

In book 7, Confessor Augustine distinguishes progress toward *confessio* by showing how catechumen Augustine discovers *confessio* is man's proper disposition. Fed up by his sordid state, Augustine once again resolves to analyze Catholic teaching. By the end of book 7, catechumen Augustine knows, with almost certainty, that the Catholic account of Wisdom is true. How does he arrive at this conclusion? First, his quest to achieve indubitable knowledge of Wisdom is aided not only by the truth claims concerning Wisdom made by the Milanese Church and by upholding that God is immutable and incorruptible but also by studying the "Platonist books." Aided by the claim that God is immutable since incorporeal, Augustine is given, he says by God's aid, an intimate experience of Wisdom (7.10.16). Consequently, he sees, with certitude, that Wisdom is immutable and offers humanity the means to enjoy Him forever.

Next, catechumen Augustine discovers that the Catholic doctrine of "the Word made flesh" articulates Wisdom because He offers man the means to enjoy Him forever. Augustine begins his process of verification by drawing through various implications of the claim that Wisdom is the immutable God. As such, he understands conceptually, among other things (7.11.17–16.22), that (i) God has made all things good, (ii) evil is a privation rather than a substance, and (iii) humans sin by choice of will rather than by necessity.

But what about the Catholic religion's cardinal claim that God gives man the ability to enjoy Him forever through "the Word made flesh"? Although Augustine recognizes the need for divine mediation (e.g., 7.10.16; 21.23), it takes him a while to verify

Catholic doctrine. He initially thinks Catholic doctrine instructs that God became a man—in which case are contradicted both of his (i) intimate experience of Wisdom and (ii) philosophical knowledge of God. Augustine prefers the pagan Platonist teaching since it upholds divine immutability (7.20.26) but realizes, however, that imitating excellent character does not match up with his indubitable experience of Wisdom wherein God promised direct mediation so man can enjoy Him forever—and this is exacerbated by his awareness of sexual lust. This motivates Augustine to reconsider Catholic doctrine. With the aid of St. Paul's epistles (7.21.27), he sees that Catholicism teaches God takes to Himself a human nature so that, by His infinite goodness, man is made fit for permanent divine union. Hence, Confessor Augustine shows that the Catholic religion's claim concerning Christ is reasonable and that *confessio*, requiring man's acknowledgment of dependence on and gratitude toward Wisdom, is man's proper disposition.

Hence, Confessor Augustine's universal and progressive confession in books 5–7 explains that his younger self came to understand (i) how the Catholic religion's account of Christ is Wisdom and (ii) that man's proper disposition toward God consists in *confessio*. In this regard, Confessor Augustine, continuing from books 3–4, distinguishes key stages in his *reditus* toward God. By focusing on young Augustine's universal and progressive intellectual and moral development, Confessor Augustine leaves his principal audience with several cardinal insights. First, catechumens should follow Church teaching since "faith leads to understanding"; they should not be *radically* skeptical, since that sort of skepticism breeds misery. As pagan Platonist philosophy helps to show, there is available cognitive certitude concerning the Catholic religion's account of Wisdom as divine "Word"—including that He offers man the means to share forever in Him. Moreover, since the Catholic religion's account of Christ is grounded in the aforementioned certitudes, it reasonably claims He is the way to attain permanent union with God. Consequently, Confessor Augustine claims Catholic teaching provides an account of Wisdom fulfilling man's (i) intellectual capacity for truth and (ii) practical desire to live truly. Accordingly, man's proper response to God and neighbor consists in *confessio* since he can know, with certitude, that he has from God his being for the sake of fulfillment in Him and, with "next to certitude," that God in Christ provides the means whereby that can be accomplished.

Thus, Augustine's confessional standpoint in books 5–7 includes universal and progressive elements instructing that *confessio* is man's proper disposition. Since Augustine's confessing his past is always to *return* himself and his audience to present *confessio*, everything recounted in books 5–7 is set within an *exitus-reditus* structure. In light of and to develop *confessio* (e.g., 5.1.1, 6.1.1), Augustine turns from present to past (*exitus*) to present (*reditus*) (e.g., 6.16.26, 7.21.27). He thereby teaches that God incarnate, by his infinite goodness, guides human life toward *confessio*.

But, as the remainder of *conf.* clarifies, Augustine holds that (i) *confessio* is existential, i.e., cognitive *and* affective, and (ii) the pattern of confessing God's infinite goodness participates in the Godhead—matters implied since *conf.*'s outset.

Further Study

Book 5: What cognitive conditions govern the study of astronomy?

How does Augustine's study of the liberal arts help him notice deficiencies in the Manichean religion?

Do you think Augustine's decisions to pursue teaching positions first at Rome but later at Milan are related to his disaffection with Manichean religion? Please explain.

How does Augustine's listening to the sermons of Bishop Ambrose at Milan help him see the reasonableness of the Catholic religion?

How does Augustine's acquaintance with the skeptical doctrines of the Academics help him make the decision to reenroll as a Catholic catechumen?

Book 6: According to Confessor Augustine, what is the primary cause of catechumen Augustine's miserable lifestyle as a catechumen?

Do you think Augustine's pursuit of money, honor, and friendship is more miserable to him than ever before? Please explain.

Book 7: By what principles does catechumen Augustine assess the Catholic religion's teachings about God and His effects?

Why does catechumen Augustine see that trying to understand God and His effects by the mode of body brings irrational conclusions? Please explain.

How is catechumen Augustine helped by studying pagan Platonist philosophy? Please explain.

Why does catechumen Augustine understand that the Catholic account of Christ as Wisdom is cogent? Please explain.

Articles

Beatrice (1989), 248–81
Cary (2003), 107–26; (2020), 227–41
Crosson (2003), 71–87, 237–9
Crouse (2000), 37–50
King (2014), 6–27
MacDonald (2006), 85–105
Plumer, 89–105

Books

BeDuhn (2010), 106–302, 329–60
David (2019A), 67–110
McMahon (1989), 74–102
O'Donnell, 2@281–489
O'Meara (1965), 92–159
Starnes (1990), 113–211
Stock, 52–74, 77–89
Vaught (2003), 115–54, 172; (2004) 25–65, 145–9

3

Confessions 8–10, Living *Confessio*

Introduction

Confessor Augustine now instructs that Wisdom's lifestyle means being *existentially*, i.e., cognitively *and* affectively, united with Christ. First, in book 8, catechumen Augustine prepares to be joined with Christ by embracing existentially what he learned intellectually, and this eventually leads from presumption, i.e., claiming he has the resources to join himself with Christ, to humility, i.e., recognizing that Christ alone can join him with Himself. Then, by the good fortune of being offered and receiving Christ's grace, catechumen Augustine converts. Second, book 9 shows how God governed Augustine's preparation for baptism and life afterward so he instantiated *confessio*. In particular, we see how the newly baptized Augustine, especially through the example of Monnica and his response to her death, became clear on life's *telos* (9.10.23–6) and developed charity (9.12.29– 13.37). Finally, Augustine confesses his present life in book 10. This includes a brief explanation, at the end, for why he became a priest (10.43.70) but, more important, book 10 distinguishes the profound depth Augustine now knows and loves Wisdom. By considering his relationship with Wisdom according to its principal psychological dimensions, Confessor Augustine identifies soul's ontological (10.24.35–27.38) and active (10.41.66–43.69) dependence on Wisdom's presence, thereby offering existential proof that *confessio* is man's proper lifestyle.

All told, Augustine teaches in books 8–10 that, by Christ's infinite goodness, *confessio* consists in loving God and neighbor. This requires conforming to God's providence, wherein temporal reality is loved in God's eternal plan. Additionally, *confessio* is fortified by recognizing not only that the soul's innate pursuit of happiness ("joy in the truth"/in God [10.22.32]) represents a fixed orientation toward c*onfessio* but also that attaining Him requires cultivating Christ's present *and* future activity upon the soul. Therefore, while immutable divinity is spiritually present to each, cultivating His presence is decisive since that is the purpose of soul's ontological structure and inchoate spiritual union with God. Thus, book 10's conclusion contains these important words concerning Christ's mediation:

> With good reason my firm hope is in him. For you will cure all my diseases (Ps. 102: 3) through him who sits at your right hand and intercedes with you for us (Rom. 8:34). Otherwise I would be in despair. Many and great are those diseases, many and great indeed. But your medicine is still more potent. We might have thought your Word was far removed from being united with mankind and have despaired of our lot unless he had become flesh and dwelt among us. (Jn 1:14)[1]

In books 8–10, then, Augustine details that through Christ, he embraced the lifestyle of *confessio*. However, looking ahead to *conf.* 11–13, that lifestyle's center is Christ (11.2.4) regarding what He points to as the incarnate Word, viz. to God in Himself, the Trinity—Father, Word, and Holy Spirit. In this respect, Christ is the gateway to what stands beyond. God's goodness is, in one way, more transcendent and, in another way, more intimate to man than book 10 discloses.

Conf. 8

In *conf.* 8,[2] Confessor Augustine begins showing why the Catholic religion's claim that Christ provides a proper way of life is cogent. By explaining his conversion to Christ and some of its immediate effects, Augustine argues that conversion is congenial with the disposition of "natural" humility or "natural" *confessio* but determined by Christ's grace.³ Until catechumen Augustine embraced natural *confessio*, his mindset, though moving toward Wisdom, was yet opposed to it. However, once his intellect *and* will embraced natural *confessio*, he was *open to receiving*⁴ Christ's grace and, therefore, (supernatural) *confessio* and its beneficial effects.

An important clarification is required. I said "open to receiving" since as Confessor Augustine holds that immutable causes mutable being⁵ natural *confessio* does not cause (supernatural) *confessio*. A relationship of causal necessity, as thunder produces sound, does not exist between natural and supernatural *confessio*. Rather, by Augustine's principles,⁶ it is the other way around, meaning that supernatural causes natural *confessio* or, put differently, what is, in this instance, later in time causes what is prior. Hence, to the extent there is a causal relationship between the natural and the supernatural, it is because of the latter. Augustine's confessing his past in *conf.* is likewise structured, for he advocates the meaning of his past, present, and future is understood through the prism of *confessio*.

Until just before his conversion, then, catechumen Augustine contradicts, to varying degrees, the knowledge of Wisdom displayed in *conf.* 7 since he holds, albeit implicitly, that mutable causes immutable reality. Although Augustine wants to become a Christian, and book 8 depicts progressive stages of wanting, his inveterate presumption gets in the way. The problem is that catechumen Augustine's desire for vain delight blocks him from becoming Christian. The point is not that Augustine lacks real desire to join the Church. He has that, and it grows until the moment he is converted.⁷ However, until conversion, his desire to embrace Wisdom is weaker than his desire for vanities. Throughout book 8, then, Confessor Augustine presents us with a sequence of starts and stops, including interactions with Simplicianus, Ponticianus, and Alypius that bring catechumen Augustine closer to Wisdom. Conversion to Christ, however, is God's gift rather than the result of personal effort. Yet Confessor Augustine claims that catechumen Augustine's effort helped bring about *confessio*. How so? Since God, in His infinite Wisdom, used that sequence of events for catechumen Augustine to embrace *confessio*.

As Confessor Augustine remarks at the outset,⁸ catechumen Augustine's problem had nothing to do with achieving knowledge of Wisdom. Rather, his difficulty concerned embracing His lifestyle:⁹

"My desire was not to be more certain of you, but to be more stable in you."[10] Augustine preferred joining the Church as a celibate instead of as a married member. Yet he maintained his impending Christian marriage and the secular activities needed to support a married lifestyle, though he disliked them. Presumably, this is because, as past events show[11] and future events will make clear,[12] he desired secular goods more than he wanted to join the Church. Confessor Augustine describes his mindset at that time like this:

> My secular activity I held in disgust. . . . By now those prizes gave me no pleasure in comparison with your gentleness. . . . But I was still firmly tied by woman . . . and because of this one factor I was inconstant in other respects and was wasting away with nagging anxieties.[13]

For aid, young Augustine visits Simplicianus, a counselor to Bishop Ambrose. Simplicianus's advice motivates Augustine but not enough. Although Simplicianus encourages him to embrace "the humility of Christ"[14] by describing Victorinus's conversion,[15] and Augustine is thereby motivated to join the Church,[16] he ultimately refuses because of his greater love for secular delights: "The burden of the world weighed me down with a sweet drowsiness such as commonly occurs during sleep."[17]

However, since Augustine wants to become a celibate Christian, he is especially inspired by Ponticianus's account of monasticism.[18] Nevertheless, this motivation also proves inadequate since, although Augustine is more disgusted than ever by his vanity,[19] he discovers *he* does not have the native power to desire celibacy. Hard as he tries,[20] his will to become celibate cannot overwhelm his "old" will: "The body obeyed the slightest inclination of the soul to move the limbs at its pleasure more easily than the soul obeyed itself, when its supreme desire could be achieved exclusively by the will alone."[21] Although he progressed, Augustine could not "leap" from the one lifestyle to the other due to the weight of past actions and habits.[22] He writes:

> The nearer approached the moment of time when I would become different, the greater the horror of it struck me. But it did not thrust me back nor turn me away, but left me in a state of suspense. . . . Vain trifles and the triviality of the empty-headed,

my old loves, held me back. They tugged at the garments of my flesh and whispered: "Are you getting rid of us?".... They held me back. I hesitated to detach myself, to be rid of them, to make the leap [*transilire*] to where I was being called. Meanwhile, the overwhelming force of habit was saying to me: "Do you think you can live without them?"[23]

At this point, catechumen Augustine finally recognizes he cannot unite himself with Wisdom. To consider a key distinction from *Simpl.* 1.2, Augustine sees that *choice of will* cannot cause *free choice of will*. Therefore, in agreement with insights into Wisdom he had earlier learned (e.g., *conf.* 7), viz. that immutable governs mutable being, Augustine sees he requires Wisdom's aid. Since Augustine now recognizes his finitude existentially (cf. 7.10.16), he finally *imitates* Christ's humility.[24] Accordingly, in his garden at Milan,[25] Augustine hears the encouraging counsel of Lady Continence[26] and cries tears of confession.[27] While this is occurring, he interprets words spoken by nearby children, viz. "*tolle lege, tolle lege*," as God's command—like Saint Antony once did—to pick up the scripture at his side "and read the first chapter ... [he] ... might find."[28] Fortunately Augustine, by divine grace Confessor Augustine says, interpreted things correctly for, upon reading Rom. 13: 13-14, he was converted to Wisdom.[29] Confessor Augustine writes: "At once, with the last words of this sentence [i.e. of Rom. 13: 13-14], it was as if a light of relief from all anxiety flooded into my heart. All the shadows of doubt were dispelled."[30]

Immediately thereafter Alypius, encouraged by Augustine's remarks, does something similar so that he too is converted; and they speak of their conversions to Monnica, who "was filled with joy."[31] As a result, catechumen Augustine is a celibate Christian. Moreover, as his friendship with Alypius and mother Monnica shows, Augustine also partakes in a Christian community. Confessor Augustine writes:

> The effect of your converting me to yourself was that I did not now seek a wife and had no ambition for success in this world. I stood firm upon that rule of faith on which many years before you had revealed me to her [i.e. to Monnica—*cf.* 3.11.19–20].[32]

Hence, when Augustine embraced a rational disposition toward God he was soon thereafter converted. But we need to remember that by Confessor Augustine's principles, while the former is temporally prior to the latter, the relationship between them is effect to cause. Since Augustine understands that immutable (and therefore, Christ, the immutable-mutable God-man) causes mutable reality, he instructs that God's determination to share Christ's grace causes what is temporally prior. Accordingly, God's infinite goodness, being prior in origin, causes the events leading to catechumen Augustine's conversion in the Milanese garden.

Book 8 shows, then, how catechumen Augustine passed from *presumption* (through natural humility) to *confessio*. He transitions, by God's gift, *from* man's improper state apart from Christ's grace *to* man's proper state apart from that grace *to* man's proper state with Christ's grace—wherein and whereby Confessor Augustine composes *conf.* itself. Indeed, since Confessor Augustine understands that the Sabbath rest is creation's final cause, he confesses Christ's infinite goodness so each can be led there—but more on that later.[33]

Conf. 9[34]

It is one thing, however, to be newly established in *confessio*, i.e., "to be without the sweets of folly" and "talking with God," but quite another to live *confessio*. Therefore, as 9.1.1 states, Augustine's fresh "problem was to reject . . . [his] . . . own will and to desire . . . [God's]."[35] What does that entail? In key respects, Confessor Augustine answers this question by recounting significant developments in young Augustine's life whereby he achieved the disposition of *confessio*. In this matter, Augustine had much to learn as God "entered to take . . . [the] . . . place"[36] of the habitual orientations of his intellect and will. For his past thirty-two years, Augustine had directed himself toward pursuing secular success. Hence, he now learned that his heart should properly know and love like God and, consequently, his love for people and things should be governed accordingly.[37] Augustine pursues his eternal end with God[38] so that that alone guides his temporal objects and the means by which these are attained.

How did young Augustine learn this? Especially through pious reflection upon his (i) departure from secular society,[39] (ii) effort(s) to establish a Christian monastic community,[40] (iii) writing philosophical books,[41] (iv) Bible study,[42] (v) being cured of a nasty toothache,[43] (vi) baptism at Milan and its aftermath,[44] (vii) interacting with mother Monnica—including their shared vision of heaven at Ostia,[45] and (viii) learning, through Monnica's death, the Christian response to death.[46] After deciding, with Alypius and others, to become a monk, catechumen Augustine resolved to resign his job as *rhetor* and teacher in a manner seeking to avoid drawing attention to himself. But God helped with this in an unexpected way. By His providence, Augustine fell sick as the appointed time drew near and that made it easier for his students' parents to accept his resignation.[47] All told, catechumen Augustine aims to conform to God's way, but He helps him in an unexpected manner. As such, Augustine learns to employ God's means to accomplish God's ends.

Catechumen Augustine also discovers more about the primacy of God's plan while attempting to found a Christian monastery. He has in mind that its members will include Alypius, Verecundus, and Nebridius. However, while God looked favorably on Augustine's decision to establish a monastery,[48] He deigned this community would include those whom He selected, would be established according to His schedule, viz. after Augustine and his friends returned to Africa, and where He wills, viz. in Thagaste.[49] Hence, while the wealthy Verecundus, married to a Christian wife, refused to become a Christian unless he could join Augustine's monastery as a celibate, God willed otherwise. Confessor Augustine reports that Verecundus soon takes ill but, happily, is baptized on his deathbed.[50] Hence, God prohibits Verecundus from membership in Augustine's community but grants Verecundus's wish to attain eternal life. Likewise, Augustine wanted Nebridius to join his monastery but God planned otherwise; although Nebridius became "a baptized Catholic believer" he never joined Augustine's monastery, hesitating on the matter while in Italy and dying once back in Africa.[51] So, Augustine learns to conform to God's will.

In a similar vein, book 9's account of catechumen Augustine's preparation for baptism shows how the latter's intellect *and* will, i.e., love, were schooled by Wisdom. When Augustine finished his responsibilities as *rhetor*, he and his friends retired to a villa at Cassiciacum,[52] where he wrote books in philosophy, read portions of the Bible (especially David's Psalms), and, while praying with friends, was cured of a painful toothache. By these events, Confessor Augustine describes how God educated his heart. Although Alypius maintained that Augustine's books, written in Christ's service (but, to Confessor Augustine's mind, "still breathe the spirit of the school of pride"[53]) should not include "Christ's name,"[54] young Augustine thought otherwise.[55] Contrary to Alypius's counsel, Augustine's judgment was oriented toward divine eternity. Likewise, reading David's Psalms enflames Augustine's love for God and neighbor (particularly for his Manichean acquaintances)[56].[57] By this, we see reorientation occurring in Augustine's soul since the aforementioned response to the Psalms evinces he was learning to know and love himself and others as God knows and loves each. Finally, Confessor Augustine recounts catechumen Augustine's being cured of a painful toothache through communal prayer.[58] Why is this significant? Probably because it shows, first, Augustine's belief in divine omnipotence, i.e., no temporal event stands outside of God's plan. Second, it discloses Augustine's growing humility—he petitions God for aid in this matter and ecclesial spirit—because he prays for relief in conjunction with like-minded friends. Hence, Confessor Augustine claims young Augustine's heart was orienting toward Wisdom. He is Augustine's end and means.

Confessor Augustine describes the events following young Augustine's baptism at Milan in a similar manner. He is baptized by Bishop Ambrose and thereafter is deeply moved both (i) while reading Isaiah, by the "profundity" of God's plan for the human race's salvation, and (ii) while enjoying the hymns and songs at worship, allowing "feelings of devotion to overflow. Tears ran, and it was good for me to have that experience."[59] Augustine's understanding and love continue to develop. Moreover, God enables him to establish his desired monastic community but, as mentioned earlier, He populates and locates it as He sees fit. Although Verecundus and Nebridius are excluded, God provides Alypius, Adeodatus,[60] and Evodius[61] and, seeking to consider the place where they "could be of most use in . . . [God's] . . . service," the community resolves to establish itself back in North Africa.[62] Since Augustine's project to establish a monastery is for Wisdom, Wisdom governs its accomplishment. In all things, then, Augustine eagerly conforms himself to God's plan.

Based on the volume of pages Confessor Augustine devotes to the topic, it is evident that mother Monnica had a profound influence on young Augustine's reorientation.[63] Several matters in the remainder of book 9 show this, viz. (i) Monnica's *vita*, (ii) Monnica's shared vision of Wisdom with Augustine at Ostia, (iii) Monnica's last wishes, (iv) Augustine's decision concerning the burial of Monnica's body, and (v) Augustine's response to Monnica's death. Confessor Augustine presents these matters so that by reflecting on them we can both (i) see how her example encouraged young Augustine and (ii) be likewise encouraged ourselves. While the *vita* describes how Monnica came, by God's influence, to embrace charity,[64] the other matters describe aspects of her charity. Looking ahead some, it seems that the vision of Wisdom shared with Augustine at Ostia[65] shows both her profound contemplative capacity and remarkable friendship with Augustine. Moreover, her decision for burial at Ostia, rather than next to husband Patricius's gravesite back in Africa,[66] and her request that Augustine "remember her at the altar of the Lord"[67] depict her fervent trust in God's providence.

How, though, was newly baptized Augustine's character well influenced by Monnica? Confessor Augustine highlights two matters of profound significance, viz. young Augustine's (i) shared vision of Wisdom with Monnica at Ostia and (ii) response to her death. Concerning Ostia, Confessor Augustine explains that young Augustine and his mother philosophized in unison to understand "what quality of life the eternal life of the saints will have"[68]—note how different this is from Augustine's ascent(s) at Milan! In unison, their minds moved beyond external and psychological things to Wisdom, described as "the region of inexhaustible abundance where you feed Israel eternally with truth for food."[69] This vision helps young Augustine understand better (i) the communal aspect of Christian contemplation, (ii) that the Christian's proper object is communal life in heaven, and (iii) that this life, as Monnica's response to the vision shows, is preparatory.[70]

What does Monnica's death teach young Augustine? He discovers that the same heaven he tasted with Monnica at Ostia is also the proper object of his love. How so? At first, a stoic Augustine refrained from weeping at Monnica's death, thinking that tears might cause "weaker" brethren to overvalue temporal life.[71] But Augustine later discovers the Christian should weep since (cf. Augustine's weeping at his friend's death in *conf*. 4[72]) tears can be grounded in loving Christ and, likewise, in Christ's love.[73] One weeps over losing Christ's presence in one's friend, i.e., for not having nearby that Christian witness,[74] and, above all else, over one's friend's and one's possible separation from Christ because of personal sin and imperfection.[75] Hence, weeping a loved one's death is licit on a Christocentric basis.

All told, Monnica's presence in young Augustine's life is immensely salutary since she helps him learn, through her Christian witness, that the heart's proper object is heaven and, therefore, its primary activities can and should be ordered accordingly. Consequently, while young Augustine's shared vision of Wisdom at Ostia with Monnica shows that heaven, consisting in the communal enjoyment of Wisdom, is intellect's proper object, his response to Monnica's death instructs that heaven, in the company of Christian brethren, is will's proper object.

In book 9, then, Confessor Augustine shows how young Augustine became firmly established in Wisdom. By conforming his projects to God's will, and especially by the influence on him of Monnica, Augustine adapts his knowing and loving to God. His projects order temporal to eternal reality rather than, as he had done prior to conversion, the other way around. Consequently, Augustine's inveterate vanity no longer dominates his personality as he recognizes, with real assent, that the Christian's proper approach to persons and things is incarnational.[76] Since young Augustine's end is Wisdom, the temporal means to accomplish that properly conform thereto; and Wisdom helps Augustine in these matters in what, to him, are unexpected ways. By the end of book 9, Augustine finally has "the wind at his back." Since his lifestyle accords with "the Word made flesh," he is now "stable"[77] in Wisdom. He practices *confessio*.

Conf. 10[78]

Confessor Augustine, now a Catholic priest and bishop who avidly reflects upon, receives, and shares God's word and eucharist (10.30.41; 43.70),[79] confesses his state of *confessio* to his brethren (10.2.2–4.6) while wanting to know himself, i.e., his soul, as known by God (10.1.1). In this respect, Augustine's essential project is the same as before, viz. to encourage himself (10.1.1) and his audience to praise and thereby conform to Wisdom as far as possible (10.1.1–5.7).[80] Unlike before, however, Confessor Augustine's material is mostly his soul's present Christian relationship with God. Augustine's focus is decisively inward since, unlike the movement from historical events to spiritual meaning we encountered in books 1–9, book 10 focuses on soul's interior relationship with

Christ. Therefore, the veracity of what Augustine reports depends, as before, on the goodwill of confessor and audience.

This need for trust has been present from *conf.*'s beginning, but now the events Confessor Augustine reports only concern his present mindset as a Christian. For example, whereas certain persons could verify that Augustine was once a Manichean (3.4.8) and later baptized into the Christian religion by Ambrose (9.6.14), no one but Augustine can verify the content of his dreams (10.30.41–2).[81] There is a difference—but it should not be exaggerated.[82] Why not? In both instances, Augustine interprets the meaning beneath the events he reports. Moreover, while he now speaks at length of *strictly* spiritual matters constituting *his unique* relationship with God (10.27.38–43.70),[83] Augustine gives an objective basis to his examination of conscience. This is by (i) presenting it in light of both 10.6.8–25.36's account of soul's structure[84] and teaching on temptation found in 1 Jn 2:16 (10.30.41; 41.66); and (ii) subsequently appealing to Christ as mediator (10.43.67–9). As before, Augustine urges his reader to focus on confessing's universal character. Therefore, although Augustine alters his parameters, his discourse about *confessio* continues.[85]

Accordingly, my analysis of book 10 concentrates on the universal dimension of Augustine's confessing. After introducing his subject matter in 10.1.1–5.7, Augustine focuses on two principal parts belonging to his quest for Wisdom. These are how Wisdom (i) can be known indubitably and what that means concerning the human person (10.6.8–25.36), and (ii) provides a divine lifestyle and what that means for both Augustine and others (10.28.39–43.69). By this manner, Augustine teaches two closely related doctrines. First, that each is structured by Wisdom and can have an indubitable knowledge thereof. Second, that Wisdom's lifestyle is fruitful but incomplete—not only for the new convert but also for the veteran. While one can live wisely, one cannot live perfectly, but this is divinely ordained to teach soul to embrace charity. Above all else, it must rely on Christ's mediation both for aid here and to achieve perfect union with Him in the hereafter (10.42.67–43.69). For this reason, the person Augustine became a priest (and bishop) (10.43.70). Hence, Augustine confesses to encourage *confessio*.

Augustine's first teaching commences with the question "What do I love when I love God (10.6.8)?" and finishes with characterization of his past, present, and (hopefully) future response to God's presence

(10.27.38)—which presence, Augustine teaches, can be known with certitude (10.20.29–26.37). Augustine reaches the latter by his familiar pattern of reasoning, viz. *exteriora-interiora-superiora* (cf. *conf.* 7.10.15; 7.17.23; 9.10.23–5). Augustine begins from soul's acquaintance with bodies and, finding the latter mutable (for which reason they cannot be God), he turns into the soul. But since he finds, through considering what is adventitious, that nothing soul places within itself can be God, and also that soul (even viewed as the home of consubstantial matters) is mutable, he turns elsewhere, through considering soul's permanent, since consubstantial, and most fundamental drive, viz. its pursuit of happiness. This leads him to find what is above soul, viz. the immutable God from Whom soul's aforementioned innate disposition, and therefore everything already considered, derives. This raises four obvious questions. First, how does this occur? Second, in what sense is Augustine's conclusion indubitable? Third, what does this say about soul's quest for Wisdom? Fourth, what light is shed on Augustine's quest for Wisdom?

How does this occur? As mentioned previously, Augustine first considers whether bodies are God. But since the soul knows bodies through the senses, it is claimed, since "What is inward is superior"[86] and soul (*anima*)[87] gives life to the body, that God gives life to the soul (10.6.10). Hence, Augustine introduces his ascent through the soul like this: "What then do I love when I love my God? Who is he who is higher than the highest element in my soul? Through my soul (*ipsam animam meam*) I will ascend to him."[88] While marveling at soul's mysterious expanse, and his inability to introspect thereon[89] (cf. Augustine's account of mind in 8.9.21), Augustine's ascent through soul, identifying soul in key respects with memory (*memoria*),[90] has several stages. It passes *from* images gathered through the bodily senses[91] *to* "the skills acquired through the liberal arts"[92] *to* the ideas or notions in mind signified by words[93] *to* mind's affections—including "cupidity, gladness, fear, sadness"[94]— *to* mind's knowledge of numbers and principles of mathematics[95] and *to* mind's remembrance of its "forgetfulness."[96] Here Augustine pauses his ascent since, unlike previous distinctions, "forgetfulness" means mind has self-knowledge. Most important, since God is "the life of the mind," Augustine considers whether he needs to transcend mind (which is impossible since mind is subject!) to know God.[97] However, since knowing God requires being "mindful" of Him[98] it follows, as considering forgetfulness shows,[99] mind cannot know

God unless He is somehow present. As such, Augustine considers the nature of God's presence in the soul whereby He makes Himself known,[100] discovering what permanently structures each of soul's activities is innate love "for the happy life (*beata vita*)."[101] Augustine ultimately distinguishes the latter as "joy based on the truth"[102] which (as already shown in *conf*. 7.10.16; 7.17.23; 9.10.23–5) properly consists in taking "joy in God."[103]

Therefore, after considering how persons seek "joy in the truth,"[104] Augustine distinguishes that God, known to be immutable (e.g., 7.10.16; 7.17.23; 9.10.23–5), is permanently present to each through their permanent quest for "joy in truth."[105] Hence, Augustine claims the immutable God is present as each pursues happiness. Hence, the divine presence Augustine analyzed in *conf*. 1.1.1–5.6 and has been cultivating throughout *conf*. is shown to include soul's pursuing God. Augustine's claim, then, is that God is none of (i) what soul adds to itself through experience, (ii) what belongs to soul, or (iii) soul itself.[106] Rather, He is immutable, i.e., above all created things, yet present to soul spiritually—for which reason soul has permanent orientation toward happiness. Accordingly, Augustine finishes this portion of his argument by considering his relationship with God before his conversion and afterwards[107]— which entails his identity as he writes *conf*. and longing for God's "peace."[108]

Although commonly overlooked,[109] Augustine has provided another claim (cf. 7.10.16; 7.17.23; 9.10.23–5) that Wisdom, in part, can be known with certitude. How so? While only some identify God as proper object,[110] it is obvious that each seeks happiness and identifies happiness with truth. (Since each claims that happiness consists in this or that, each identifies happiness as the quest for truth.) Moreover, this quest structures the human as such (note how Augustine claims this belongs to soul's objective character) and underlies every activity (past, present, and future). Finally, since the "quest for happiness in truth" is something each can know with certitude by introspection, each can have, in principle, an indubitable knowledge of seeking "happiness in truth." Consequently those, like Augustine and pagan Platonist philosophers, who rightly identify God as Wisdom (e.g., 7.10.16; 7.17.23) can have another form of indubitable knowledge of Wisdom—really, it is what their original knowledge of Wisdom implies—by seeing that each, objectively speaking, is seeking God. Confessor Augustine's famous claim at

conf.'s outset (1.1.1), that "the heart is restless until it rests in God," has significant philosophical ground.
Augustine's second consideration in book 10, viz. 10.28.38–43.70, explains the extent to which he lives the happy life.[111] Certainly, Augustine's account of his inner life is highly personal but, as mentioned earlier, he analyzes it publicly for reasons simultaneously personal and universal. Augustine certainly has four things in mind. First, by showing his present relationship with Christ, he wants to encourage living wisely. Second, he identifies the "slow growth" aspect to Wisdom's lifestyle[112] to demonstrate how, in the end, that lifestyle is governed by charity. Third, the previous considerations help Augustine explain why he transitioned from being a monk to a priest.[113] Fourth, by focusing on the universal aspects of his examination of conscience, Augustine implies general proof that Christ is Wisdom.

In what sense? While Confessor Augustine has just showed how one is structured by Wisdom, one might wonder whether one can have a secure knowledge of Wisdom's lifestyle? Analysis of *conf.* 7 showed one can have certain knowledge concerning the existence of divine mediation and that the Catholic religion's account of Christ is cogent. And we can add to this (from 10.20.29–23.34) that each intrinsically seeks God (because He is present to each). One can know with certitude that Wisdom has created man and provides him with a way to beatitude; the doctrine of "the Word made flesh" subordinates mutable to immutable reality; and all persons seek God by seeking happiness. However, the Catholic religion's "made flesh" component cannot be indubitable since it refers to sense experience. Nevertheless, the claim "Christ is Wisdom" can have existential credibility if Augustine's experience with Christ shows his heart has progressed. In other words, the Catholic religion's claim that Christ is Wisdom can have merit if the aforementioned cognitive evidence is supplemented by existential evidence.

Regarding Augustine's principal focus in 10.28.39–39.64, he explains his standing in the happy life by analyzing himself according to the standard, found in 1 Jn 2:16,[114] concerning temptations of the flesh (does one succumb to sensual pleasure?),[115] the world (does one succumb to vain curiosity?),[116] and the devil (does one succumb to temptations for fame and power?).[117] Augustine thereby shows he has progressed since becoming a Christian but also that he is far from perfect.[118] For example, while he no longer pursues sexual activity, he is beset by dreams about the matter.[119] And while he no longer pursues secular power, he struggles with lust for power as a priest and bishop[120]—to such an extent, he calls it "the main cause why I fail to love and fear you [i.e. God] in purity."[121] In short, Augustine finds he has progressed but also that he sometimes sins and is, in certain matters, beset by temptation and ignorance. As he remarked at the outset, "Is not human life on earth a trial in which there is no respite?"[122]

Regarding Augustine's second purpose in 10.28.39–39.64, it is important to recognize the significance of the prayer commencing his examination of conscience, viz. to "Grant what you command, and command what you will (*Da quod iubes et iube quod vis*)."[123] Considering this prayer in light of Augustine's examination of conscience reveals a weighty perplexity. Since God is good, He has the power and motive to cure completely and immediately Augustine (and all humans in the *saeculum*) of sin, temptation, and imperfection. But God chooses otherwise.

Augustine makes it clear he would prefer to enjoy perfect unity with God. In fact, he spends spare moments pursuing divine union. He writes:

> in all these investigations which I pursue while consulting you, I can find no safe place for my soul except in you. There my dispersed aspirations are gathered together, and from you no part of me will depart. And sometimes you cause me to enter into an extraordinary sweetness. If it were brought to perfection in me, it would be an experience quite beyond anything in this life. But I fall back into my usual ways under my miserable burdens. I am reabsorbed by my habitual practices. I am held in their grip. I weep profusely, but still I am held. Such is the strength of the burden of habit. Here I have the power to be, but do not wish it. There I wish to be, but lack the power. On both grounds I am in misery.[124]

However, Augustine implies that God's ordination of "slow growth" encourages charity.[125] Presumably, this is to (i) promote thanksgiving toward God for the good He has accomplished in one's life, (ii) love God so more can be accomplished, and (iii) encourage proper self-love and love of neighbor by exhibiting holy patience concerning progress along Wisdom's way.

Most important, juxtaposing this consideration with Augustine's previous conclusion provides existential evidence that Christ is Wisdom for it is apparent that Augustine's union with Christ has caused him to grow in Wisdom. When this testimony is joined with the aforementioned cognitive evidence found in 10.6.8–25.36, the claim that "Christ is Wisdom" has significant warrant.

It is also possible that Augustine's perseverance helps explain why he became a priest (10.40.73). How so? As it is through Christ's self-sacrifice in laying down His humanity to redeem the human race[126] that Augustine grows in Wisdom, he (i.e., this person, Augustine—who already enjoyed celibacy) judges it is by sacrificing himself, in Christ's manner, that he best serves Him in the *saeculum*.[127] Hence Augustine's extraordinary zeal for Christ seems to have motivated him to become a priest[128] and, in this respect, he identifies himself with Christ in the same manner as the priest(s) described back in *conf*. 1.1.1. Just as Augustine had received the gift of faith through Christ's priests preaching, i.e., through those sharing in Christ's humanity, he now shares Christ with others. Hence, priest (and bishop), Augustine now mediates Christ to others as Christ had been (and continues to be) mediated to him. As Ambrose, for example, was to Augustine, now Augustine is to others.

In book 10, then, Confessor Augustine confesses his present state, i.e., his lifestyle of *confessio*, by showing three things: first, his psychological or inward knowledge of Wisdom; second, his status in Wisdom's lifestyle; and third, that he serves Christ as priest. Augustine shows that he *knows* himself, and therefore each human, to be structured by God to pursue and enjoy Him. Concerning this matter, Augustine distinguishes the psychological dimension of the indubitable knowledge of God first manifested in *conf*. 7. In one way, what 10.6.8–26.38 discloses depends on the knowledge of God articulated in *conf*. 7 but, in a more profound way, it depends on God's presence. For how can one attain an indubitable knowledge of God apart from spiritual unity with Him (cf. 1.1.1–5.6)? Hence, that God the creator implants Himself in each person, and adds to this in Christ, is the ultimate ground of the forms of knowledge Augustine articulates. Augustine's second principal teaching in book 10 is that he progresses in Wisdom but has a long way to go; and that he will only enjoy fullness in the afterlife. In each respect, Augustine shows dependence on Christ.

Finally, as if completing a circle of sorts, Confessor Augustine's recounting his priesthood signals the end of both book 10, i.e., analyzing his present relationship with God, and the first major confession constituting *conf*. First, Augustine shows something of the cause behind his mature knowledge and practice of Wisdom, viz. being a priest requires knowing the soul. Second, by mentioning his priesthood, Augustine completes his teaching on the nature of *confessio* by describing (i) the stages whereby he embraces *confessio*, (ii) *confessio*'s content, and (iii) that he promotes *confessio*. Moreover, by evincing that *conf*. 1–10 is produced by a priest, Augustine manifests that his reader is not only Christian laypersons, like Monnica, but also priests and bishops like himself. Therefore, since *conf*.'s audience can be certain there is Wisdom, as certain as can be that Wisdom leads to beatitude, and that the one confessing these matters is a priest, Augustine's spiritual biography is completed.

Yet Augustine is also looking forward in *conf*. First, he mentioned meditating on God's law in 10.40.70. Second, he detailed in books 8–10 that, through Christ, he embraced the lifestyle of *confessio*. From this perspective, Augustine has written *conf*. 1–10 to show how those sharing his circumstances attain *confessio* and how God's goodness leads them thereto. However, that lifestyle's center is not simply Christ but what He points to as incarnate Word, viz. to God in Himself, the Trinity—Father, incarnate Word, and Holy Spirit—Who is immutable creator. In this respect, Christ (e.g., 11.2.4) is the gateway to what stands beyond. God's goodness is, in one way, more transcendent over man and, in another way, more intimate to him than what Augustine has said so far.

Conclusion

In books 8–10, Confessor Augustine confesses in a universal and progressive manner that *confessio* is *existentially*, i.e., cognitively and affectively, sound. Although *conf*. 7 shows that catechumen Augustine recognizes the cognitive merit of the Catholic religion's account of Christ, and prepares to embrace Him, *conf*. 8–10 show that how he embraced Christ and the cognitive but especially affective augmentations that subsequently occurred. Consequently, Augustine augments his account of *confessio*'s merit.

How is Augustine's confession universal? It is because he continues to focus, especially for the benefit of his principal audience, on key aspects of soul's relationship with infinite divine goodness. It is true that Augustine details portions of his personal experience in these books. He wanted to become a Catholic Christian; preferred to be a celibate Catholic; was beset by sexual lust; sought counsel from Simplicianus; learned about monasticism from Ponticianus; converted to the Catholic religion; resigned his job as *rhetor*; retired to Cassiciacum where (among other things) he wrote books, prepared for baptism, and was healed from a nasty toothache; was baptized at Easter 386 AD at Milan by Bishop Ambrose; shared a vision of Wisdom with mother Monnica at Ostia just before her death; learned much about the Christian lifestyle from Monnica's death; established a monastery in North Africa; became a priest and bishop; confessed how he now knows and loves God; and strived, in all things, to embrace His goodness. Therefore, as mentioned previously, Augustine selects the aforementioned events to illustrate his mindset toward participating in Christ. Moreover, since Augustine's primary goal is to explain how he attained *confessio* and what that entails, he now concentrates on his relationship with divine goodness from the time immediately before his baptism through his present state as priest (and bishop) in the Catholic church.

But Confessor Augustine has also, in principle, a subaltern audience. As he discloses at the heart of *conf.* 10, he thinks happiness consists in conforming to divine goodness (i.e., to "joy in the truth/God"—10.23.33) and, consequently, that all persons embrace truth or falsity and, therefore, do good or evil. Augustine certainly thinks, then, that everyone pursues happiness by embracing what they think to be true and good. So while his subaltern audience may not agree that happiness consists in following Christ, it will likely agree that everyone pursues happiness. Hence, because of Augustine's *confessio* perspective, *conf.*'s biographical elements are conjoined with universal concerns. The historical events he recounts and analysis of his present spiritual state help to encourage *confessio*.

How, though, is Augustine's confession in books 8–10 progressive? This is because its conclusion that *confessio* is a reasonable lifestyle is arrived at by consecutive stages. We remember *conf.* 7 presented us with a younger Augustine who (i) thought the Catholic religion's claim that Christ is Wisdom is cogent and (ii) wanted *to* experience

Christ to overcome his moral and ontological differences from Him. Accordingly, the progress visible in books 8–10 pertains principally to Augustine's embracing the lifestyle of Wisdom and, in this respect, we see he grows in *confessio* and ultimately provides us with a profound analysis, in book 10, of his *confessio* mindset as he writes *conf*. All told, Augustine gives his reader significant evidence that *confessio* is cogent.

In book 8, Confessor Augustine distinguishes progress toward and in *confessio* by showing how young Augustine is initially joined with Christ. Looked at in one way, this is by embracing the existential aspect of the speculative knowledge of Wisdom (book 7 shows) he had already achieved. It is only when Augustine recognizes both cognitively *and* affectively, i.e., with intellect *and* will, that he must *live wisely* that he has a proper disposition toward God (i.e., the disposition of natural humility or *confessio*). Previously, he gave notional rather than real assent to the lifestyle of Wisdom. Moreover, soon after Augustine embraces the proper disposition toward God, he has the good fortune of being converted to Christ—whereupon he helps his friend Alypius convert and joins with him and Monnica in Christian community. So, book 8 is about progress, by God's aid, from presumption to natural humility to *confessio*, i.e., from presuming upon divine goodness *to* humbly seeking divine goodness *to* humbly embracing infinite divine goodness in Christ.

In book 9, Confessor Augustine distinguishes progress by showing how young Augustine put on "the mind of Christ" while joining His church. Augustine left behind his secular ambitions, embraced the heavenly Jerusalem as proper object, and governed accordingly his temporal life. Augustine progresses as he prepares for and receives baptism, establishes his monastic community, is enamored with the scriptures (especially with David's *Psalms*), shares a vision of Wisdom at Ostia with mother Monnica, and eventually responds to her death with charity. So, book 9 shows how Augustine, by God's aid, embraced the lifestyle of Wisdom.

In book 10, Confessor Augustine marks progress by analyzing his present mindset. In particular, he shows in a twofold manner how he has grown intellectually and morally since the events related in book 9 (approximately thirteen years prior). This is by detailing, first, his indubitable knowledge concerning Wisdom's presence to the soul and, second, how he has grown in loving

Wisdom. Augustine's initial project consists in an ascent *exteriora-interiora-superiora* showing that soul's pursuit of happiness is really the pursuit and enjoyment of God. Each person, knowing it or not, has immediate relationship with God (hence Augustine's subaltern audience). Augustine's second project (moving *superioria-exteriora-interiora*) examines his place in the happy life, i.e., the extent of God's presence, by analyzing the latter in light of his relationship—under the condition of "slow growth"—to (1 Jn 2: 16) the temptations of the flesh, world, and devil. Consequently, Augustine shows his *knowledge* that Christ is Wisdom and *love* of Wisdom have grown. God is more present in his heart than before his conversion and is welcome even more. How so? This is because as Augustine's first project shows, he is surer than ever that Christ is Wisdom and, as his second project discloses, he has overcome vanity in certain respects and strives to overcome it further. Hence, Augustine enjoys and cultivates God's presence so (cf. 1.5.5–6) he can become happy.

Moreover, *conf.* 10 contains a book-related, retrospective *reditus* dimension since Confessor Augustine has reached the end (as *retr.* says) of *conf.*'s spiritual biography (books 1–10). Book 10 implies *reditus* in three related ways. First, Augustine is now confessing his present life. While the earlier books return from past to present, book 10 is almost entirely about the present. Second, since Augustine discloses at book 10's conclusion that he became a priest, there is suggested a significant symmetry with *conf.* 1.1.1. How so? This shows that he who received the gift of faith through Christ's priest is now a priest sharing that same gift. As priest (and bishop), Augustine now mediates Christ to others as Christ was mediated to him. Hence, Augustine's confessing his present life returns us to the teachings stated at *conf.*'s opening. Third, the nature of divine presence Augustine described in 1.2.2–5.6 is detailed. Augustine explains divine presence by distinguishing its spiritual conditions and his general relationship thereto (10.6.8–27.38); and his profound examination of conscience in 10.28.39–43.69 that culminates with confessing Christ the mediator shows his experience and continued pursuit of God's presence. In these respects, book 10 returns us to *conf.*'s beginning.

All told, books 8–10 explain why Confessor Augustine thinks man's proper disposition is *confessio*. This is by arguing, through distinguishing stages in his spiritual development, that the Catholic doctrine of Wisdom has intellectual and practical merit. Augustine instructs that Catholic teaching provides an account of Wisdom fulfilling man's intellectual capacity and, especially by his personal witness, man's practical desire for a true lifestyle. Therefore, since man can know with (i) certitude that his existence is from God to attain complete fulfillment in Him and (ii) "next to certitude" that "the Word made flesh" helps him live wisely, his proper response is *confessio*.

Finally we note, as earlier, that Augustine sets the universal and progressive elements in books 8–10 confessions within an *exitus-reditus* framework. Augustine's confessing, whether focusing on his past or present, is always for *returning* himself and his audience to *confessio* (e.g., 8.1.1, 9.1.1, 10.1.1–2.2). By this manner, Augustine confesses that *confessio* is cognitive *and* affective. Augustine's confessing has had that character since *conf*.'s beginning. However, while *conf*. 1–7 have shown, through young Augustine's development, that *confessio* is grounded in certitude, *conf*. 8–10, focusing on (i) catechumen and newly baptized Augustine's developments, and (ii) Confessor Augustine's present psychological state, disclose that *confessio* properly guides mind *and* will. This gives more evidence to Augustine's claim that *confessio* is reasonable.

But there is more to *confessio*. As the remainder of *conf*. (viz. books 11–13) will clarify, Augustine thinks, through Christ (11.2.4), his pattern of confessing participates in the Godhead and, therefore, in His infinite goodness toward men. This augments Augustine's account of *confessio*'s merit.

Further Study

Book 8: At the outset of book 8, what keeps catechumen Augustine from being baptized?

Why is catechumen Augustine not sufficiently inspired by (i) the counsel of Simplicianus and (ii) Ponticianus's account of Christian monasticism?

Does Confessor Augustine recount his conversion, in book 8, as the passage from presumption to humility to c*onfessio*? Please explain.

Book 9: Why does Confessor Augustine recount young Augustine's transition from resigning his role as *rhetor* and teacher to the events following his baptism?

What does newly baptized Augustine learn from the shared vision of Wisdom with Monnica at Ostia?

What does newly baptized Augustine learn from Monnica's death?

Book 10: What is the object and chief circumstance of Augustine's confessing in book 10?

What, in the end, does Augustine "love when he loves God," and how does he arrive at that conclusion?

Is Augustine's account of his standing in the happy life scrupulous or realistic? Please explain.

Why does Augustine judge that Christ is responsible for the progress he has made in the lifestyle of Wisdom and for the progress that remains?

How is Augustine's becoming a priest related to his confession in book 10?

Does Augustine's confession in book 10 provide a fitting conclusion to book 1–10's general confession? Please explain.

Articles

Bright, 155–66
Couenhoven, 23–44
Ekenburg, 28–45
Helm (2006), 147–60
Ferrari (1983), 232–45; (1989), 235–50; (2003), 127–36
Paffenroth (1997), 141–54; (2003), 137–54
O'Donnell (1979), 280–303
Starnes (1987), 95–103; (1992) 51–65
Wills (2006), 195–208
Wolterstorff (2014), 46–70

Books

BeDuhn (2013), ix–163, 429–55.
David (2019A), 95–160
Kenney (2005), 73–86, 89–128
McMahon (1989), 102–13, 127–9

O'Donnell, 3@3–259
Starnes (1990), 213–76
Stock, 89–121, 207–32
Vaught (2004), 67–138; (2005), 27–99
Hochschild, 137–54
Wills (2011), 58–111

4

Confessions 11–13, *Confessio*'s Ultimate Ground is the Godhead

Introduction

In books 11–13 Augustine instructs, through Christ (11.2.4), that *confessio* is universal and progressive by the mode of *exitus-reditus* because it is structured so by God's infinite goodness and properly imitative thereof. Augustine's principal task in books 11–13 is accomplished in three stages and culminates in the exegesis of Gen. 1:1–2:3,[1] explaining God's creating His church unto "the Sabbath rest." Book 11 concentrates on divine creating, arguing it is grounded in the Father's eternal begetting of His Word and therefore that mutable being depends on immutable divinity. Book 12 focuses on the ontological nature of creatures and exegesis' character as motivated by divine goodness and properly carried out in His Spirit. Here Augustine distinguishes God's Spirit in conjunction with love and consequently as Cause of man's *reditus* to God. Finally, book 13 concentrates on the divine motive for creation, viz. God's goodness (specially related to His Spirit), since He creates only for creatures' benefit.

However, 13.11.12 alerts us to another development in books 11–12 central to book 13's conclusion and, therefore, to *conf*. itself. Augustine's account of divine creating contains doctrine concerning divine presence. Taking its proximate cue from 10.20.29–27.38's instruction on divine presence (but its ultimate prompt from 1.1.1–5.6), this teaching develops through books 11 and 12, and reaches its zenith in 13.11.12. There, Augustine, starting with Church teaching on the Godhead (13.5.6), distinguishes core activities of mind, viz. of being, knowing, and willing, as distant instantiations of relationship in the Godhead between Father, incarnate Word, and Holy Spirit. Hence, it is now claimed, through Christ and His scriptures, that divine presence is trinitarian, so that man's proper response to God (as Augustine's exegesis in 13.12.13–38.53 discloses) is trinitarian.

Therefore, while books 11–12 mostly explain the created order's coming forth and how the exegete properly understands scripture, book 13 primarily distinguishes creation's return, i.e., *reditus* to God, through the prism of the Church's and exegete's "return" to Him. Augustine speaks predominantly of Father and Word in books 11–12 but especially of Father, Word, and Spirit in book 13, in which respect his focus, as concentrations on scripture and Church show, continues to depart from what Christian and pagan Platonist philosophical theology hold in common[2] to what the former uniquely upholds. As always, Augustine's fundamental point is that God is better and, therefore, man owes Him more praise than commonly thought.

Finally, Confessor Augustine's exegesis of the Church in 13.12.13–38.53 brings *conf.* to a fitting conclusion. Obviously, the Sabbath rest is, at once, the purpose for (i) God's creating and (ii) Augustine's writing *conf.* In these matters, Augustine's account of the Church places his personal development (*conf.* 1–10), including his trinitarian activity as exegete (*conf.* 11–13), within a universal and progressive framework having its *telos* in the Sabbath rest. Moreover, the Church is placed within a universal and progressive account of God. For Augustine, the *exitus-reditus* pattern structuring both (i) the Church—its coming into existence, development, and attaining its *telos*—and (ii) selfhood—its existing, knowing, and loving of God—is intrinsically universal and progressive because it imitates the relationships between Father, incarnate Word, and Spirit. Augustine thereby implies that *conf.* itself has God in Himself, through His Christ, as origin, governor, and goal.

Conf. 11[3]

Introduction: Augustine commences *conf.*'s second major confession, viz. books 11–13, by claiming it is universal and progressive. First,

Augustine discloses, as aforementioned, he confesses so each can grow in knowing and loving God.[4] This confession, however, is explicitly universal (in the sense of "collective" or "general"[5]) since its topic is the Church, i.e., the body of believers priest (and bishop) Augustine serves. In one way, then, Augustine's aim is identical to books 1–10, but now he is less concerned with biography. Once again, Augustine confesses personal details to distinguish spiritual meaning—but in this instance his object consists in a shared zeal for scripture.[6] On that topic, moreover, Augustine's confessing is targeting not just laypersons but also, following from his clerical role,[7] Catholic leaders so they may obtain knowledge concerning divine providence (including Church development).

Additionally, Augustine's topic, viz. "from the beginning in which ... [God] ... made heaven and earth until the perpetual reign with ... [God] ... in ... [His] ... heavenly city,"[8] is progressive since tracing Church development. It is also structured by *exitus-reditus* since it begins with the Church's coming forth from divine eternity (in principle in 11.4.6)[9] and finishes, in 13.38.53, with a brief account of her eternal union with God. Moreover, Augustine confesses his progressive discoveries since—as believer, priest, and bishop—that is a microcosm of the created order. Consequently, while confessing God's creating His church, Augustine focuses on *his own* relationship with God as exegete. Hence, Augustine's *confessio* concerns not only the objective realities he discovers, i.e., the Godhead, the mode of divine creating, and the principal structure of God's providence, but also his own relationship with Wisdom as these are discovered. Since *confessio* is principally concerned with soul's relationship with God and neighbor it is *fitting* Augustine focuses simultaneously on God in Himself, understood as triune, His scriptures, and His creating His church, together with the nature of and his attitude toward God's trinitarian presence as he practices exegesis.

Moreover, it is after Augustine achieves adequate accounts of the Godhead, God's creating, interpreting the scriptures, and the nature of divine presence (13.11.12) that he provides his account (found in 13.12.13–38.53) of God's creating His church unto the Sabbath rest. Augustine's depiction of the Sabbath rest in 13.35.50–38.53 constitutes a *fitting* end to his confession for books 11–13 in particular and for books 1–13 in general since the *terminus ad quem* of the Church is, simultaneously, personal development's *telos*. In this respect, the universal and progressive dimension of Augustine's confessing, including the latter's *exitus-reditus* aspect, is made clear.

Analyzing Conf. 11: After Augustine identifies his goals in books 11–13 and confesses how accomplishing them depends on Christ's grace—in Whom, as mediator,[10] "'are hidden all the treasures of wisdom and knowledge' (Col. 2:3)"[11]—he focuses on distinguishing "how in the beginning . . . [God] made heaven and earth (Gen. 1:1)."[12] However, since Augustine lacks Moses's explanation and since, even if Moses were present, he would need to verify Moses's claims, Augustine interprets Gen. 1:1 based on his present conceptual resources. By employing key insights originally obtained with Platonist philosophy's aid (7.9.13–16.22), Augustine advances two points. First, he argues Gen. 1:1 means "God" is immutable creator, i.e., self-sufficient and consequently possessing the plentitude of perfections found in mutable reality (i.e., in creatures).[13] Second, Augustine claims, based on previous discussion, that God creates by His immutable speaking.[14] Appealing next to scripture, Augustine asserts Gen. 1:1 must mean by God's immutable speaking His Eternal Word, i.e., the Trinity's Second Person; and He is signified by the term "beginning" in Gen. 1:1 (11.6.8–9.11): "In this Beginning, God, you made heaven and earth, in your Word, in your Son, in your power, in your wisdom, in your truth speaking in a wonderful way and making in a wonderful way."[15] Hence, Augustine recognizes, through Christ, that scripture contains truth about God including what is found in pagan Platonist philosophy.[16]

Augustine maintains, moreover, that the aforementioned understanding is capable of answering: "'What was God doing before he made heaven and earth?'"[17] In the remainder of book 11, Augustine responds to this question to defend the earlier claim that God (the Father) creates by His immutable Word. For Augustine, the opponent's question presupposes mutability so that God's "activity" entails both that His will to create and the created order are everlasting.[18] Eternity is identified with everlastingness, perpetuity, or enduring for the whole of time rather than with a transcendent mode of being. Hence, the question denies Augustine's cardinal, indubitable (7.10.16) doctrine of divine immutability (11.4.6–5.7)—and, consequently, scripture's distinction between God the Father and Word (11.6.8–9.11). In short, the question reduces God to the mode of mutability and makes a mockery of scripture.

Augustine's solution is twofold.[19] First, he responds analytically, claiming that holding Gen. 1:1 signifies God is creator of "every created being," i.e., of "heaven and earth," brings the conclusion He was not making before He made.[20] Likewise, if God has "made time itself," it is rightly inferred, since time signifies change, that God was not "doing" anything "before" creating since "There can be no 'then' when there was no time."[21] Augustine underscores this response by asserting both divine immutability and scripture's account of God the Father's immutable speaking of His Word (11.13.16).

Second, Augustine longs to provide an existential solution to the problem (11.11.13; 14.17) only since he thinks it more effective—likely because it belongs to his *confessio* perspective concerning divine-human relationship. Augustine writes:

> Who will lay hold on the human heart to make it still, so that it can see how eternity, in which there is neither future nor past, stands still and dictates future and past times? . . . Can the hand of my mouth by mere speech achieve so great a thing?[22]

To explain divine eternity, Augustine offers his famous (commonly misunderstood) account of time in 11.14.17–28.38.[23] For Augustine, man measures time by a "stretching out of the mind/soul" (*distentionem . . . animi*[24]) since mind is stretched out, i.e., mutable,[25] and therefore in need of healing and augmentation.[26] By contrast, the healed mind, like God, measures time apart from experiencing mutability.

Augustine arrives at his conclusion in five steps. First (11.14.17–20.26), he argues mind has awareness of time-periods. But this is problematic since mind's awareness thereof is based on its present awareness of things. Hence, the durations (e.g., minutes, days, years, and millennia) mind distinguishes are not present to it as such. So mind speaks of "time," i.e., the measure of mutation in mutable things, as if it is something objective (i.e., present, in its entirety, to consciousness). However, mind's notions and measuring of time(s) depend on bringing before its present awareness what it (i) remembers (*memoria*) and (ii) anticipates (*expectatio*); and it considers present things by immediate awareness (*contuitus*).[27]

Augustine's second analysis (11.21.27–24.31) stems from the above: if time is not "objective," why does mind measure things' movements by the same? It seems, then, that time is objective, i.e., that mind uses mutable things' mutations to measure mutable things because of, and perhaps to overcome, its own intrinsic temporality. However, analysis shows that mind gives durations to the movements it uses to measure movements. Mind, in other words, uses things' movements, like sun and moon, to measure things' movements like sitting or standing. Augustine claims, therefore, that since mind recognizes it measures times, time cannot be bodily movement.[28] (This does not deny the value of using movements as measures, but Augustine's principal point is mind does so because, being subject to temporality yet somehow being capable of measuring it, it uses these movements to signify duration.)

What therefore does mind mean by "time"? Augustine now maintains (his third analysis—11.25.32–26.33) since mind has awareness of measuring times, and therefore time cannot be something *external,* mind means by time mind's measuring itself, i.e., its own temporality.[29] Hence mind, not body, is the measure of mutability. If so, the obvious question is this: How does mind distinguish time? Accordingly (Augustine's fourth analysis—11.27.34–28.38), using mind's recitation of a familiar psalm, Augustine claims that mind's awareness of past, present, and future times results from measuring the duration of its present awareness of events. Put simply, mind assigns durations to things based on measuring its present consciousness of some things and by considering others by that measure.[30] Augustine writes:

> So it is in you, my mind, that I measure periods of time. . . . The impression which passing events make upon you abides when they are gone. That present consciousness is what I am measuring, not the stream of past events which have caused it. When I measure periods of time, that is I what I am actually measuring. Therefore, either this is what time is, or time is not what I am measuring.[31]

Augustine is not denying external reality—or else, to make this point obvious, he would be negating his fundamental account of God the creator (11.4.6). Rather, Augustine shows that, by contrast with divine immutability, mind's relationship to things—including to itself—*is conditioned by temporality.* Since mind is limited it experiences things, whether created or uncreated, accordingly.

Mind can be sure its experience of things is colored by its limited mode. But this, of course, does not negate the existence or natures of mutable things or that mind knows them. Rather, it means mind experiences objects by the mode of mutability. (For example, mind can know the nature of a cow but cannot have present the entire life of a particular cow.) Hence, mind's awareness of anything (whether mutable or immutable) is determined by its mutability.

Most important, mind's attempt to know things via present consciousness requires imitation of divine immutability (considered the eternal source and governor of temporality [11.11.13–14.17]). But mind fails at this since present consciousness encompasses neither the whole of mutable reality nor the whole of its experience of mutability.[32] Mind would better know mutable reality, including itself, *and* immutable reality, i.e., God, if it participated more in God's immutability.[33] Why so? Because mind's present consciousness would be expanded to know mutable things and God (as present). In this respect, mind, *by its mode of being*, would know things not only conceptually (i.e., in terms of their nature[s]) and as it experiences them but also in their own substance since they (God and, in a way, participated immutable things excepted) would be entirely present. Once again, therefore, mind recognizes its dependence on God, knowing its relationship with Him is privative and hopes for a cure.

Next, Augustine (his fifth and, in a way, most important step) directly considers his mutability and expresses gratitude that Christ[34] will heal him by causing him to participate fully in His immutability.[35] Augustine writes:

> You are my eternal Father, but I am scattered in times whose order I do not understand. The storms of incoherent events tear to pieces my thoughts, the inmost entrails of my soul, until that day when, purified and molten by the fire of your love, I flow together to merge into you.[36]

For our long-term purpose,[37] another important aspect to Augustine's consideration of time is that he defends divine immutability by introducing another mode of indubitable self-knowledge. Whereas in *conf.* 10.22.32–3 mind's pursuing "happiness in truth" is a corollary of mind's certitude that God is immutable, here mind's knowledge that its making is mutable, because its mode is mutable, is a corollary of mind's knowing divine immutability. Accordingly, the consecutive analogies, the first is false while the second is true, *conf.* 11 finishes with are highly significant. Augustine's first analogy considers God's knowing on the model of temporality, as if (like 11.10.12's questioners presuppose) He knows the whole of time in a temporal manner prior to time's unfolding. Augustine writes:

> Certainly if there were a mind endowed with such great knowledge and prescience that all things past and future could be known the way I know a very familiar psalm, this mind would be utterly miraculous and amazing to the point of inducing awe. From such a mind nothing of the past would be hidden, nor anything of what remaining ages have in store, just as I have full knowledge of that psalm I sing. I know by heart what and how much of it has passed since the beginning, and what and how much remains until the end.[38]

Augustine's second analogy, however, considers God's knowing and making according to His immutable eternity so that, in agreement with mind's indubitable knowledge of divine immutability (7.10.16; 7.17.23), it is recognized that divine "activity" occurs apart from any change in His substance. Augustine writes:

> But far be it from you, Creator of the universe, creator of souls and bodies . . . to know all future and past events in this kind of sense. You know them in a much more wonderful and . . . mysterious way. A person singing or listening to a song he knows well suffers a distension or stretching in feeling and in sense-perception (*affectus sensusque distenditur*) from the expectation of future sounds and the memory of past sound. With you it is otherwise. You are unchangeably eternal (*incommutabiliter aeterno*), that is the truly eternal Creator of minds. Just as you knew heaven and earth in the beginning without that bringing any variation into your knowing, so you made heaven and earth in the beginning without that meaning a tension (*sine distensione*) between past and future in your activity.[39]

Therefore, since God immutably creates, there is no temporal distinction in Him, as there is in soul, between knowing what will be made and making. God, of course, has something akin to ontological distinctions but these, and therefore His knowing and making, belong to His immutability. Moreover, in God's knowing, all created things are present in their natures according to when He deigns they be present in time. This helps to explain, then, what Augustine means (11.13.15) that God is creator of time.

Conclusion: What does all this signify concerning Augustine's larger projects in book 11 and in books 11–13? First, it shows, through Christ, that scripture provides a credible account of God. Augustine's exegesis supports the doctrine of divine immutability and is capable of showing how God's creating occurs. Augustine manifests that scripture's account of the eternal Father eternally begetting His eternal Son, through Whom all things are created, is compelling. What scripture upholds allows one to understand, and perhaps even develops, the indubitable knowledge of God and creation obtained through pagan Platonist philosophy. Second, Augustine's argument shows that knowledge of God's presence can be expanded. If immutability's creating entails the Father's eternal begetting of His eternal Word, His presence is by the mode of Father and Word. Soul's "pursuit of happiness in truth" represents the Father's begetting His Word—perhaps in terms of (i) *truth* signifying the Father and (ii) *pursuing of happiness* representing the Word. Hence, even though 13.11.12 shows Augustine is dissatisfied with hitherto accounts of divine presence, he certainly implies that *conf.* 11 is more representative of divine immutability than 10.22.32–3.

What does book 11 signify concerning *confessio*? It shows that analyzing scripture in Christ provides more evidence He is Wisdom. First, it is made evident that confessing scripture elicits certitudes concerning (i) God in Himself and (ii) mind. Second, Augustine's exegesis shows soul can consider His presence in a more profound manner. Whereas in 10.22.32–3, God's presence was found in soul's pursuing the happy life, it is now understood that the latter is somehow grounded in God's inner life, according to the distinction between Father and Word. Moreover, Augustine's account of mind's awareness of past, present, and future suggests something significant about his activity of confessing for his present awareness brings before itself his past and present, according to its awareness of past, present, and future. While Augustine's confessing is structured by separation from God, its purpose is to overcome that separation so that in heaven confessing will be apart from temporality.

Confessor Augustine implies that awareness' regulation of past, present, and future (in which respect he is making) is not for the end of knowledge. Rather, Augustine carries it out so he can, through Christ's mediation, achieve eternal union with God; and he can thereby see—by the mode of present awareness—his entire life and the life of humanity. Moreover, Augustine's present awareness acts according to the immutable standard who is God. From beginning to end, Augustine presents God's immutable knowing and making as the ultimate source, medium, and goal of his own knowing and making. Augustine confesses, by God's grace, to become like Him. Christ (11.2.4 and 11.29.39), therefore, gives Augustine insight into the Godhead and his own psychological structure because He gives Augustine opportunity to participate immutably in God. Thus, Augustine's insight into Christ's wisdom and knowledge belongs to Christ's gift of mediation.

All told, Confessor Augustine has shown God should be praised for His scriptures since the latter, rightly interpreted, evinces that Christ is Wisdom. Explicitly, this is because scripture explains how divine immutability creates; implicitly, scripture instructs concerning the nature and object of *confessio*. Just as *conf.* 10 provided proof by showing intellectual and moral progress, *conf.* 11 offers evidence by displaying the same.

However, Augustine's project constituting *conf.* 11–13 is incomplete since, regarding its principal goal (e.g., 11.2.3), it has mostly told us about the mode of God's creating and things' *exitus*. We lack an account of God's creating His church unto His Sabbath rest, i.e., the complete *exitus-reditus* Augustine had promised. Thus, more needs to be said about God in Himself, the nature and object of His creating (especially His church) and presence, the value of confessing scripture and, therefore, *confessio* itself.

Conf. 12[40]

Introduction: Book 12 considers the meaning of "heaven and earth" in Gen. 1:1 and, in a related vein, the nature of exegesis. First, Augustine confesses what God initially creates. This is (i) the "heaven of heaven" (*caelum caeli*), understood as the place of eternal bliss[41] (i.e., the object Augustine longs for in Christ [11.29.30–30.40] because it is the Church's *telos*)[42] and (ii) formless matter (*informis materia*),⁴³ conceived as the principle of mutability in creatures—underlying book 11's analysis of time.⁴⁴ But Augustine notices his conclusion's interpretation of "heaven and earth" is not indubitable since he cannot be sure what Moses, inspired by God's Spirit, meant by these words. By his own principles, Augustine knows there are several plausible interpretations thereof. Hence, Augustine's proof, through exegesis, that Christ is Wisdom appears to have "hit a wall" since, contrary to book 11's account of Gen. 1:1's "In the beginning, God created," interpretation of the remainder of Gen. 1:1 eludes certitude.

This leads to book 12's second major consideration, concerning the nature of exegesis. Augustine's study brings the conclusion that, as man and (therefore) *confessio* are developmental, God's knowledge and love (i.e., His goodness) is both beyond human comprehension yet shared out. Since exegesis is governed by the command to "love God (Who is Truth) and neighbor," and men can be at different stages in loving "God and neighbor," two related implications follow. First, scripture has many possible interpretations and, second, the charitable exegete will acknowledge a plurality in truth to encourage others toward (what *conf.* 12 identifies as) "heaven of heavens." To Augustine, moreover, the exegete's activity is specially affiliated with God's Spirit since He motivates man's love for God and neighbor. And this, it is implied, plays an important role in Augustine's ongoing accounts of God in Himself (now considered, in some measure, as Father, Word, and Spirit) and the nature of His presence (now considered, to some degree, as trinitarian). Augustine finishes book 12 by asking God's Spirit to help him provide a plausible and economical account of His creating His church.

In book 12, therefore, Augustine confesses more of creation's *exitus* and the beginning of its *reditus*. While *exitus* is visible in God's creating creatures' formal principles, *reditus* is visible in Augustine's account of the rational creature's *telos* in the "heaven of heavens" and appeal to the connected topics of God's Spirit, scriptures' liberality, and, consequently, of exegesis. For those reasons and more, the entirety discloses key aspects of *confessio*.

Analyzing book 12: Augustine commences book 12 by considering the meaning of Gen. 1:1's "heaven and earth." He analyzes the words' literal meaning as "sky above" and "soil below," but wonders, based on Ps. 116:13, whether "heaven" refers to the "heaven of heavens," i.e., the blessed's eternal abode and, therefore, if "earth" signifies "sky above" and "soil below."⁴⁵ Next, Augustine scrutinizes the meaning of "earth" and surmises, by considering Gen. 1:2 description of "earth" as "invisible and unorganized," that it probably refers to formless matter,⁴⁶ i.e., *to what he understands philosophically*⁴⁷ is not a substance but a principle within each creature.⁴⁸

Is Augustine's notion coherent?⁴⁹ As he explains both here and later (12.29.40), each creature, created from nothing, is a formed (i.e., made) reality. Moreover, as making shows, whatever is formed is a composite of form and matter (or subject) that is obviously capable of being brought into existence, taken from existence, or modified. A statue, for example, can be formed from marble, destroyed, or scratched. Hence, the statue, as formed, is composite and, likewise, the marble is also composite, having the form marble and some appropriate material(s) as its subject. What Augustine has noticed, however, is since each composite is intrinsically mutable, i.e., can be modified, has received existence, or can cease existing, each composite must contain some principle of mutability, i.e., ability to change, as its subject. Moreover since form is what causes things to be, distinguishes things, and "provide[s] the originating cause of the time process,"⁵⁰ then the matter, or subject, must be potential to change. That matter, furthermore, cannot be formed, since that would be a substance rather than the cause of mutability. Instead, the matter must be *formless*, as what is found in all created things, and "is," therefore, not a thing (substance) but some intrinsic potentiality found therein.⁵¹

This may help. Augustine later returns to his notion of formless matter by distinguishing between various forms of priority, viz. priority "in eternity (*aeternitate*)," "in time (*tempore*)," "in preference (*electione*)," and "in origin (*origine*)."⁵² He claims formless matter is prior to things, i.e., to composite substances, by the mode of origin. Since formless matter is not a created substance, it cannot be prior in eternity to form (like God is to creatures), prior in time to form (as parent is to offspring), or prior in preference to form (as one prefers bagels to sliced bread). Rather, formless matter's priority is by origin as sound is related to song—for song is formed sound and sound is song's subject. Therefore, sound is prior to song. Sound, though, is not prior to song as sound belonging to song exists prior to that song. For then two different "substances" are being designated, viz. (i) the song to be and (ii) the sound—which, since existing, must be some kind of formed reality. Rather, since song *is* formed sound, sound belonging to song must be prior in origin, rather than temporally prior, to the song. Therefore, since form gives being and intelligibility to things, and things are composites of form and subject, the mutability in mutable things depends on the priority in origin of matter to form. Put simply, there must be a priority of subject to form not only concerning mundane making but also, more significantly, regarding the existing of mutable substance as such. Hence, Augustine claims there is priority of formless matter to form. Based on that, and on what Genesis says in subsequent lines about creatures, Augustine thinks Gen. 1:1 means formless matter by "earth."

Augustine implies, then, that analysis of "earth" brings knowledge concerning scripture's veracity and proof, therefore (since scripture manifests Christ), that Christ is Wisdom. How so? Just as Gen. 1:1 adds to the indubitable knowledge that God is immutable creator by distinguishing between Father and Word, its claim that formless matter is prior in origin within God's creating adds to the aforementioned understanding of God as creator.[53] Otherwise, one denies divine immutability, the Father's eternal begetting of His Son, and that God is creator, by maintaining creatures are divine substance.[54]

Moreover, Augustine's account of "heaven" as "the heaven of heavens" is reasonable since if Genesis speaks after 1:1 of the creation of mutable things, then "heaven" in 1:1. is some kind of non-mutable reality.[55] But this cannot be God, as He alone is immutable.[56] Rather, it is some formless creature, to Augustine's mind the place of eternal blessedness, the eternal Jerusalem, where creatures are immutable by participating in God (12.9.9; 12.10.12–12.15).[57] Augustine's point is not that creatures become God but become, by His goodness, immutably united with His immutability.[58] Hence, if "heaven" designates a timeless created reality, Augustine thinks that is "the heaven of heavens," the eternal abode of the blessed where, through Christ, Monnica, for one, now dwells.

Augustine maintains his interpretation of Gen. 1:1 is philosophically accurate since, in conjunction with Genesis' subsequent verses, it upholds divine immutability and creating.[59] Yet, Augustine remarks in 12.13.16 that his understanding of "heaven and earth" is "provisional (*interim*)."[60] Why say this? It is not because Augustine thinks his interpretation is wrong[61] but because he cannot be *certain* it is what Moses, led by God's Spirit, means.[62] Exegetes might agree with Augustine's interpretation yet hold that Moses had other things in mind that were appropriate to either his audience's mindset or his own.[63] In addition, Augustine recognizes many other licit interpretations of Gen. 1:1.[64]

Accordingly, Augustine "waves a white flag" for while knowing his previous interpretations of formless matter and heaven are philosophically accurate, he cannot know, *with certitude*, if Moses meant the same.[65] Augustine maintains, then, that "two areas of disagreement can arise when something is recorded by truthful reporters using signs."[66] First, "the truth of the matter in question" and second, "the intention of the writer."[67] Augustine opposes false interpretations of Gen. 1:1 and/or claims Moses promulgated something "untrue."[68] Therefore, while Augustine agrees he cannot know exactly what Moses meant by those words, he can be sure that whatever Moses meant "was true and that his articulation of it in words was appropriate."[69]

How does Augustine sort this out? By appealing to charity, i.e., to the love of God and neighbor.[70] Above all else, Augustine opposes the presumptuous, i.e., those claiming to *know* what God and/or Moses meant by Gen. 1:1.[71] Rather, the charitable, i.e., *confessio*, mindset strives to know and share truth while acknowledging its limitations.[72] Since *confessio* will not claim to know what it cannot, it will not assert identity with God's or Moses's mind, and, following these minds,[73] it will encourage true interpretations to inspire others in truth.[74] In short, the exegete will love God and neighbor. Therefore, while Augustine maintains his earlier interpretation's (12.28.38–29.40) legitimacy, he promises to propound it charitably.[75] Accordingly, a humble Augustine finishes book 12 by asking God's help to understand His scriptures and, in particular, to confess some economical interpretation concerning the project begun in 11.2.3 regarding God's creating His church.[76]

Conclusion: How does this apply to Augustine's projects in book 12 and in books 11–13? First, Augustine confesses "formless matter," "heaven of heaven," and exegesis' nature, in a manner analogous to book 11's confession of time and eternity, to encourage *confessio*. By considering "formless matter" and "heaven of heavens," each can recognize their mutability and need to participate, through Christ, in divine immutability. On this basis, each will transcend mutability by dwelling in the "heaven of heavens"—where (following *conf.* 11's distinction between time and eternity) *confessio* will be structured by an a-temporal *exitus-reditus*. Hence, the human agent, becoming like God, will know and love His presence apart from duration. Moreover, since charity governs exegesis, it shows both the way to "heaven of heavens" and something of the latter's character. First, the exegete reaches toward heaven by performing exegesis according to *confessio*. Second, "heaven of heaven" is a community of love wherein, as Augustine's shared vision of Wisdom with Monnica at Ostia implies, each shall love others in perfect agreement with God's love.[77]

Additionally, Augustine encourages *confessio* by showing that scripture's account of God is credible. Augustine suggests that even if the meaning of "heaven and earth" is mysterious, the claim it is divinely created is coherent. This is not because the latter stands upon the indubitable knowledge of God mind can obtain with Platonist philosophy's aid (cf. 7.11.17), but since it shows the fundamental structure of mutable reality. Furthermore, Augustine's argument discloses that God's presence can be expanded beyond book 11's concluding analogy. There Augustine implied divine creating entails that God's presence is somehow in likeness of the Father's begetting His Word. Soul's pursuing "happiness in truth," then, represents the Father's begetting His Word—perhaps in terms of (i) "truth" denoting the Father and (ii) "pursuing happiness/truth" denoting the Word. Book 12's consideration of the Holy Spirit, however, changes things for Spirit's affiliation with love implies that soul's pursuing truth better represents the Spirit than the Word. But we notice here an asymmetry. Relative to *conf.* 10, the divine side of God's presence is loosely distinguished into Father, Word, and Spirit, while the human side is only distinguished into mind and will/love. Something is obviously missing on the human side. Except perhaps for Spirit and will, we lack correspondence between God in Himself and mind in itself. Progress is apparent since Augustine implies divine presence is more sophisticated than stated in 10.22.32-3 and 11.31.41. However, as 13.11.12 shows, Augustine realizes a coherent account of divine presence is lacking.

Conf. 12 also shows that analyzing scripture provides more evidence that Christ is Wisdom since, as Augustine reminded us in 11.2.4 and 11.29.39, Christ is the Mediator through Whom the "heaven of heavens" is attained. First, *conf.* 12 has shown that confessing scripture elicits new certitudes concerning God in Himself and mind in itself. Love of God (Who is Truth) and neighbor governs exegesis as it governs everything else in the lifestyle of Wisdom. Second, Augustine's exegesis shows soul can consider His presence more profoundly. In 10.22.32–3, God's presence was found in soul's pursuing the happy life, in 11.31.41 pursuing the happy life is grounded in kinship to aspects of the Godhead, understood in terms of distinction between Father and Word. Book 12, however, shows that pursuing the happy life is grounded in kinship to the entire Godhead, distinguished as Father, Word, and Spirit—though, as mentioned previously, the matter is somewhat inchoate.

Thus, Confessor Augustine has shown that each should praise God for scripture since the latter, rightly interpreted, gives more evidence that Christ is Wisdom. Just as *conf.* 10–11 provided proof by showing us intellectual and moral progress, *conf.* 12 offers proof by disclosing intellectual progress in 12.2.2–13.16 and moral progress in 12.14.17–32.43.

Nevertheless, Augustine's exegesis is incomplete since, to consider its principal object stated in 11.2.3 (viz. to distinguish God's creating His church), he has hitherto told us more about the mode of God's creating, and therefore concerning creatures' *exitus*, than about the mode of God's returning creation to Himself, i.e., regarding creatures' *reditus*. Augustine has now explained creatures' origin, including how and why they are mutable. Moreover, he has considered the rational creature's *telos* in "the heaven of heavens," and his exegesis claims that "love" belongs to the rational creature's return to God. However, as 12.32.43 evinces, we lack an account of God's creating unto His Sabbath rest, i.e., of the complete *exitus-reditus* promised in 11.2.3.

Thus, Augustine has much more to say about God in Himself, His creating, the nature of His presence, the value of confessing His scriptures, and, therefore, about *confessio*.

Conf. 13[78]

Introduction: Augustine confesses God's goodness (*bonitas*) since that is divine creating's raison d'être. God's goodness in Christ is responsible for God's creating His church, God's presence, the proper mode of scriptural exegesis, Augustine's spiritual exegesis in 13.12.13–38.53 (wherein he finally promulgates [11.2.3] God's creating His church), and the reason why, concerning *conf.* as a whole, Augustine practices *confessio*.[79] Since Augustine's *telos* as confessor coincides with those of (i) the created order and (ii) God's church, Augustine's concentration on God's goodness in book 13 makes a fitting conclusion to books 11–13 and to *conf.*

Analyzing book 13: In concert with 11.1.1's final words,[80] Augustine commences book 13 with discussion of God's goodness (*bonitas*), and book 13's remainder, *conf.*'s final confession, is guided accordingly. This is because Augustine's activity as confessor, and therefore *conf.*, explicitly participates in God's goodness. Augustine claims God's goodness is His motive for creating and, therefore, for producing humanity. Accordingly, Augustine confesses that book 11–13's exegesis participates in God's goodness. The primacy of divine goodness, moreover, implies that creatures' *exitus*, and therefore scripture's existence (already highlighted in books 11–12), is traced to *reditus*, i.e., because God creates (rational) creatures for their benefit—to be eternally established with Him.[81] *Exitus* is because of *reditus*, i.e., for creatures' return to God. Augustine's exegesis in 13.12.13–38.53 will describe that and, consequently, the reason for exegesis.

In 13.1.1–2.3 Augustine transitions, following *conf.*'s major divisions between books 1–10 and 11–13,[82] from microcosm to macrocosm, from personal to universal development, showing thereby that biography is instantiated and disclosed within theology. First, Augustine recalls God's mercy upon him, chastising him for evildoing before conversion, converting him, and placing in him a longing for eternal union.[83] Viewing things next from a metaphysical perspective, Augustine confesses that his existing, conversion, and orientation toward beatitude (cf. 10.27.38) is caused by God's goodness (*bonitas*).[84] God does not create him because He lacks but *entirely* for Augustine's benefit: "I serve and worship you so that from you good may come to me. To you I owe my being and the goodness of my being."[85] Second, Augustine claims the entire created order, even the ultimate subjects of spiritual and corporeal creatures, viz. formless "whatever" for spirits and formless matter for bodies, and the conversion to Wisdom of spirits and humans, depend on God's goodness (*bonitas*).[86]

To make his point, Augustine maintains Gen. 1:2 signifies the Holy Spirit, which the Catholic religion identifies as the Godhead's third Person. (Gen. 1:3, Augustine says, signifies God's creating His angels.[87]) At first, Augustine evinces that creation, including creatures' constituting principles, depends on God's goodness. Hence, a corollary of His goodness is displeasure with creaturely imperfection. Just as He could not have made formless "matter" apart from making creatures, so He makes creatures for their perfection. Augustine writes:

> You made it not because you needed it, but from the fullness of your goodness, imposing control and converting it to receive form—but not as if the result brought you fulfillment of delight. The corollary of your perfection is that the imperfection of created things is displeasing. So they seek perfection from you that they may please you, yet it is not that otherwise you would be imperfect and need to be perfected by their perfection.[88]

Most important, Augustine finds this signified in Gen. 1:2, where he also distinguishes the Trinity's third Person, Who leads things to their ends. Augustine writes: "'Your good Spirit' (Ps. 142:10) 'was borne above the waters' (Gen. 1:2), but not borne up by them as if resting weight on them."[89]

Augustine teaches, then, that creatures owe their being to God's goodness and depend, therefore, on God the Father, Word, and Spirit.[90] Moreover, God's Spirit has special responsibility for creatures' sharing in His goodness since He leads them to their *telos*. Augustine, therefore, views God's Spirit as responsible for creatures' formation and, in the case of spirits and humans, especially for their enjoyment of God.[91] Put differently, Augustine claims that God's Spirit (i) shares responsibility for creatures' existing[92] and (ii) motion, also named love,[93] toward their *telos*.[94]

Reflecting on his ongoing exegesis, Augustine remarks (13.5.6) that the Trinity, i.e., the Catholic religion's account of the Godhead, is distinguishable in Gen. 1:1-2:

> And now where the name God occurs, I have come to see the Father who made these things; where the "Beginning" is mentioned, I see the Son by whom he made these things. Believing that my God is Trinity, in accordance with my belief I searched in God's holy oracles and found your Spirit to be borne above the waters. There is the Trinity, my God—Father and Son and Holy Spirit, Creator of the entire creation.[95]

Augustine implies that the Catholic religion's account of God as Trinity is cogent since the Spirit is immutable. This also gives evidence that scripture and, therefore, the Catholic religion's claim that Christ is Wisdom are credible.

In 13.11.12, Augustine supports Catholic doctrine of the Godhead by showing mind has a trinitarian structure and, consequently, that divine presence is trinitarian.[96] Beginning with belief that God is triune, Augustine considers three aspects of mind easily accessible upon introspection, viz. mind's being (*esse*), knowing (*nosse*), and willing (*velle*).[97] This, then, is consubstantial with, since structuring (rather than adventitious to), mind; its character, moreover, is akin to each of mind's (i) pursuing happiness, distinguished in book 10, (ii) knowing and making, manifested in book 11, and (iii) knowing and loving, briefly detailed in book 12. Hence, Augustine distinguishes something structuring mind about which it can have certitude. Moreover, he urges this triad be considered as activity: "For I am and I know and I will. Knowing and willing I am. I know that I am and I will. I will to be and to know."[98] None of these can be present without the other since each is co-implicate; to be is to know and to love; to love is to know and to be; and to know is to love and to be.

Augustine likes two things about this analogy. First, those reflecting on this triad see something simultaneously one and many. The three activities mind sees structuring itself are "inseparable in life ... they are one life, one mind, and one essence."[99] Additionally, each activity is distinguishable—knowing can be demarcated from willing and being, etc. Augustine remarks: "The fact [i.e., the unity and distinction] is certain (*Certe coram se est*) to anyone by introspection (*videat qui potest*). Let him consider himself and reflect and tell me what is there."[100] Second, those reflecting on trinitarian mind should see that the insight it brings concerning the Trinity is imperfect. It is not only that mind is mutable but also that the aforementioned activities structuring mind probably belong to each divine Person rather than to any Person alone.[101] Augustine writes:

> So the divine being is and knows itself and is immutably sufficient to itself, because of the overflowing greatness of the unity. Who can find a way to give expression to that? Who would venture in any way whatever to make a rash pronouncement on the subject?[102]

Hence, this account of mind works by wide rather than by narrow analogy. Mind can learn something about the Trinity but since the

Trinity transcends human nature and comprehension, that learning is minimal.

There are two reasons why this passage is important to analyzing Augustine's *confessio*. First, it provides philosophical evidence for the Catholic account of the Godhead and therefore that Christ is Wisdom. Second, in a related vein, it gives a satisfactory account of divine presence. On this score, we see not only, contrary to 10.25.36–26.37's implied parallel between divine immutability and mind's pursuing happiness, that divine presence parallels God in Himself with mind in itself but also, contrary to what was implied in books 11–12, these parties are paralleled in a generally coherent manner. In the former instances, either God the Father and Son are affiliated with human intellect and will (book 11) or Father, Son, and Spirit are somehow associated with intellect and will (book 12). In 13.11.12, however, Father, Son, and Spirit are paralleled with mind's being, knowing, and willing. As such, Augustine has identified something in mind known with certitude through which it pursues God and by which (though Augustine does not make that connection here) His immutable existing can be known. In these respects, Augustine's reasoning implies proof of divine immutability and that the Catholic religion's account of Wisdom is cogent.

Most important, now that Augustine has distinguished God as triune and His presence as trinitarian, he finally provides, by the mode of spiritual exegesis, his account of God's creating His church (13.12.13–38.53). This has threefold importance. First, Augustine's exegesis is spiritual since it interprets the scriptures (while acknowledging scripture's literal elements—13.24.35–7) to increase his knowledge and love. For Augustine, Christ, the mediator between God and man in Whom "is found all the treasures of wisdom and knowledge" (11.2.4), guides his exegesis. Second, although the words Augustine focuses on in Gen. 1:1–2:3 do not mention the Church, he interprets them to signify her for two reasons. There is not only what Church tradition and scripture says elsewhere about the Church[103] but also that Augustine considers God's creating His church roughly analogous to the universal elements found in his own relationship with God (13.1.1). The latter, consisting in an essentially progressive relationship with divine goodness,[104] is viewed as microcosm of God's creating His church (cf. 13.1.1–2.2.3).

Since Augustine summarizes, within 13.32.47–34.49, his exegesis of God's creating His church (13.12.13–31.46)[105] in advance of his concluding depiction of the Sabbath rest, we cite his exegesis of Gen. 1:1–2:3 to show his exegesis' principal distinctions.[106] After describing Gen. 1:1-31's literal meaning in 13.32.47, Augustine begins his summary, in 13.33.48, by stating that Gen. 1:1 signifies God's eternal decision to create His church. Following this, Augustine makes these seven claims. First, Gen. 1:2-5 (day 1: 13.12.13–14.15) bespeaks God's creating His church by separating the godly from the ungodly. Second, Gen. 1:6-8 (day 2: 13.15.16–18) describes God's placing His scriptures over His church. Third, Gen. 1:9-13 (day 3: 13.17.20–1) means God's growing His church from among the Gentile nations. Fourth, Gen. 1:14-19 (day 4: 13.17.22–19.25) signifies the elects' spiritual and corporal acts of mercy. Fifth, Gen. 1:20-23 (day 5: 13.20.26–8) bespeaks the Church's conversion of nonbelievers through preaching, the sacraments, and miracles. Sixth, Gen. 1:24-31 (day 6: 13.21.29–31.46) means God's developing His church's leaders in wisdom and, through that, her other members. Finally, Augustine describes the Sabbath rest (day 7: Gen. 2:1-3) in 13.35.50–38.53 by claiming the Church's *telos* consists in eternal rest. The Sabbath rest is why God creates His church.

Therefore, by reading the earlier distinctions in light of Augustine's account, in 10.27.38 and 13.1.1, of the principal divisions constituting his relationship with God's goodness, viz. (i) before conversion, (ii) after conversion, and (iii) the afterlife, we see a rough parallel between Augustine's analyses of personal experience and Church development.[107] Gen. 1:2-13, describing God's establishing His church, corresponds with Augustine's life prior to his conversion (since he was then outside the Church). Gen. 1:14-31, detailing the Church's activity, signifies Augustine's conversion to and subsequent role in the Church, first as monk but now as priest and bishop. Finally, Gen. 2:1-3, concerning the Sabbath rest, represents what to Augustine's mind is one and the same, viz. his and the Church's *telos*. Hence, just as Augustine finds in the Godhead, microcosm and macrocosm, particular and universal, are one.

Third, Augustine's exegesis represents a fitting conclusion to *conf.* since his activity has loving of God and neighbor (completed in the Sabbath rest) as its origin, medium, and goal. How so? Augustine's desire, implanted in Him by God's goodness (in particular by His Spirit) for the Sabbath rest, is his exegesis' motivation and guide because these cause him to confess, i.e., to write *conf*. Hence, Augustine's activity as confessor directs and, consequently, coincides with his activity as exegete; each activity instantiates and therefore aims to share divine goodness. From beginning to end, then, *conf.* belongs to Augustine's *reditus* to God.

Conclusion

In *conf.* 11–13, Augustine confesses in a universal and progressive manner that *confessio*, centered in the humble worship of Christ,[108] is existentially sound. In one way, this is identical to his confession in *conf.* 8–10 but in another, and significant, manner it is distinct. As mentioned, Augustine's *confessio* is grounded in God incarnate's mediation.[109] Now, however, Christ is considered concerning His place in the Godhead in which all creatures participate—including the Church and some of her content: like scripture, Augustine himself, Augustine's scriptural exegesis, man as *imago trinitatis*, and (by implication) *conf.* Augustine continues to uphold Christ but adds to this a significant portion of the knowledge and love that the path toward beatitude brings by presenting Christ as the One in Whom "'is hidden all the treasures of wisdom and knowledge' (Col. 2:3)."[110] As such, Augustine leads from microcosm, viz. from his attaining *confessio*, to macrocosm, viz. to considering, through Christ's creating His church, the ultimate cause of *confessio*. Although Augustine's formal object is God's creating His church (11.2.3), confessing his knowledge and love of Christ's knowledge and love gives *confessio* additional existential warrant.

In what sense is Augustine's confession "universal and objective"? Certainly, it is so by analogy, but there is also a way it is universal and objective as such. To begin, Augustine's confession is explicitly "general" (and therefore "universal and objective") since, unlike his confessing in *conf.* 1–10, exegesis of God's creating His church from Gen. 1:1–2:3 obviously distinguishes aspects of divine goodness only shared with some. It is true, then, that Augustine engages much more his principal, rather than subaltern, audience and, furthermore, we note it is *this* Augustine who engages in *this* exegesis of *these* words in *this* way. Particularity is everywhere. Consequently, the principal medium Augustine engages, the foremost object of his exegesis, and his goal in confessing to his Christian brethren are "universal" in the sense of "general."

However, everything Augustine confesses in these books—viz. his knowledge and/or opinion concerning God and His actions, the ontological structure of creatures, the scriptures, and trinitarian mind—is *qua* knowledge or opinion, applicable to each. As Augustine sees it, his central account of divine goodness (disclosed in 13.1.1–2.3) and everything flowing therefrom can apply, in principle, to anyone. Augustine's confession in *conf.* 11–13 is certainly "universal and objective" analogically since it appeals to matters Augustine holds in common with his principal audience; but it is "universal and objective" period if Augustine is right about the nature of happiness.

Books 11–13's confession is overtly progressive because it details a series of closely related cosmic developments participating in the Godhead. Concomitant with Augustine's project to distinguish God's creating His church (11.2.3) are progressive accounts of the Godhead, God's creating, scriptural exegesis, and divine presence. Each teaching develops throughout books 11–13. Book 11 concentrates on the immutable mode of divine creating (grounded in the Father's eternal begetting of His Word) and on creaturely but especially human mutability, made evident in considering time. The latter, moreover, is especially significant since implying certain matters concerning divine presence's nature (that look backward and forward in *conf.*) while focusing on mind's imperfection and need, therefore, of Christ's mediation (11.29.39–30.40). Book 12 also concentrates on God and creature toward considering man's participation, through Christ, in immutable divinity. It focuses on the first "things" God creates *de nihilo*, viz. (i) the subject (formless matter) of corporeal creatures and (ii) the elect's eternal home, viz. the "heaven of heavens," ultimately obtained through Christ's mediation. Book 12 also considers scripture—especially as affiliated with God's Spirit so the *ecclesia* can thereby attain heaven and participate immutably in God. Here too, Augustine implies certain things regarding divine presence's nature, but his focus on "heaven" and the proper attitude toward exegesis shows his preeminent concern with achieving immutable participation in and through Christ.

Book 13, *conf.*'s final confession, follows suit but in a special way since it summarizes key doctrines from books 11–12 to exhibit, by exegesis in 13.12.13–38.53, that the entirety has its origin and goal in the Sabbath rest—which book 12 identified as "heaven of heaven." *Conf.* 13 begins by reviewing, in its early chapters, the relationship between creaturely mutability (especially human mutability) and divine immutability. It considers (i) *creatio*, *formatio*, and *reformatio/conversio* and (ii) mind as trinitarian along with (a) divine goodness, (b) the Spirit, and (c) the Trinity. Moreover, once human selfhood, viewed as *esse-nosse-velle*, is formally matched up with the Godhead (13.11.12), book 13 presents a spiritual exegesis of the seven days of creation in Gen. 1:1–2:2/3 as the origin and development of the Church unto the Sabbath rest.

Hence, Augustine's exegesis, begun in book 11 by explaining creatures' origin in God, is completed in book 13 by depicting the Church's *telos* in eternity. In general, books 11–13 are progressive since Augustine's confession has an *exitus-reditus* structure applying to and, for this reason, concluding *conf.* entire. Augustine now praises God for His creating, i.e., for His production of all things and return thereof in His Sabbath rest. Augustine's focus on macrocosm, viz. on God's creating His church, converges with (as subordinate to) his concentration on microcosm, God's creating Augustine. In both instances, book 13's account of divine goodness (*bonitas*) is decisive since that is God's motive. God, Augustine claims, chooses to create mutable reality in general and human beings in particular, and forms and reforms them (13.1.1–10.11), entirely for their benefit.

God creates, then, because, as Christ shows, He shares infinite goodness. Hence, the *reditus* Augustine describes in book 13, already signified in book 11's account of temporality and book 12's accounts of the "heaven of heaven" and exegesis, governs the *exitus* Augustine distinguished in books 11–12 and in book 13's early part. From beginning to end, books 11–13 confess Christ as mediator (11.2.4); Augustine displays Christ's "knowledge and wisdom" while embracing Him as way to beatitude.

How, though, does Confessor Augustine's doctrine of infinite divine goodness guide *conf.* as a whole? As stated earlier, Augustine (whether viewed as writer or as narrator[111]) produces *conf.* to encourage loving God and neighbor. Book 13's cosmic scope implies, therefore, that Augustine's motive to confess participates in God's motive to create, viz. to share goodness. Hence, Augustine's confessing *reditus* in book 13 implies that *conf.* belongs to[112] God's infinite goodness.

For Augustine, *conf.*, as its account of divine presence in 1.1.1–5.6 shows, has an *exitus-reditus* structure. That, however, is only the most general implication. Particular implications include Augustine's account of *confessio* as trinitarian (e.g., 13.11.12) since his introduction in *conf.* 1.1.1 is loosely trinitarian and also his concluding with the Sabbath rest in 13.35.50–38.53 since, in this respect, Augustine distinguishes that rest, initially identified in *conf.* 1.1.1, for which the human heart and, consequently, God's church long. And there are many more implications including considering the temptations of flesh, world, and devil according to the standard of 1 Jn 2:16, teachings on concupiscence, *conf.* 1–9's ostensible chiastic structure, and *conf.*'s focus, specifically considered in *conf.* 11, not only on memory but also on the triad of present expectation, awareness, and remembrance.

But these are essentially secondary since proceeding from Augustine's disposition of *confessio*. What, then, is primary? Augustine implies that everything above ultimately participates, through Christ, in the Godhead. Indeed, Augustine's *exitus-reditus confessio* continually praises God for His creating and claims to participate in divine creating's *exitus-reditus* and therefore in some sort of *exitus-reditus* constituting the Godhead. Augustine attaches himself to God incarnate so others might follow suit and ultimately confess (in heaven) by a manner of *exitus-reditus* transcending temporality. From beginning to end, then, *conf.* is governed by participating explicitly in Christ's knowledge and love. In this regard, Augustine gives evidence that *conf.* is motivated by Christ.

Why, then, does Augustine confess? And why do we study *Confessions*? As Augustine sees it, this is because God in Himself, as Christ shows, is *confessio* and invites us to share therein.

Further Study

Book 11: What is the purpose of Augustine's confession in books 11–13? Please explain.

Why does Augustine maintain Gen. 1:1 shows that an immutable God creates mutable reality?

How does Augustine answer the question, "What was God doing before He made heaven and earth?"

Does Augustine's concluding analogy in book 11 improve on the account of divine presence articulated in 10.22.32–4?

Book 12: Why does Augustine think the words "heaven and earth" in Gen. 1:1 signify "the heavenly Jerusalem" and "formless matter"? Please explain.

Why does Augustine maintain his interpretation of "heaven and earth" is uncertain? Please explain.

Why does Augustine hold that the principle of exegesis consists in "loving God and neighbor"? Please explain.

What is the importance of Augustine's introduction of the Holy Spirit into his exegesis in book 12? Please explain.

Book 13: What is the immediate importance of Augustine's distinguishing divine goodness (*bonitas*) at the outset of book 13? Please explain.

How does Augustine's account of divine goodness represent the *reditus* element in books 11–13's exegesis? Please explain.

What is the nature and importance of Augustine's discussion of the Godhead in 13.11.12?

How is Augustine's exegesis of the Church in 13.12.13–38.53 related to his accounts of personal conversion in 10.27.38 and 13.1.1?

Why is Augustine's exegesis of the Sabbath rest in 13.35.50–38.53 a fitting conclusion to both his (i) exegesis of the Church in 13.12.13–38.53 and (ii) general exegesis in books 11–13?

Articles

Jordan, 255–79
Karfíková, 175–90
Helm (2014), 135–54
Kennedy, 167–83
Kenney (2010), 145–65
Martin, 185–206
McMahon (2003), 207–23
Peters, 53–74
Teske (2000), 29–45; (2008), 254–79
Tornau, 181–218

Books

BeDuhn (2013), 369–402, 468–91
David (2019A), 161–252
O'Donnell, 3@250–421
Hochschild, 155–88
Vaught (2005), 101–226
Kenney (2005), 102–9, 113–28
Wills (2002), xi–26, 147–87; (2011), 111–32
McMahon (1989), 38–41, 117–41, 145
Stock, 232–42
Rigby, 204–12

5

Conclusion

Confessions is about *Confessio*—and *Confessio* Imitates Divine Incarnation

Introduction

This chapter argues three things and strongly suggests another. First, *conf.* has a formal unity grounded in *confessio,* i.e., of praising God incarnate for His infinite goodness so one's innate union with Him can ultimately become immutable. Second, this chapter claims, in a related vein, that *confessio* is reasonable. Third, it is maintained that *confessio*, looked at doctrinally, embodies the Christian doctrine of incarnation and, through that, the doctrine of Trinity and virtue of charity. Therefore, if *conf.* is grounded in *confessio*, and *confessio* is guided by divine incarnation, *conf.* is fundamentally incarnational. In short, CC maintains that whereas *conf.*'s proximate cause is *confessio*, its exemplar cause is likely divine incarnation.

Confessions' Formal Unity is *Confessio*

Commentators agree *conf.* has a material unity, consisting in thirteen confessions, but only some assert Augustine composed *conf.* with a plan so that his text is *teleological*.[1] While those claiming *conf.* has only a material unity[2] maintain it should be studied apart from considering formal unity, those ascribing formal unity can be divided into two groups. While some claim Augustine's intention is *definitive and discoverable*, others maintain it is "probably" beyond comprehension. The latter express two views: one is that studying *conf.* from the perspective of some formal unity absconds from insight into the text's essential message;[3] another holds that studying *conf.* in that light can be beneficial.[4] This party shares the former's skepticism about discovering *conf.*'s "actual" unity but holds that studying *conf.* by attempts to distinguish formal unity can enable more insight than if the text is viewed otherwise. By contrast, those claiming *conf.* has a *definitive and discoverable* formality commonly hold the text has an *exitus-reditus* pattern, and studying *conf.* in that light enables the reader to better comprehend it. These interpreters differ, however, concerning Augustine's intention. One party grounds *exitus-reditus* in "affective mimesis," tracing Augustine's growing love for God that culminates in the Sabbath rest (13.35.50–38.53). A second party centers *exitus-reditus* in the Prodigal Son parable (Lk. 15:11-32) so Augustine gives a progressive account of his journey away from and then toward God. A third party locates *exitus-reditus* in the Trinity so Augustine's turning away from and then toward God is, in various ways, guided by the relations in the Godhead between Father, Word, and Spirit.[5] On this view, Augustine interprets his own life, including his exegesis, to instantiate the Godhead.[6]

Despite the differences between those asserting *conf.*'s material and/or formal unity, we find significant overlap regarding their approaches. Each holds (at least implicitly) to two things. First, that certain matters can be discovered about *conf.* by study—everyone, for example, encourages analysis, viz. to "pick up and read." Second, as I argued in *CC*'s "Introduction" and elsewhere,[7] *conf.*'s unity is found in Augustine's activity of *confessio*. In these respects, each party emulates the exemplary attitude toward exegesis Augustine expresses in *conf.* 12:

> May all of us who, as I allow, perceive and affirm that these texts contain various truths, show love to one another, and equally may we love you, our God, fount of truth—if truth is what we are thirsting after and not vanity.[8]

CC, taking its cue (albeit selectively) from the opinions enumerated earlier, asserts not only that *conf.* has a formal unity which (i) careful study can distinguish and is insightful, and (ii) employs an *exitus-reditus* pattern but also, more importantly, its unity consists in *confessio*.[9] CC has arrived at this conclusion by following Augustine's lead. First, it upholds Augustine's claim in *retr.* 2.6.1 that *conf.*'s unity lies in praising divine goodness—for which reason Augustine names his text *Confessiones*. But there is more since *retr.* 2.6.1 also discloses that Augustine divides *conf.* into two major parts, viz. (i) books 1–10, concerning how God's goodness has governed his life so he now cooperates with Him, and (ii) books 11–13, wherein interpreting scripture's account of God's church (the macrocosm containing Augustine's personal development) is guided by divine goodness. According to Augustine, then, *conf.*'s biographical and exegetical components praise God's goodness. Hence, *conf.*'s method and content are fundamentally one; its medium is congruent with its message.

To show how *conf.*'s formality lies in Augustine's notion of *confessio* I divided *conf.* into four parts. This can appear arbitrary, but these divisions follow Augustine's principal partition since I left alone his second division while distinguishing his first, viz. books 1–10, into three parts to disclose the aforementioned unity. I divided books 1–10 into books 1–4 (Chapter 1), books 5–7 (Chapter 2), and books 8–10 (Chapter 3) to detail Augustine's coming to embrace *confessio*. Analysis of books 1–4 commences with Augustine's account of the principal causes and nature of *confessio* in 1.1.1–5.6 and follows by considering young Augustine's descent to an anti-*confessio* mindset and the first stages in his ascent toward *confessio*. Therefore, while analysis of 1.6.7–2.10.18 distinguished reasons for and the nature of young Augustine's embracing an anti-*confessio* mindset, my study of 3.1.1–4.16.31, including Augustine's conversion to Wisdom while reading Cicero's *Hortensius* and subsequent joining the Manicheans, details his movement toward *confessio*. Hence, Confessor Augustine begins *conf.* by providing, in 1.1.1–5.6, an account of the *confessio* mindset he aims to share within *conf.* as a whole and, thereafter, commences *conf.*'s "biographical" aspect, explaining his embracing *confessio* and, to some extent, the latter's nature.

But what is that ideal? Helped now by viewing 1.1.1–5.6 in retrospect, we see Confessor Augustine tried to explain and validate the Catholic doctrine of *confessio*. In particular, Augustine argues his reader properly shares (i) certain ontological claims and (ii) a preeminent spiritual claim. The former includes that (i) man, a soul-body composite, is spiritually connected with God (1.1.1–5.6; cf. 7.10.16; 7.17.23); (ii) God is unchanging and therefore incorporeal (1.3.3–4.4; cf. 7.9.14; 7.11.17); and (iii) man has orientation toward immutable participation in God (1.1.1; 1.5.5; cf. 7.10.16) ultimately achieved in the afterlife (7.21.27; 9.10.24). Augustine's preeminent spiritual claim is that man, guided by divine incarnation (1.1.1; cf. 7.21.27), properly strives to cultivate and augment divine union in this life (1.5.6) toward attaining complete union in an afterlife (9.10.24). Augustine claims, then, the Catholic account of divine-human union is reasonable because it holds that man is structured for complete union with God (1.1.1; 1.5.6). Augustine supports his assertion in two complimentary manners. First, he argues that mutable man requires special physical and/or mutable media to attain his *telos* (hence 1.1.1's account of divine incarnation and the related means whereby Augustine has "faith"). Second, Augustine contends the Catholic view of divine-human union is that the latter is not ultimately mutable, i.e., physical (1.2.2–3.3) or durational (1.3.3–4.4), because God is immutable (1.2.2–4.4). Stated positively, the Catholic view is, as Christ's mediation via special mutable reality implies, that God offers man immutable participation in Himself (1.4.4–5.6). Mutable reality is not man's end but, in Christ, the divinely appointed medium whereby he attains his end.

In retrospect, *conf.*'s narrative of young Augustine's coming to Wisdom shows that the first view, being materialist, has a Manichean provenance (e.g., 3.6.10–7.14); the second, being durational, has a Platonist provenance (e.g., 7.10.16; 7.17.23); and the third, pointing toward and culminating in immutably enjoying God (e.g., 7.21.27–13.38.53), has a Catholic provenance. However, the specific views of divine-human union Augustine employs in 1.2.2–4.4 toward validating the Catholic view are neither Manichean nor Platonist since neither party shares Augustine's teaching (taken as a whole) concerning God, man, and Christ's mediation. The Manicheans hold that (i) God is mutable in one respect yet immutable in another (7.2.3); (ii) man, composed of divine and anti-divine particles, is mutable and perishes (4.4.9–5.10); and (iii) Christ's "mediation" brings the divine particles partly constituting man back to God after man dies (7.2–3).[10] The Platonists (taking certain writings by Plotinus and Porphyry as the principal non-Catholic "Platonist books" Augustine reads in 386 AD[11]) agree with Augustine that supreme divinity is immutably incorporeal (e.g., *conf.* 7.9.13–17.21; *Ennead* 5.1.5). However, the Platonists disagree by holding that (i) man, the soul-body composite, ultimately perishes (i.e., man is made for mutable rather than for immutable participation in God—e.g., *Ennead* 1.1.9–10) and (ii) divine mediation (whereby immutable divinity takes to itself mutable humanity) is not needed. This is because they think that *nous*, i.e., the human power of intelligence, and/or the rational soul containing *nous* is akin to supreme divinity and can achieve unity with Him in an afterlife resulting from some combination of (i) *nous*-centered philosophical activity in this life and (ii) bodily death (e.g., *Ennead* 1.1.10).[12]

Additionally, the earlier discussion implies that *conf.* 1.1.1–5.6 has a developmental character disclosing something of the *exitus-reditus* dimension governing *conf.* and therefore of Augustine's *confessio.* 1.1.1–5.6's developmental aspect is visible in two related ways. Obvious is Augustine's account of man's proper unity with God. This commences with the claim that God has both created and stirs the human heart to rest in Him (1.1.1), but transitions to an account of how the heart's proper unity with God occurs (1.1.1–5.6). The latter considers divine incarnation, mediated through His church (1.1.1), to show that although God's mediation employs special mutable means (1.2.2–3.3) the union He promises, entirely for man's welfare (1.5.5), is ultimately immutable (1.4.4–5.5). Hence, Augustine's teaching in 1.1.1–5.6 develops by considering (i) the origin and purpose of man's desire to rest in God, (ii) the medium whereby that desire is fulfilled, and (iii) fulfilment's nature. All told, Augustine's *terminus* refers back to and, to some extent, explains his starting point in 1.1.1.

Viewed accordingly, we notice a subsidiary development in Augustine's philosophical theology. This begins with his vague, but pregnant,[13] account of God's power, wisdom, and goodness (1.1.1); continues with his depiction of divine incarnation, whereby God makes Himself present to man according to the mode of mutability (ibid.); considers why God cannot be material (1.2.2–3.3); and finishes with the claim that God is immutably incorporal (1.4.4–5.5–6). It is thereby implied that God's goodness, power, and wisdom, spoken about in 1.1.1, are immutable, and that He makes His power, wisdom, and goodness present to man under the condition of mutability. Since Augustine's account of God as immutable implicitly refers back to and explains the philosophical theology he enunciated in 1.1.1, we recognize more of 1.1.1–5.6's *exitus-reditus* structure. In agreement, though, with books 1–4, *CC*'s study of books 5–7 distinguished how young Augustine came to understand that *confessio* is man's proper mindset. Therefore, while book 5 showed reasons for which Augustine left the Manicheans and reenrolled as a Catholic catechumen, book 6 claimed that Augustine's life as a catechumen was miserable because his quest for certitude was misplaced. While pursuing certitude played an important role enabling Augustine to become a catechumen and see the futility of his secular pursuits, it also kept him from adhering to Wisdom's noncontradictory lifestyle (exemplified by Monnica's belief) since that was not something about which he had certitude. Hence, Augustine's life as a skeptical catechumen was rife with contradiction since his skepticism condemned him to pursue futile secular goods. Finally, analysis of book 7 showed how catechumen Augustine's encounter with key aspects of Christian doctrine and Platonist philosophy enabled him to know (indubitably) key aspects of Wisdom and subsequently recognize as cogent the Catholic religion's claim that "the Word made flesh" is Wisdom. Therefore, man's rational mindset "almost certainly"[14] consists in *confessio* since (i) it is indubitable that the divine Word is man's proper object and (ii) reasonable that Christ is the way thereto. Hence, books 5–7 showed how Augustine learned that *confessio* is cogent.

Next, analysis of books 8–10 disclosed how Augustine embraced *confessio* and found out *existentially*, i.e., by intellect *and* will, that *confessio* is rational. In book 8, Augustine eventually and fortunately becomes joined with Christ, i.e., after he finally embraces humility (understood as man's proper disposition toward God—8.1.2) and receives Christ's grace. Book 9 shows how Augustine, by adhering to Christ, became established in Wisdom's lifestyle. And, the profound book 10 discloses Confessor Augustine's present life as a Christian priest (and bishop). It explains Augustine's certitude of God's presence in his heart (cf. 1.1.1–5.6) and his successes (e.g., 10.35.56) and sometimes perplexing shortcomings (e.g., 10.42.67) in "the happy life." Therefore, while books 5–7 revealed *confessio*'s cognitive nature, books 8–10 detailed *confessio*'s cognitive *and* affective character. All told, *conf.* 1–10 depict how Augustine came to embrace *confessio* and something of its content.

Study of books 11–13 (Chapter 4) also followed Augustine's lead since it distinguished his encouraging *confessio* through providing an exegesis of the Church from its origin in divine eternity to its *telos* sharing therein. Books 11–13 manifest more about Augustine's *confessio* in the context of a Church-centered scriptural exegesis of Gen. 1:1–2:2/3. Here, Augustine displays God's goodness by explicitly employing, through worshipping Christ (11.2.4), an *exitus-reditus* structure. Book 11 details God's creating by showing, first, that it falls beneath the Father's eternal begetting of His eternal Word and, second, that creatures are intrinsically mutable. Book 12 shows the ontological status of mutable reality by both (i) detailing God's creating "formless matter" and the "heaven of heavens," and (ii) highlighting the Spirit's role inspiring exegetes to interpret scripture with charity (so they seek the "heaven of heavens"). Hence, God creates man participating in divine eternity so he can willingly participate therein. However, book 13 both summarizes the teachings in books 11–12 and caps the entirety by employing a distinctively Christian *exitus-reditus* structure. This is visible in two obvious ways. First, Augustine reviews, beneath the guise of divine goodness, the principal doctrines in books 11–12. Then, after distinguishing God as Trinity and mind as trinitarian (whereby the divine presence spoken about in *conf.* 1.1.1–5.6, focused on in 10.20.29–27.38, and developed within books 11 and 12, is formally specified[15]), Augustine provides a spiritual exegesis of creation's seven days in Gen. 1:1–2:2/3 showing God's creating the Church in eternity and guiding it to His Sabbath rest. So, exegetes should practice *confessio* since it enables them to know and love God.

But there is more for we now see that *conf.* 13's conclusion in the Sabbath rest shows *conf.* has an *exitus-reditus* structure taking its cue from 1.1.1–5.6's *exitus-reditus confessio*. In general, we notice that *conf.* aims to explain, support, and develop the principal claims enunciated in 1.1.1–5.6 by spiritual biography (books 1–10) and scriptural exegesis (books 11–13). *Conf.* 1–13, then, not only show the nature of divine-human union (including how divine immutability brings that about by special mutable means) but also how this is progressively discovered by man and effected in him by God so that his restless heart (1.1.1) can be cured. Thus, we learn that Augustine's *exitus-reditus confessio* in 1.1.1–5.6 governs his *confessio* in the remainder of *conf.* so that *confessio* functions, in a way, as *reditus* to 1.1.1–5.6 as *exitus*.

This is visible in two ways. First, we notice a progressive account of divine immutability. Just as 1.1.1–5.6's *confessio* led toward understanding divine immutability, so *conf.* progresses toward distinguishing divine immutability. We see this by juxtaposing Augustine's approaches to divine immutability in the four sections we distinguished of *conf.* Within books 1–4 Augustine does not offer proof for immutability since, by the materialist ontology he ascribes to Manichean theology, it is impossible to attain. Although the Manicheans acknowledge divine presence (and Augustine implies they are right about that—e.g., 1.2.2–3.3), their interpretation thereof contradicts its reality. This is because while divine presence is incorporeal, and therefore presupposes that God and soul are incorporeal, the Manichean theology Augustine embraces holds that God is corporeal and consequently mutable (3.6.10–7.14). Hence, Manichean ontology is unable to support the phenomenon of divine presence Manichean religion upholds. Toward the end of books 5–7, long after recounting how he had embraced certitude, in a modified way, as his principal criteria of judgment (5.10.19; 6.4.6), Augustine presents (7.17.23) a Platonist-aided proof for divine immutability that moves from sense *to* mind *to* divinity and shows, *certissima ratione*, that an immutable God both transcends and is present to mind. In book 10's ascent to God (10.6.8–26.37), however, Confessor Augustine (as in book 9's ascent with Monnica, 9.10.23–5) presupposes divine immutability and presence (e.g., 10.1.1) while transitioning *from* sense *to* mind *to* immutable divinity to disclose that immutability's presence causes mind's cardinal activity to seek happiness (10.20.29–23.34). Finally, in 13.11.12 Augustine assumes (i) 11–13.10.11's doctrine of immutability and (ii) immutability's presence to mind in books 10–12. However, he now (i) holds by faith that God is immutably triune and thereby (ii) asserts that mind can achieve self-certain knowledge it exists, knows, and loves, to argue that God's triunity, which specifies His goodness, structures and is spiritually present to mind. Hence, the development we see in Augustine's account of immutability in *conf.* both takes its cue from and augments the development toward immutably participating in divine immutability presented in *conf.* 1.1.1–5.6.

As the earlier discussion shows, however, ascent to divine immutability belongs to an incarnational ascent to God, and ultimately to the Godhead, as *Summum Bonum*. In 1.1.1–5.6 Confessor Augustine detailed *confessio*'s nature and encouraged its practice by transitioning, through Christ's mediation (1.1.1) and therefore in His likeness, from mutable to immutable reality (1.2.2–5.6). Similarly, the remainder of *conf.* ascends *from* (books 1–4) sense (first descending and then ascending), *to* mind (books 5–7), and subsequently *to* God via mind's principal powers, viz. intellect and will joined together in union with Christ (viz. books 8–10). Then, in books 11–13, with intellect and will united in Christ (e.g., 13.11.12–12.13), Augustine goes higher by meditating on the scriptures, divine creating, human selfhood, and God's church, while considering the incarnate Godhead Who is above and in all. Hence, *conf.*'s overall account of divine-human union, taking its cue from 1.1.1–5.6's *confessio*, is progressive because it moves, through Christ, "the Word made flesh," from mutable to immutable reality, first embracing *corporeal reality* then *mutable mind*, but finally embracing *God in Himself* as *Summum Bonum*—first in Christ and then, through Him (e.g., 11.2.4), in a triune Godhead. Confessor Augustine teaches, therefore, that God offers humanity immutable union through His mutable-immutable Christ. In this regard, Augustine's *confessio* constituting 1.6.7–13.38.53 relates to his *confessio* in 1.1.1–5.6 as *exitus* to *reditus*.

The latter claim, moreover, helps us consider *conf.*'s essential structure, for we now see that Augustine's handling of man's participating in divine immutability transitions *superiora-exteriora-interiora-superiora* to illustrate that divine immutability, ultimately disclosed as triune, both structures and is present to mind.[16] In this regard, we remember that Augustine's handling of immutability began with a relatively sophisticated account of spiritual union between an immutable God and mutable man that offered progressive evidence for the latter teaching. How is that paralleled in *conf.*'s remainder? After Augustine presents his account of spiritual union in 1.1.1–5.6, *conf.* moves from viewing God and man as spiritually united: (i) yet incomprehensible (*conf.* 1.6.7–4); (ii) ultimately comprehensible— and whereby man, through Christ, is motivated to seek greater unity with Him (*conf.* 5–7); (iii) growing in unity through Christ (*conf.* 8–10); and finally (iv) growing in unity, through Christ, with the Godhead (*conf.* 11–13). In a rough manner, then, the distinctions stated earlier parallel Augustine's treatment of divine presence in 1.1.1–5.6. While *conf.* 1.6.7–4 have kinship with 1.2.2–3.3, *conf.* 5–7 have likeness to 1.3.3–4.4, *conf.* 8–10 have kinship with 1.5.5 (since Augustine appears to invoke Christ, "the Word made flesh"[17]), and *conf.* 11–13 have likeness to 1.5.6 (because Augustine seems to invoke God's Spirit[18]). In general, Augustine's original *confessio* in 1.1.1–5.6 sets the agenda for what follows.

We see, therefore, that *conf.* has a progressive structure rooted in Augustine's intention to encourage *confessio*. Moreover, the relationship between *conf.* 1.1.1–5.6 and the spiritual biography (books 1–10) and exegesis (books 11–13) that follow shows that *conf.*'s progress is more circular than linear. Augustine's text has an *exitus-reditus* structure wherein linear progress is built into circular progress. Hence, the biography Augustine presents in books 1–10 and the exegesis manifested in books 11–13 are grounded in encouraging and developing the doctrine of *confessio* stated at *conf.*'s outset.[19]

Our retrospective study makes it evident that *conf.*, and therefore, *confessio*, has an *exitus-reditus* structure. Augustine encourages his audience to embrace *confessio* by showing its cognitive and closely related existential (i.e., cognitive *and* affective) value. Hence, Augustine (in agreement with 1.1.1–5.6) endeavors to confirm *confessio* by arguing, explicitly in *conf.* 7, that its proper object, viz. Wisdom, is grounded in the claims (i) that God is immutable substance, (ii) that man, composed of soul and body, is a mutable substance with orientation toward immutable participation in divine immutability, and (iii) that God offers man opportunity to participate immutably in Him through His mediation in "the Word made flesh." This teaching has central importance in *conf.* 1–7 and is augmented in books 8–13 by Augustine's respective focuses on Christ and Godhead. Viewed in light of upholding immutable divinity as Wisdom, *conf.*'s speculative argument transitions, as stated earlier, *from* divine immutability presupposed (books 1–4) *to* immutability recognized (books 5–7), *to* immutability enjoyed in Christ (books 8–10), *to* immutability enjoyed in the Godhead (books 11–13).

Of course, as Augustine's focus in books 8–13 highlights, *conf.*'s overall argument for Wisdom is cognitive *and* affective. Throughout *conf.*, Augustine exhorts his audience to know *and* love what he himself everywhere *confesses*, viz. that, through Christ, he is stably united with God and seeks the Sabbath rest. Stated cognitively, Augustine constantly confesses (i) that God, as made known through "the Word made flesh," is good, (ii) that he is created and governed by Him solely for his welfare, and (iii) that man's end is achieved by conforming to God's immutable goodness. As such, *conf.*'s determining *exitus-reditus* pattern, to which

Augustine introduces his reader at the outset (1.1.1–5.6), depicts man *in relationship* with God, according to his proper mode of conformity to divine goodness. Whether Augustine considers (i) his past, present, and hoped-for future, (ii) biography or scripture, (iii) or divine immutability—either, as such (e.g., *conf.* 7), in Christ (e.g., *conf.* 8–10) or in Trinity (e.g., *conf.* 11–13)—the disposition of *confessio* centers his activity. This notion of *confessio*, consisting (as 1.1.1–5.6 shows) in mutable man's spiritual union, given through the immutable-mutable Christ, with immutable divinity is the text's baseline account of man's relationship with God.

Consequently, what gives unity to *conf.*, and therefore to its thirteen confessions, is not simply what or who Augustine confesses—whether that is divine goodness, divine immutability, divine incarnation, the Trinity, or God's creating His church—but *his confessing that object*. This does not negate *confessio*'s principal component, which *retr.* and *conf.* claim is divine goodness. Rather, the point is that *confessio*'s essential structure is governed by divine goodness but is not that goodness. *Confessio* is comprised by two components, viz. (i) divine goodness and (ii) Augustine's confessing thereof. Hence, Augustine's *confessio* is essentially incarnational since, by God's grace, Augustine's humanity cooperates, for its own benefit, with its divine creator, governor, and *telos*. (I will say more later about the incarnational character of Augustine's *confessio*.)

Moreover, as it is misleading to emphasize the divine object to the exclusion of the person's disposition toward it, it is also misleading to emphasize disposition to the exclusion of divinity. It is helpful but inaccurate, therefore, to maintain that *conf.*'s key is humility, worship, battling concupiscence (1 Jn 2:16), or warring against the temptations of the world, flesh, and devil. Why is this inaccurate? These claims focus only on *confessio*'s human side. *Confessio*, however, consists in a human mindset praising divine goodness by participating therein. Augustine presents his confessing as an explicit participation in God's creating and redeeming, showing that *confessio* cooperates with God's creating (*creatio/formatio/recreatio*) both of Augustine himself and, since he belongs to the Catholic religion, of His church. All of this, Augustine implies, is happening "right before the reader's eyes"; and the reader can experience it if he/she embraces *confessio*.

Confessio, moreover, is intrinsically dynamic because it is, in one way, its own origin and goal. As soul's spiritual union by God's grace, with God, *confessio* is where Augustine's analysis begins; *confessio* is his motive to analyze; *confessio* is the prism by which analysis occurs; and *confessio* is analysis' goal since the latter aims to augment spiritual union—for which reason *confessio* guides *conf.*'s progress. Hence, Augustine's *confessio* has an *exitus-reditus* structure because it actively enjoys and strives to augment itself (i.e., its spiritual unity with divine goodness). But, although this properly adumbrates aspects of the Trinity (and shall, in eternity, be immutable in the Trinity's likeness—e.g., 11.29.39–30.40), this dimension of *confessio* is grounded in Augustine's fundamental claim that, by God's goodness, man participates in His goodness.

Confessor Augustine began *conf.* with the teaching that "the heart is restless until it rests in God" because, to his mind, God has created and governs man "to rest in Him." Augustine speaks of each heart, as he does everywhere in *conf.*, from the depth of his heart as, by teleological spiritual union with God, it enjoys and strives to rest immutably in Him. While narrating *conf.*'s biographical and exegetical segments, Augustine presupposes, employs, validates, and develops his incarnational paradigm of *confessio*, highlighting it at *conf.*'s end to explain something of *confessio*'s origin in the Godhead and consummation in God's Sabbath rest. *Confessio*'s restlessness, Augustine instructs, motivates it to know its origin and pursue its *telos*.

Study shows, then, that Confessor Augustine guides his text, from beginning to end, to encourage *confessio*.[20] While original analysis of *conf.* 1–13 shows that *conf.* intends to display the reasonability and encourage practice of *confessio*, retrospective study discloses additional details concerning *confessio*'s character. Thus, Augustine's description, in *retr.* 2.6.1, of *conf.*'s method and content can be confirmed.

Confessio is Reasonable

It is one thing to claim *confessio* constitutes *conf.*'s formality but quite another to show it is compelling. One commentator, for example, asserts that *conf.* has a "protreptic-paraenetic communicative purpose"[21]—by which is meant that Augustine's text "displays qualities of a specific genre (the ancient protreptic)" and "targets a specific segment of its audience (the Manicheans)."[22] To that mind,

Augustine's principal aim consists in showing the Catholic religion's veracity to a Manichean audience. Although CC maintains this is included in Augustine's *confessio*, the fundamental issue, whether one limits Augustine's protreptic purpose to the Manicheans or extends it, following other commentators,[23] to additional audiences, is whether *confessio* is reasonable? In agreement with Augustine, I believe so and, to disclose why, I analyze in order five passages from *conf*. While the first three passages, (i) part of 7.17.23, (ii) 11.4.6, and (iii) 13.11.12, show Augustine's doctrine of divine goodness is coherent, the last ones, (iv) 10.28.39–39.64 and (v) the gist of 13.12.13–38.53, evince that participating in Christ improves lifestyle. All told, Augustine gives significant evidence supporting *confessio*.

I begin with Augustine's doctrine of divine goodness. First, I study part of 7.17.23, where Augustine describes how the "Platonist books" helped him see, with the mind's eye, that God is immutable. Second, I scrutinize 11.4.6, where Augustine argues, from a cosmological perspective, that God is the immutable creator. Finally, I probe 13.11.12, where, beginning with Church doctrine that God is Trinity,[24] Augustine argues that selfhood is fundamentally triune—which, viewed in a certain way, gives evidence for the Church claim that God is Trinity. These passages are important because, as Augustine sees, showing divine immutability discloses divine goodness—and therefore that *confessio* and, by implication, Augustine's account of *conf.*'s unity have cognitive merit.

Within 7.17.23, Confessor Augustine's description of catechumen Augustine's philosophical ascent to God moves from mind's consideration of bodies to mind's contemplation of its powers of perception and, finally, to mind's consideration, through studying its power of intelligence, of immutability. The pattern of discovery is *exteriora-interiora-superiora*. Beginning with recognition of making value judgments on mutable things, viz. that X is or is not beautiful or that X ought to or not be like that,[25] catechumen Augustine scrutinizes his judgment-making and notices he possesses powers of perception that are hierarchically related and generally parallel to external reality. Therefore, whereas in external reality he discovers mutable substance (i.e., bodies and perhaps intelligent bodies like himself) and immutable divinity, in mind/soul he discovers the powers of sensation, reasoning, and intelligence.

How does Augustine arrive at immutable divinity? Concentrating on mind's ability to make value judgments, he notices that the process begins by encountering bodies *via* his sensitive power. His sensation, however, reports its experience (*via* the power of imagination)[26] to his rational power[27] which, as part of its knowing, considers its experience in conjunction with intelligence (which seems to provide some kind of intelligible form to reason).[28] Intelligence, moreover, enables reason to make a value judgment on the original body, viz. that it is or is not beautiful. I consider this at greater length later but Augustine notices, by reflecting on this activity, that mind's power of intelligence "touches" immutable reality,[29] which he ultimately names God, since it provides reason with the unchanging principles whereby it makes the aforesaid value judgments.[30]

How, then, is God attained? First, Augustine notices that since none of his higher powers of perception is body, it follows that his soul cannot be a body. Rather, it is incorporeal. Second, Augustine infers two kinds of substance, viz. mutable and immutable. While the bodies he encounters through his senses are mutable and he, having a body and soul (which houses his powers of sensation, reason, and intelligence), is mutable, that his intelligence (which is mutable) can know immutable principles implies being in touch with immutable substance. (Otherwise, if intelligence produces these immutable principles, then incorporeal mind, and human being, is both mutable and immutable.) Therefore, since Augustine's introspection discovers that his mind is incorporeal and mutable, it follows that his intelligence, being incorporeal but less mutable than reason, is in contact with immutable substance. To hold otherwise both (i) denies the value judgments he makes and (ii) means, again, that mind in particular and/or Augustine is both mutable *and* immutable substance, i.e., man and God.

Finally, the previous discussion also shows that immutable substance must be God, upon whom all substance and all powers of perception depend for, by definition, there can be nothing greater than or equal to immutable substance. Consequently, since God is intrinsically self-sufficient, all mutable substance must depend on Him for its being and, therefore, activity. Augustine writes: "So in the flash of a trembling glance (*in ictu trepidantis aspectus*) it came to that which is (*ad id quod est*). At that moment I saw 'your invisible nature understood through the things which are made' (Rom. 1: 20)."[31] Therefore, since all primary characteristics structuring creatures are found preeminently in God, creaturely goodness is from Him. Insofar, then, as 7.17.23 shows God is immutable, it implies He is good[32] and creatures participate in His goodness.

11.4.6's argument is cosmological, rather than psychological, and explicitly claims God is good. Augustine begins with the reality of change, and since whatever changes is mutable, and therefore (from 7.17.23) dependent on immutable being, there must be immutable being upon whom the changes in mutable being depend. Augustine writes: "See, heaven and earth exist, they cry aloud that they are made, for they suffer change and variation. But in anything which is not made and yet is, there is nothing which was not previously present. To be what once was not the case is to be subject to change and variation."[33] Next, Augustine firms up analysis of mutable beings' dependence by arguing that mutable depends on immutable being not only for its mutations but also for its existing (in the sense of "be-ing"). Since mutable being depends on God for its being, its changes also depend on Him: "They also cry aloud that they have not made themselves. . . . [']For before we came to be, we did not exist to be able to make ourselves.'" Augustine's final distinction pertains especially to God's nature. He infers that since God is responsible for mutable being's existing and mutations, the primary characteristics distinguished therein, like beauty and good and being, are found preeminently in Him. So God is beauty, good, and being:

> You, Lord, who are beautiful, made them for they are beautiful. You are good (*bonus*) for they are good (*bona sunt*). You are, for they are. Yet they are not beautiful or good (*bona sunt*) or possessed of being in the sense that you their Maker are. In comparison with you they are deficient in beauty and goodness (*nec bona sunt*) and being.[34]

Hence, Augustine offers proof that God is good.

Our third argument, developed from 13.11.12, studies mind in light of Church teaching that God is triune (e.g., 13.5.6; 13.11.12). Hence, Augustine both begins and finishes with teaching that God is good. Looking at mind by a trinitarian account of God, Augustine claims mind is akin to God in its co-implicate, and therefore consubstantial and co-equal, activities of being (*esse*), knowing (*nosse*), and willing (*velle*).[35] Although Augustine notes this likeness is subject to qualification, since divinity is very different from humanity,[36] he keeps his original claim that mind has an ontological kinship to God.[37] Therefore, since man has being from the good God, it follows that both (i) man is good and (ii) God is good as triune. Here Augustine's account of God depends on earlier philosophical theology found in 7.17.23, 11.4.6, and thus far in *conf.* 11–13 for, under such conditions, he can argue from God to His effects and imply, in that light, some kind of analogy from mind to God. What, then, does 13.11.12 add to Augustine's doctrine that God is good? It shows how divine goodness is present at the very core of man's being.

But that only considers divine goodness' *theoria* dimension. What about the benefit of Augustine's explicit and, therefore, special participation in God through Christ? *Conf.* presents this matter from beginning to end, but specific evidence for Augustine's existential relationship with divine goodness begins with his conversion in 8.12.29. What follows show not only that God is good toward Augustine and, therefore, toward humanity in general but also how humanity benefits by confessing His goodness. Looked at in this way, Augustine's account of divine goodness, that Christ is Wisdom, is evinced by positive character developments. To display this, I focus on two passages, viz. (i) 10.28.39–39.64, wherein Augustine's examination of conscience gives proof his character has improved; and (ii) 13.12.13–38.53, where Augustine's spiritual exegesis does likewise from a trinitarian perspective.

First, we consider Confessor Augustine's examination of conscience in 10.28.39–39.64. While judging himself according to 1 Jn 2:16, i.e., by the standard of the flesh, world, and devil (10.30.41 and 10.41.66), Augustine discloses that although he remains beset by temptation, sin, and imperfection, his lifestyle is less vain than before he joined the Catholic religion. For example, Augustine is plagued by lascivious dreams (10.30.41–2), but his conscious life is no longer subject to sexual lust. He does not pursue sexual pleasure for its own sake (2.1.1) and/or for power and praise (2.3.7). Additionally, Augustine has neither a concubine with whom he raises a child (4.2.2) and/or to satisfy his sexual urge (6.15.25); nor is he engaged (to be married) to gain future regular sexual satisfaction and/or social status and/or sufficient wealth to pursue Wisdom (6.12.22–15.25; 8.1.2; 8.7.17). What Augustine said about celibacy upon conversion to Christ can be validated, viz. he did not "now seek a wife and had no ambition for success in this world."[38] Augustine's decision to embrace celibacy, initially to become a monk, has been maintained. Moreover, while Augustine finds himself occasionally succumbing to curiosity (10.35.57), he reminds us (10.35.56) that he no longer attends the theatres (3.2.2–4) or practices astrology (4.3.4–5). Lastly, although cleric Augustine finds himself tempted by lust for power and praise (10.36.59–39.64), he no longer pursues these ephemeral objects, like he once did (e.g., 4.1.1; 6.6.9; 8.1.2; 9.2.2–4.7), as life's meaning. Hence, Augustine's account of his existential relationship with Christ as he writes *conf.* gives evidence that *confessio* improves character.

Additionally, Augustine's profound exegesis of the Church in 13.12.13–38.53 shows, like everything else in *conf.*, his active love for God and neighbor. This is because Augustine's exegesis encourages confessing God's goodness. First, he recognizes his (and therefore each created) selfhood as *imago trinitatis* (e.g., 13.11.12). Second, Augustine's exegesis includes not only his entire audience but also, by beginning and ending in divine eternity, all persons. It seems impossible to portray the active love of God and neighbor in a greater way than Augustine does here. This is because (i) the one confessing and the ones and One to w/Whom confession is made, and (ii) the object confessed, viz. the Church's development unto the Sabbath rest, are united, in the confessor, by the bond of love. Augustine confesses the best for him and others, viz. that, through God, each shall forever be one in Him. This is like Monnica's requesting Augustine "to remember her at the altar of the Lord (9.11.27)." Here, however, Augustine wants the optimum for Christians and, in principle, for everyone. Hence, Augustine's exegesis provides more evidence his character has improved since he became united with Christ (8.12.29).

All told, Augustine offers significant cognitive *and* existential evidence that (i) God is good and (ii) confessing Christ specially participates in His goodness. While study of *conf.* 7.17.23, 11.4.6, and 13.11.12 gives confirmation, through the prism of Augustine's experience, that God is good, analysis of *conf.* 10.28.39–39.64 and the core of 13.12.13–38.53 disclose, through that same prism, why confessing God's goodness improves character. As such, Augustine gives evidence that his intimately related accounts of *confessio* and *conf.* are reasonable.

Conclusion

I finish this book, however, by connecting Augustine's *confessio* of man's special unity with divine goodness to his appropriation, initially as a catechumen (5.14.25), of key aspects of Nicene Christianity.[39] Based on our analysis, Augustine's grounding *confessio* in divine love represents an imitation both of the divine incarnation, understood as fully God and fully man (i.e., the "Word made flesh") without any mixing of the divine and human substance, and of the Trinity, understood as three divine persons (including "the Word made flesh") having the same divine substance.[40] Looked at in one way, these accounts of divine-human relationship differ by degree since the former more concerns man's fundamental union with God, whereas the latter, considering God as Trinity, more concerns the nature of man's ultimate union with God. While focusing on Christ, then, teaches the nature of God's goodness toward man, considering the Trinity instructs regarding the extent of His goodness toward man. Therefore, as human thinking progresses from discovery to insight, the incarnation is a stepping stone to the Trinity.

How does *confessio* imitate the divine incarnation?[41] To begin, Augustine confesses so each can become united with God through Christ Who, as God *and* man, is Wisdom. Unlike Christ, whose divine nature is completely God, and whose human *nature* is completely united with God, i.e., is *confessio*, Augustine is a human *person* created by God seeking immutable unity with Him by practicing *confessio*. Christ, therefore, is Augustine's paradigm, such that confessing has Christ as its *proximate* exemplar, and help since what Christ *is* and shares by His humanity, viz. complete unity with God, Augustine is and seeks by participation.

Various matters in *conf.* support Augustine's deference to the doctrine of divine incarnation. He maintains his experience of God began by considering divine incarnation, thanks to his mother's influence, he grew up in a Catholic household (1.11.17) and always associated Wisdom with Christ (3.4.8; 5.14.25). Moreover, *conf.* shows how young Augustine's loyalty to the claim that "Christ is Wisdom" motivated him to attain indubitable knowledge of God (*conf.* 7) and recognize how claims that God is incarnate (*conf.* 7–10) and triune (*conf.* 11–13) are reasonable. Furthermore, the assertion that "Christ is Wisdom" includes a lesson in humility (7.18.24; 20.26) rejected by young Augustine because of pride

(3.5.9), but that Confessor Augustine thinks properly disposes one toward God (7.18.24). Accordingly, while *conf.* 1–8 explain Augustine's movement, through Christ, toward unity with God, *conf.* 9–13 distinguish the nature of that unity, through Christ, with God. Moreover, just as Augustine's spiritual biography in *conf.* 1–10 takes its cue from Christ (1.1.1), so his exegesis in *conf.* 11–13 is grounded in Christ (11.2.4). Of course, as *conf.* 11–13 manifest, man's unity with God is ultimately trinitarian. Since God is Trinity, that structures Christ's human nature and what that nature, through its union with the Word, ultimately enjoys. Certainly, then, Augustine claims that God the Father, incarnate Word, and Holy Spirit, as first cause, determine his nature and activities (e.g., 13.11.12), and he hints at that from the outset (e.g., 1.1.1–5.6). It is obvious, however, that *conf.*'s explicit account of man's unity with God moves from the incarnation to the Trinity.

Why does Augustine have special regard for divine incarnation? Building on this, he thinks this teaching better manifests *the order of discovery within the order of being* than the doctrine of Trinity. In one respect, the incarnation is identical to the Trinity for each signifies both that and how man's *telos* is God. But as the Trinity, in a way, causes the incarnation, it represents more the order of being. However, Augustine emphasizes that discovery moves from incarnation to Trinity as from what is proximate to understanding to what is remote (which, in this instance, is considered the highest cause). Therefore, although *confessio* (in league with Church doctrine) upholds enjoying the Trinity as man's ultimate goal (*conf.* 11–13), it also claims (as *conf.* 1.1.1 and 11.2.4 show) it is by the Word's humanity that God's unity with man, i.e., the nature of His goodness toward man, is *first known*. Likewise, while Augustine thinks divine presence is trinitarian (13.11.12), he focuses on confessing divine presence as such (1.1.1–5.6) before confessing it as trinitarian (13.11.12). Although Augustine maintains divine presence causes humans to seek happiness (10.25.36–27.38), he confesses man's pursuing happiness in God (1.1.1) before confessing divine presence (1.1.1–5.6). Moreover, while Augustine ultimately holds that rejoicing in the Trinity guides his forays into past, present, and hoped-for future (13.11.12–12.13), he initially attributes these to divine goodness (13.1.1). Since Augustine maintains God is present to man before he properly cultivates divine union, Augustine obviously thinks man attains knowledge by transitioning from the proximate to the remote. Hence, Augustine describes his union with God by distinguishing, in order, implicit union, explicit union (which depends on cooperating with divine grace given in Christ[42]), and the complete union he hopes to enjoy in heaven. Of course, the entirety begins with God, i.e., with the order of being, but through His Christ man discovers the nature of God's goodness toward him, and therewith cooperates. Augustine writes:

> Late have I loved you, beauty so old and so new.... And see, you were within and I was in the external world and sought you there, and in my unlovely state I plunged into those lovely created things which you made. You were with me, and I was not with you. The lovely things kept me far from you, and though if they did not have their existence in you, they had no existence at all. You called and cried out loud and shattered my deafness. You were radiant and resplendent, you put to flight my blindness. You were fragrant, and I drew in my breath and now pant after you. I tasted you, and I feel but hunger and thirst for you. You touched me, and I am set on fire to attain the peace that is yours.[43]

Furthermore, Augustine repeats, from *conf.*'s beginning to end, that it is through divinely established mutable means—found, among other things, in Christian friends, the sacraments, scripture, and the Church—that he is led to explicitly participate in God's immutable goodness. In each instance, Augustine's confessing the order of discovery places the proximate before the remote cause. Yet, as if imitating Christ's ontological structure, Augustine also instructs that mutable reality is from immutable reality for man's attaining unity with immutable goodness. Even though Augustine's focus on divine incarnation entails commencing with the order of being, that same focus reveals his commitment to *the order of discovery within the order of being* since he judges the incarnation is the proximate cause of man's knowing and enjoying both "the Gospel" and, therefore and ultimately, the Trinity. Hence, as the previous passage discloses, Augustine maintains that conversion begins and finishes with God, and God connects man with the order of being through His Christ, i.e., through disclosing and sharing His goodness toward man, so man can conform thereto. In short (as I explain later), Augustine views divine incarnation as Wisdom leading to Wisdom.

The most obvious evidence showing *confessio*'s deference to the divine incarnation is found in Confessor Augustine's account of learning from the "Platonist books." He plainly states that studying the philosophical texts therein had the advantage of providing him, for the first time, with knowledge of God shared with the Christian religion (7.9.13). Augustine, however, also maintains that such learning left him, and therefore could leave anyone in similar circumstances, without an explicit account of his *telos* and how it is attained, i.e., without a clear account of the order of being.[44] Moreover, Augustine explains this through the prism of the divine incarnation rather than through the Trinity. While the "Platonist books" spoke of the Word's (i) divinity, (ii) responsibility for divine creation, and (iii) presence (7.9.13), they did not speak of "the Word made flesh" (7.9.13–14).[45] Accordingly, in 7.10.16 and 7.17.23, Augustine traces the steps from sense experience to discovering God, but these ascents[46] leave out an account of how man can rest with God, i.e., an account of what belongs to the nature of His goodness toward man. Augustine obviously values man's philosophical ascent to God and what that implies concerning human destiny yet, to his mind, that is less important than discovery, through scrutinizing the divine incarnation, both that *and* how man's *telos* is God. Augustine shows, therefore, that people can learn of God's goodness by philosophical reasoning, but this is ultimately limited because it fails to teach *both* that man can and what he must do to rest immutably with God. Hence, the Platonist texts Augustine studied do not disclose the nature of God's goodness toward man and, therefore, the length to which man should love God. Augustine famously writes:

> It is one thing from a wooded summit to catch a glimpse of the homeland of peace and not to find the way to it, but vainly to attempt the journey along an impracticable route. . . . It is another thing to hold on to the way that leads there, defended by the protection of the heavenly emperor.[47]

Augustine judges, therefore, that man's philosophical discovery of God is valuable because it can help toward recognizing the order of being—but the latter properly includes an account of how man attains immutable divine union.

Augustine implies, then, that divine incarnation is vital because it instructs concerning the order of being and certain details about that order depending on embracing it. In the former regard, the doctrine of divine incarnation presupposes the philosophical pursuit of Wisdom—it operates as the *terminus* of human discovery; in the latter regard, it functions as the order of discovery toward embracing the Trinity—it operates as medium. So, after learning the nature of God's goodness toward him, man can discover the extent of that goodness. Hence, the doctrine of divine incarnation is Wisdom leading to Wisdom. Either way, it emphasizes *the order of discovery within the order of being*.

Augustine certainly maintains, then, that *conf.* (and therefore *confessio*) points toward and has its ultimate source and goal in the Trinity. However, as our discussion shows, Augustine's emphasis on divine incarnation (1.1.1; 7.9.13–15) alerts his reader to what he thinks is the fundamental truth concerning man's relationship with God, viz. that man's *telos*, because of God's goodness, is God. My point, therefore, is not that *conf.* subordinates what the Christian religion claims is the highest truth, i.e., the Trinity, to proximate truth. Augustine does not think divine incarnation discloses more about God and man than the Trinity *and/or* that focusing on the Trinity is not a gateway to greater knowledge and love of God. Rather, Augustine emphasizes the incarnation since it both contains a portion of the highest truth, viz. that *and* how man's *telos* is God, and is the indispensable vehicle through which more of highest truth, such that God is Trinity, is reached. For Augustine, then, Christ functions as Wisdom's hinge; He is both man's end and means therein.

But there is more. Based on Augustine's account of the intellectual *and* affective nature of *confessio*, his reason for emphasizing divine incarnation can be fruitfully developed. This is because Augustine implies that grounding *confessio* in divine incarnation both instantiates and discloses something significant about charity. In what sense? Stated cognitively, *confessio*'s pronounced focus on divine incarnation (e.g., 7.9.13–15) can be attributed to Augustine's desire to share with his diverse audience (made up of beginners and veterans alike—i.e., 10.4.5–6) a baseline teaching that *and* how man's *telos* is God. There is parallel, here, with Augustine's instruction (in 12.30.41) that the law of charity governs biblical exegesis. Just as the exegete knows there are better interpretations of "heaven and earth," so Augustine thinks the doctrine of Trinity teaches more about the order of being than divine incarnation. However, just as the exegete encourages all persons toward loving Truth, since the law of charity demands this in the face of a multiplicity of truth-loving interpretations of "heaven and earth," so Augustine upholds the doctrine of divine incarnation since charity requires this in the face of plural, truth-loving accounts of the order of being. Therefore, by appealing to what is common to beginners and veterans, rather than to veterans alone (which might be found in exclusive appeal to divine Trinity), *confessio* shows a pronounced devotion to *the order of discovery within the order of being*. This implies, then, that *confessio*'s preference for divine incarnation is rooted in Augustine's determination to share truth with persons at any state in their relationship with God. In this regard, Augustine's notion of *confessio* both displays and teaches what he instructs about charity.

To Confessor Augustine's mind, then, man's explicit relationship with God properly commences with embracing Christ since imitating His will, by His aid, encourages piety and leads to greater piety. Confessing, Augustine strongly implies, properly imitates the divine incarnation, and thereby progresses—including to the Trinity. So Augustine writes:

> Your Word, eternal truth, higher than the superior parts of your creation, raises those submissive to him to himself. In the inferior parts he built for himself a humble house of our clay. By this he detaches from themselves those who are willing to be made his subjects and carries them across to himself, healing their swelling and nourishing their love. They are no longer to place confidence in themselves, but rather to become weak. They see at their feet divinity become weak by his sharing in our "coat of skin" (Gen. 3:21). In their weariness they fall prostrate before this divine weakness which raises and lifts them up.[48]

In fine, Augustine views *confessio* as the way to love God and neighbor. Augustine's willingness, throughout *conf.*, to embrace divine incarnation, and therefore instruct his audience both that *and* how man's *telos* is God, discloses his disposition, in agreement with his counsel concerning biblical exegesis in *conf.* 12.25.35–30.41, to love as he knows he is loved by God (10.1.1). Man, Augustine maintains, should know and love the Truth, i.e., the God Who Is Trinity (13.11.12). But, Augustine's deference to Christ implies this is fittingly accomplished by helping man know and love first that portion of Truth proximate to his soul. In this regard, Augustine's *confessio* instantiates the Trinity's charity as He communicates His intimacy to man's "restless heart," decisively in Christ.

NOTES

Introduction

1 For *conf.*'s background, see, inter alios, Hammond, 11–27; Conybeare, 4–9; Wills (2011), 1–25; Brown, 158–81, *idem.*, in Sheed, xv–xxxii; O'Donnell (2005), 35–86, *idem.* (vol. 1), xli–li (1@xli–li); Solignac, 26–36; Chadwick, xi–xiii; and TeSelle (1970), 189–91.
2 This generic account of *confessio* is rooted in David (2019A), 7.
3 *Conf.* 1.1.1, 3—Chadwick.
4 Ibid., 10.23.33, 199—Chadwick.
5 Distinguishing Augustine's specific audience and preoccupations helps show why he wrote *conf*. However, as essays by Partoens, Saak, Ettenhuber, Riley, and Vessey (245–334) disclose, people have been reading *conf.* in every era. How can *conf.*'s perennial appeal be explained if the text is a particular response to particular concerns? Answering this implies not only that each reader's particular concerns are linked with some kind of universal concern but also that Augustine's concerns are similarly connected. Study of *conf.* shows Augustine joins these matters for, as 1.1.1 and 10.20.29–27.38 evince, he allies particular concerns with pursuing happiness. For Augustine, the objective character of pursuing happiness consists in taking "joy in t/Truth; i.e. in God" (10.22.32). Hence, Augustine has also fashioned c*onf.* for a broad audience because *confessio* addresses particular concerns on the plane of universality and universal concerns on the plane of particularity.

So, *conf.* appeals to general readers because these sympathize, to varying degrees, with *conf.*'s claim that man pursues happiness. Is Augustine's view of happiness reasonable? On *The Confessions* as *Confessio* (CC) argues it is.
6 *Conf.* 1.1.1, 3—Chadwick.
7 Ibid., 5.13.23.
8 See Solignac, 29–33; Chadwick, xi–xii; Conybeare, 7–8; Wills (2011), 18; Brown, 163; Kotzé (2004), 39–43; and BeDuhn (2020), 46–59,

46–8, 58–9, who views the Manichean mindset as Augustine's principal object

Martin (185–206, 196) claims Augustine's audience consists principally in Catholics, including fellow *servi Dei* and bishops responsible for preaching. Augustine views them as intellectually deficient since they hold doctrines akin to the Manicheans and/or Donatists and/or pagan Platonists. Hence, *conf.* instructs these Catholics concerning Catholic doctrine. BeDuhn (2020), 46–59; Kotzé (2020), 42–4, *idem.*, (2004); and Brown, 161–2, also discuss *conf.*'s audience.

9 While books 3–10 recount Augustine's transition from the Manichean religion to becoming a Catholic monk and priest, the exegesis in books 11–13 contains a strong anti-Manichean polemic. For commentary on *conf.*'s approach to the Manicheans, see BeDuhn (2010, 2013).

10 Following Augustine, I use the term "Platonist" instead of "Neoplatonist" (e.g., 7.9.13) because he thinks "Platonist" designates a general attitude toward reality (e.g., *civ. Dei.* 8.1–11) shared alike, albeit varyingly, by non-Catholics and Catholics. Cf. Ayres (2010), 13–20.

11 Brown, 163, writes: "He had been baptized by Ambrose; but his writings betrayed a deep acquaintance with pagan Platonists." Other commentators imply the same, e.g., Chadwick, x–xi; and O'Donnell, 1@xlv–xlvii, *idem.* (2005), 53–5. As O'Meara explains ([1965], 131–3], certain nineteenth- and twentieth-century scholars, famously Harnack (1851–1930 AD), continued to speculate about this.

12 BeDuhn (2020, 48—cf. 57) suggests Augustine had certain pagan Platonists in mind.

13 See Brown, 165–9, who notices how Platonism pervades *conf.* but does not mention how Augustine's loyalty to Nicene Christianity transforms it.

14 Based on *conf.* 7.9.13, Augustine judges that pagan Platonist and Catholic accounts of God are, to a point, identical concerning immutability and relationship, in the Godhead, between Father and Word. Here, Augustine is relying on a Porphyrean rather than Plotinian account of supreme divinity (cf. *civ. Dei.* 10.23, *c.* 416 AD) since Porphyry, unlike Plotinus, claims supreme divinity is structured by three coordinate members, viz. being, intellect, and power. For textual evidence concerning the Porphyrean triad and discussion of its influence on Christian consideration of the Godhead during the patristic era, see Lilla, 127–89, 155–8; Edwards, 14–25; Dillon, 1–13, 8–13; and O'Meara (1959), 118–22. (For recent commentary on the relation between Plotinus' account of the Godhead and Aristotle's, see Gerson [1994], 3–21.)

In *conf.*, Augustine focuses more on the pagan Platonists' fundamental account of God than on their teaching about the Godhead and, in that light, on their doctrine of divine goodness. How so? As 7.9.13–17.23 show, Augustine judges that the Catholic religion and Platonists share a doctrine of God regarding (i) immateriality and immutability, and (ii) consubstantiality concerning the Father's priority in order to His Word (cf. *conf.* 11.4.6–5.7). This theology is important for Augustine's criticism of materialist Manichean doctrine but even more so for criticism of Platonist rejecting of "the Word made flesh." The doctrine of divine incarnation implies significant difference between Catholic and Platonist notions of the Godhead—especially, as *conf.* 12–13 show, concerning the Holy Spirit (which Augustine implies [e.g., 7.9.13–15] he did not find in the "Platonist books"). This is probably because Augustine's teaching on divine incarnation, and therefore on man's opportunity to attain beatitude, entails a distinctive theology—which underlies his trinitarian consideration of the Godhead in *conf.* 11–13. (Cf. van Geest [123–37, 124–32] whose concentration on Augustine's theology in *conf.* 7–13 both (i) points out differences between Augustine's and Plotinus' theology, and (ii) implies that Augustine, following the examples of Ambrose and Origen, explicitly opposes Plotinus' theology. Unfortunately, van Geest does not consider Augustine's reliance on Porphyry.)

Augustine's instruction on divine incarnation *implies* the Christian account of God differs from pagan Platonism by its stronger notion of divine goodness. (Cf. van Geest, 128, who holds that Augustine differs from Plotinus concerning "creation" by ascribing the latter to divine goodness, associated with the divine Word, rather than to divine generosity, associated with a teaching on emanation.) For Augustine, the incarnation is both consistent with and reasonably develops the theology Platonists share with Catholics because it brings man *greater awareness* of divine goodness. Augustine's correlate focus on the disposition of *confessio* claims that belief in divine incarnation allows Catholics to *enjoy* God's goodness to a greater degree than Platonists. Augustine holds, then, that the essential difference between pagan Platonist and Christian teaching is found less in their shared view of divine immutability but more in their diverse responses to "the Word made flesh." (Cf. Catapano, 191–217, 205–6.)

15 Chadwick, xii–xiii; and Conybeare, 8.
16 E.g., *conf.* 6.7.11–10.16; 6.12.21–2; 7.19.25; 8.8.19; 8.12.30; 9.6.14.
17 See, e.g., Starnes (1990), 154; Solignac, 27–9; Chadwick, xii–xiii; Conybeare, 8; and O'Donnell, 2@358–62—who also considers Paulinus of Nola's role in Augustine's forming *conf.*

18 I say "only in part" since *conf.* features Monnica not only because of her role in Alypius's spiritual development but also due to her significant part in Augustine's development.
19 Chadwick, xii.
20 Wills (2011), 18–19; Chadwick, xii; Conybeare, 6; and BeDuhn (2020), 46–8.
21 As Brown (1967), 213, writes: "The Donatists had claimed, against the Catholics that, as the church was a unique source of holiness, so no sinner could have a part in it."
22 See Brown, 177–81, concerning the likely "shock-value" of *conf.* 10 to Augustine's Christian contemporaries.
23 Solignac, 33–5; and Teselle (1970), 182, 189. Concerning the importance of *Simpl.* 1.2 in Augustine's intellectual development, see, inter alios, Wetzel (2015), 339–52, 341, *idem.*, (2000/2), 124–41, 128–30; Cary (2008), 51–62; Bonner (2007), 42–6; Rist (1994), 14, 148–85; TeSelle (1970), 176–82; and Fredriksen, 155–89.
24 Rist (1994), 14, n. 21.
25 *The Retractations (retr.)* (*c.* 427 AD), 2.1, 370.
26 Although Augustine denies this in *retr.* 1.8.1–6 (as stated in *On Free Choice of the Will*, 151–8), many commentators hold he there embraced the view (e.g., 1.12.80–16.117) that will, since divinely created, has innate power to choose between good and evil. See, e.g., Brown, 148, and Rist (1994), 18–19.
27 *Simpl.* 1.2.3–12.
28 E.g., *conf.* 9.1.1.
29 *Simpl.* 1.2.12; 1.2.16; and 1.2.21.
30 *Simpl.* 1.2.13–16.
31 Augustine's notion of will (*voluntas*) means soul, the moral self, i.e., a mindset, a power of activity, and a wish or want. He views will neither as faculty nor, by the manner of Kant, as practical reason. For commentary, see Couenhoven, 23–44; Hollingworth, 171–203; Ekenberg, 28–45; Byers (2006), 171–89; Rist (2001), 26–39, 32–7, *idem.* (1994), 133–4, 148–77, 183–8; Stump, 124–47; Harrison, 195–205; and Djuth, 881–5.
32 Bonner (2007, 44—like David [2017, 66–81, 66–90]) overstates the matter, perhaps because he misunderstands Augustine's doctrine of will: "In the *Ad Simplicianum* every trace of human initiative, independent of God's prompting, is swept away.... the fallen human will avails only for evil, and this is just, because God is the creator of man." Cf. Rist (2020), 67–89, 84–6.

33 See Rist (1994), 18.
34 I refer to Augustine's treatises *De peccatorum meritis et remissione et de baptismo parvulorum* (411–12 AD) and *De spiritu et littera* (412 AD). For general discussion of Pelagius, and of Augustine's response to Pelagianism, see TeSelle (1999), 633–40.
35 E.g., Augustine's account of will's conversion in *conf.* 8. For recent commentary connecting Augustine's presentation of conversion in *conf.* 8 with *Simpl.* 1.2, see Drecoll, 107–220, 113, 117–18.
36 Solignac, 34–5.
37 Brown, 148–53.
38 See Brown, 138–9; Chadwick, xi; and Wills (2011), 18.
39 TeSelle (1970), 134; 186–8.
40 *Conf.* 8.12.29 and 9.4.8.
41 TeSelle (1970), 134.
42 See TeSelle (1970), 146–56; and Ayres (2010), 72–92, 128–47.
43 Kenney (2013, 93–127) discusses Augustine's quest to integrate these diverse inheritances.
44 Perhaps because he is frustrated at reconciling his biblical and philosophical inheritances Augustine had, at this time in his life, what O'Donnell (1@xliii) calls "writer's block."
45 E.g., *lib. arb.* 1.2.10–13; 2.2.8–19; 2.15.153–5 and 3.21.205–7.
46 *Conf.* 9.6.8.
47 Ibid., 9.6.8, 160—Chadwick.
48 See TeSelle (1970), 134, and Fitzgerald (2012), 491–503, 501–3.
49 Sheed, xviii. For discussion of and bibliography for Augustine's views on the Psalms, see Cameron, 290–6.
50 O'Donnell, 1@xlvii–xlviii.
51 Ibid.
52 For consideration of *conf.*'s linguistic and rhetorical dimensions, see Kotzé (2020), 28–45, 39–44; Conybeare, 32–62; and Stock, 23–121, 194–242.
53 On *confessio* as praising God, see, inter alios, Hammond, 24–6; Baumann, 208–26, 220–1; Williams, vii; David (2019A), 3–7, 9–12; Foley (2019), 425–52; *idem.*, in Sheed, 329; Wills (2001), 13–15; Rigby, 6–33; Menn, 71–107, 74–9, 94–5, 105–7; Marion (2012), 11–55; Ortiz (2012), 475–90, 488–9; O'Donnell, 1@xlii–li and 2@3–5; and Brown, 175–81. CC anchors Augustine's notion of *confessio* in Christ.

On *confessio* as *conf.*'s central doctrine, see also Ratzinger, 375–92, and Solignac, 25.

54 Since Augustine's description of *conf.* in *retr.* 2.6.1 uses the term "laudant" (from *laudare*) to designate praise, it is easily inferred, from the remainder of his statement, that his notion of *confessio* features "praising God for his salutary response to human behavior." While introducing *conf.* (1.1.1), Augustine uses forms of *laudare* several times.

55 O'Donnell (2@3–7) offers philological study of Augustine's title.

56 Augustine's *retr.* is commonly viewed as authoritative. See Cochrane (423) and Hammond (14) who remarks: "What he says in *Retractationes* about the *Confessions* . . . makes explicit some of its aims and even achievements."

57 *Retr.*, 2.6.1. I have translated this passage while consulting *The Retractations*, chapter 32, 130. The Latin text is from *Les Confessions*, 270.

58 Augustine subordinates divine justice to goodness since he thinks the latter governs the former. Augustine prominently claims that God's goodness (*bonus*, e.g., 1.7.12/*bonitas*, e.g., 13.1.1) is His preeminent characteristic—as he teaches that God creates man to share eternally in His goodness (13.2.2). God's justice (*justitia*, e.g., 4.3.4), particularly as punishment, is viewed as secondary since remedial. It encourages *confessio* by punishing the patient for vice (e.g., 1.20.31 and 2.2.4).

59 Hammond (16–17) cites ample evidence validating Augustine's division.

60 Ibid.

61 For recent bibliography, see, inter alios, Vaught, (2005), 257–63; Conybeare, 151–61; David (2019A), 273–84; and Hammond, 17–26.

62 Some (e.g., MacDonald [2006], 85–105, 99–100) might wonder why CC focuses on divine goodness (*bonitas*—e.g., 13.1.1–2.2) when *conf.* speaks more often about divine immutability (*immutabilis*—e.g., 1.4.4; *incommutabilis*—e.g., 7.10.16; 7.17.21; *qui es*—11.4.6). For Augustine, immutability focuses on divine substance as such, whereas goodness highlights something decisive concerning God's relationship with creatures. While immutability distinguishes divine from created substance, goodness signals why God creates.

63 Certainly, a trinitarian interpretation of *conf.* comes close to this since Augustine distinguishes the Trinity in *conf.* 13. However, CC argues (see *Conclusion*) that Augustine's book-long *confessio* focuses more on divine incarnation because (e.g., 11.2.4) it is proximate to human understanding.

64 Augustine implies the relationship between his notion of *confessio* and David's is akin to a seed, shrub, and something like a full-grown tree. (I say "something like" because Augustine claims *confessio*'s final state is in heaven [e.g. 10.27.38].) Augustine's notion is like the full-grown tree, David's *confessio* is the shrub, and the seed, to which Augustine's *confessio* corresponds, is God's eternal plan for divine incarnation understood as God and man, by His goodness, immutably united. Hence, the seed causes the shrub as intermediary to the almost full-grown tree—viz. to *confessio* rooted in divine incarnation. David's *confessio*, then, only partially manifests the seed since its account of God's relationship with man is indefinite; man has some unity with God but why is made clear by divine incarnation and, therefore, by incarnational *confessio*. (Cf. Rom. 11. 11-36 since Paul maintains the "shrub" plays a decisive role in God's plan, and eventually becomes equal to the almost full-grown tree and thereupon shares, he implies, in whatever stands beyond. Augustine's notion of Israel's witness, though "revolutionary" for its time [see Frederiksen, xi–xii and 316–9], appears under-developed—see *civ. Dei.* 4.34 and 18.46.)

Based on Augustine's reformation of David's notion of *confessio*, *conf.* intends to show the limitation not only of Manichean, pagan Platonist, and Donatist theology and anthropology, but also of ancient Hebrew teachings (though the writing of Philo Judaeus probably hovers in the background). On the other hand, since *conf.* is structured by Augustine's incarnational notion of *confessio,* it is also evident that *conf.*'s most pervasive debt pertains to Augustine's notion of David's *confessio*. For this reason, Augustine's writing *conf.* may have played a significant role in his achieving a relatively more positive view "of Jews and Judaism" expressed in his *Contra Faustum Manicheum* (399–400 AD) (Frederiksen, 368).

65 Following Augustine (e.g., *civ. Dei.* 8.1), I mean theological as the philosophical study of God. On this point, see also Rist (2000), 18–28, *idem.* (1994), 5–8.

Chapter 1

1 Vaught (2003, 61), MacDonald (2006), 45–69, 64; Cavadini, 25–34, 26; Starnes (1990, 37, 61); and Catapano (193) agree that Augustine "hits bottom" in his pear-theft. Some, like Crosson (1989), imply otherwise. CC holds that Augustine's pear-theft is his furthest standpoint from God, and therefore from *confessio*, since

his embracing Wisdom in 3.4.7–8 and the Manichean religion as Wisdom immediately thereafter (3.6.10) represents his intention to conform to some "objective" standard. This surpasses Augustine's standpoint in *conf.* 2's pear-theft since then he and his group determined truth and value. Augustine subsequently understands the Manicheans to be like that, but his decision to join them, unlike participating in the pear-theft, is motivated by affinity for an objective standard.

2 Vaught (2003, 22) notes these chapters disclose *conf.*'s purpose but, unfortunately, are commonly ignored. While Conybeare (27–31); O'Donnell (2@8–32); Matthewes, 7–23, 10–14; Menn (84–6); and van Geest, (132–5) consider these chapters (to limited degrees), many others (e.g., Wills [2011], Starnes [1990], and Mann [2006], 1–16) do not.

CC emphasizes these chapters disclose Augustine's essential purpose. Vaught (2003, 22) is right that Augustine's "fundamental objective is to undertake a journey that leads to dynamic and transforming interaction between God and the soul," but CC maintains the latter belongs to Augustine's notion of *confessio*.

3 Vaught (2003, 23–7) and O'Donnell (2@16–17, 21–3) rightly state that Augustine distinguishes a Catholic, rather than Manichean or pagan Platonist, account of divine presence.

4 *Conf.* 1.1.1, 3—Chadwick; latin/O'Donnell, 1@3.

5 According to O'Donnell (2@13), Augustine derives the word *cor* (i.e., heart) from his biblical inheritance; *cor* is "an expression for the indivisible, authentic center of human life, where the tensions of a sinful world are most clearly felt."

6 Conybeare (30) writes: "In these first paragraphs of the work the potent trinity of being, knowing, and willing is already in play." Cf. O'Donnell, 2@10.

7 It is, in a way, expected (since Augustine thinks that incarnation points to Trinity—e.g., 11.2.4) that 1.1.1–5.6 has some kind of trinitarian structure. As mentioned in this chapter, a vague trinitarian structure is found not only in 1.1.1's opening paragraph's identification of power, wisdom, and goodness with God but also in 1.1.1–5.6's accounts of God as (i) immutable and transcendent creator (1.2.2–3.3), (ii) transcendent and immanent (1.3.3–4.4) redeemer, and (iii) immanent in man to participate immutably in God (1.4.4–5.6). The latter adumbrate God the Father, incarnate Word, and Holy Spirit.

8 Vaught (2003), 23. Cf. O'Donnell, 2@11–12.

9 See *conf*. 8.1.2 and Starnes (1990, 198–9).
10 See Vaught (2003), 24, concerning the link between understanding and praising.
11 *Conf*. 1.1.1, 3—Chadwick.
12 Hence, Augustine remarks (in 4.12.19, 64—Chadwick) he makes confession to the Word: "To him [i.e., to the incarnate Word] my soul is making confession, and 'he is healing it, because it was against him that it sinned' (Ps. 40: 5)." Cf. 11.2.4, where Augustine addresses God the Father through His incarnate Son.
13 Philosophical theology instructs that what the incarnation teaches about divine goodness is inferable from a notion of God as self-sufficient creator, but it cannot infer divine incarnation as such—nor the assumption of *this* human nature. Certainly, one can view divine incarnation as *fitting* due to God's infinite goodness and human ratiocination's requirement of sense experience.

However, since Augustine had a direct vision of Wisdom (7.10.16) he subsequently found articulated in Catholic doctrine, he does not consider these matters in *conf*. His focus on divine incarnation shows awareness of the importance of sense experience and of faith, generally speaking (6.5.7–8), to human ratiocination.
14 O'Donnell (2@17) interprets Augustine's reference to *praedicator* generically rather than specifically. While Augustine might mean Bishop Ambrose of Milan and/or Saint Paul, one can be sure he means Catholic clergy. This underscores *conf*.'s universal dimension.
15 See Vaught (2003), 23–7, and O'Donnell, 2@18–32.
16 *Conf*. 1.2.2, 3—Chadwick.
17 Ibid.
18 Ibid.
19 Ibid., 4.
20 Ibid.
21 Ibid.
22 Ibid.
23 See Crosson (1989), 92–5.
24 *Conf*. 1.3.3, 4—Chadwick.
25 Cf. Vaught (2003), 26–7, and O'Donnell, 2@21–2.
26 *Conf*. 1.3.3, 4—Chadwick.
27 Ibid.
28 Ibid.

29 See O'Donnell (2@23–8) and Vaught (2003, 26–7) for discussion of this passage's anti-Manichean aspects.
30 *Conf.* 1.4.4, 4–5—Chadwick; latin/O'Donnell, 1@4.
31 Ibid., 1.4.4, 5—Chadwick.
32 Augustine argues in 7.10.16–17.21 that mind only knows divine immutability if it knows divine incorporeality.
33 See Introduction, n. 14 for further explanation.
34 *Conf.* 1.5.5, 5—Chadwick; latin/O'Donnell, 1@4.
35 See Cochrane, 455, and Kenney (2019), 12–14, 110–11, 118–21.
36 E.g., *conf.* 3.6.10–7.12.
37 E.g., *conf.* 7.10.16.
38 E.g., *conf.* 7.9.13–15.
39 Cf. BeDuhn (2013), 334–6. While paying special attention to Augustine's engaging Manichean sources, he notices Augustine's handling, in 1.1.1–5.6, of his Manichean and Platonic inheritances to uphold Catholic doctrine. BeDuhn writes (336): "By defining God in proper terms at the beginning of *Confessions*, Augustine set the stage for the theological arguments of book 7, by which he would map the path from Manichean error to Nicene truth."
40 *Conf.* 2.10.18, 34—Chadwick; latin/O'Donnell, 1@22.
41 For commentary on Augustine's account of infancy, see Vaught (2003), 28–37; Starnes (1990), 2–8; O'Donnell, 2@32–52; Wills (2011), 26–8; Mathewes, 17–19; and Mann (2006), 1–16.
42 *Conf.* 1.6.7. Wills (2011, 27) thinks Augustine probably develops his thoughts from observing his son, Adeodatus, as a newborn.
43 For helpful commentary, see Starnes (1990), 2–3; and Vaught (2003), 28–9.
44 Scholars debate whether Augustine is scrupulous. While some (e.g., O'Donnell, 2@44) claim he ascribes adult behavior to infants, others (e.g., Mann, 2006, 11) maintain he imputes infant behavior to infants. The textual evidence favors the latter since Augustine does not ascribe any guilt to infants (1.7.12); he is only interested in noting the tendency infant behavior displays.
45 *Conf.* 1.7.11.
46 Ibid.
47 Looked at in one way, this stands beneath the teaching of Original sin. If a self-sufficient God creates man (the species), then it must somehow be man who is primarily responsible for his orientation

toward unruliness. Consequently, if the infant inherits an orientation toward willfulness, that must originate from some first human pair.
48 *Conf.* 1.7.11.
49 O'Donnell, 1@7.
50 For commentary on *conf.* 1.8.13–20.31, see Vaught (2003), 37–52; Starnes (1990), 8–24; O'Donnell, 2@52–103; Wills (2011), 28–9; Mathewes, 19–23; Bloom, 17–29; and Matthews, 31–43. While Vaught, Starnes, Mathewes, and O'Donnell follow Augustine's lead by considering his character development and therefore motives for learning, Bloom and Matthews focus on how these passages shed light on Augustine's overall doctrines of speech and learning.
51 For commentary, see Starnes (1990), 9–10.
52 See Vaught (2003), 41–2; 49.
53 Mathewes, 19, agrees.
54 *Conf.* 1.9.14, 11—Chadwick: "in my boyhood . . . honours and . . . riches."
55 *Conf.* 1.13.20–16.26.
56 Ibid., 1.9.14; 17.27.
57 Ibid., 1.17.27; 19.30.
58 Ibid., 1.18.28–9. For helpful commentary, see Starnes (1990), 19–22.
59 Ibid., 1.9.14.
60 Ibid., 1.11.17.
61 Ibid., 1.9.14.
62 Ibid., 1.11.18. Monnica resolved to delay Augustine's baptism since, in agreement with Church teaching of her day, she feared that if he were baptized in childhood subsequent sinning might significantly weaken the sacrament's effect. See Starnes (1990, 13–14) and Vaught (2003, 44) for helpful commentary.
63 *Conf.* 1.19.30.
64 Ibid.
65 Ibid., 1.20.31. For discussion of Augustine's trinitarian analysis here, and in 1.7.12, see O'Donnell, 1@ 101–2, and David (2019A), 4–6, 29–30.
66 See O'Donnell, 2@64—"*et peccabamus tamen*"—who implies Augustine's view of childhood is scrupulous.
67 See O'Donnell (2@52–6, 104) concerning Augustine's identifying the six ages of human history with the six days of creation found in Genesis 1.

68 For commentary on *conf.* 2, see Vaught (2003), 52–65; Starnes (1990), 33–51; O'Donnell, 2@104–44; Wills (2011), 29–32; Cavadini, 25–34; MacDonald (2003), 45–69; and David (2018), 8–32.

69 Cf. Augustine's account of lust in *civ. Dei.* 14.15–26 (*c.* 418–23 AD). It is important to note he thinks there are various sorts of lust (e.g., *civ. Dei.* 14.15), and the worst (which *civ. Dei.* 14.13 implies) is spiritual lust—properly called pride (*superbia*). Augustine's focus on sexual lust in *civ. Dei.* 14.16–26 is not because of any "sexual hang-up" (e.g., Miles, 28–9) but, as he says (*civ. Dei.* 14.24), to demonstrate lust's disturbing nature.

70 As Starnes (1990, 38) writes: "What he condemns is that he broke a divine law present in man internally, as a part of his very nature, before it ever appears in the form of an external authority. He refers to something which he claims is a principle of man's very identity as a rational being."

71 See *conf.* 2.5.10.

72 Presumably, it is because he hears these matters preached at Church (O'Donnell [2@112–13]).

73 *Conf.* 2.2.3. Concerning Augustine's current options, see Vaught (2003, 53) and Starnes (1990, 35).

74 Ibid., 2.3.6. See O'Donnell (2@120) for helpful commentary concerning how Patricius's enthusiasm for Augustine's puberty was "perfectly typical of his class and station in life."

75 Ibid., 2.3.8. See Starnes's account (1990, 37) of Augustine's delicacy in characterizing Monnica. Cf. O'Donnell (2@ 121, 125).

76 Ibid., 2.3.7–8.

77 Ibid., 2.2.4; 2.3.8.

78 Ibid., 2.3.5–6. However, this also shows Patricius's paternal care for Augustine.

79 Ibid., 2.3.7.

80 Ibid., 2.1.1.

81 Ibid., 2.3.7.

82 In his words (ibid., 27–8—Chadwick): "Yet I went . . . a mark of inferiority."

83 Ibid., 2.4.9. The commentators note biblical frameworks and antecedents that Augustine relies on and/or reinterprets within *conf.* 2. These are (i) the parable of the Prodigal Son (e.g., O'Donnell [2@130–1, 143]; Cavadini [27, 33–4]; MacDonald [2003, 64]) and,

more significantly, (ii) Genesis' account of Adam and Eve's act of pride (e.g., O'Donnell [2@126–8, 139]; Cavadini [26–31, 33–4]; Wills [2011, 32]; and MacDonald [2003, 49–50]).

84 Ibid., 2.4.9–10.18.
85 Ibid., 2.8.16–9.17. As Cavadini writes (32): "The only thing one cannot have alone is praise, and there is no worthy 'similitude of omnipotence' unless there is praise."
86 Ibid., 2.6.12–9.17.
87 Ibid., 2.4.9; 6.12.
88 Ibid., 2.5.10. Perhaps Augustine continues to analyze his pear-theft because his motive transcended gaining the group's praise (see n. 92).
89 Ibid., 2.6.13; 7.16–9.17. As Starnes (1990, 41–2) writes: "[Augustine's] desire was not to imitate God in respect to any of his particular attributes, but in respect to his essential characteristic as God: his freedom and omnipotence." Therefore, as Vaught remarks (2003, 57), Augustine would not have "done it alone" since, as he pursues praise, the like-minded group, setting itself up against God, is the only thing that would praise him for the act. Hence, Augustine "loves the negative character of the act, not only for itself, but also because of the companionship of the accomplices with whom he commits it."
90 Ibid., 2.8.16, 33—Chadwick.
91 Ibid., 2.1.1.
92 My study of Augustine's crime goes further than Starnes (1990, 44–5), Vaught (2003, 60–5), and MacDonald (2003, 63–5). Since Augustine's union with "the gang" is based on utility rather than virtue, that relationship is motivated by vice. Even the gang, therefore, is a means to the self-glorification that Augustine seeks. That is not something the gang can directly give to him; rather, it is something Augustine tries to give himself since it is purely mental. Hence, the gang's praise reflects Augustine's egoism. (For further discussion, see David [2018], 17–19.) What is more distant from *confessio*?
93 O'Donnell (2@133) raises an important issue concerning *conf.* 2's analysis, prompting one to ask: Does Confessor Augustine's teaching in *conf.* 2 contradict *Simpl.* 1.2's distinction between "choice of will" and "free choice of will"?

Simpl 1.2's account of man's natural orientation toward God entails that Augustine should have behaved with humility instead of arrogance. By that standard, first set forth in *conf.* 1.1.1, Augustine would not have used women, friends, or God. Instead, he would have recognized God's truth and law, and sought His help to behave correctly. According to Confessor Augustine's principles, young Augustine was not *necessitated* to behave badly. Rather, that behavior resulted because his "choice of will" rejected God. What Starnes says (1990, 35) concerning Augustine's sexual lust applies to Augustine's entire behavior at that time: "instead of searching for God and looking for the rational order of the universe, he allowed his reason to be seduced from its proper end."

94 For helpful commentary on *conf.* 3, see Vaught (2003), 67–89, Wills (2011), 33–5; Breyfogle, 35–52; Starnes (1990), 53–87; O'Donnell, 2@145–202; O'Meara (1965), 52–83; Stock, 35–47; David (2019A), 43–53; and BeDuhn (2010, 25–105).

95 *Conf.* 3.1.1.

96 Cf. Starnes's (1990, 53–60) claim that 3.1.1–3.6 represents Augustine's lifestyle based on the pear-theft *weltanschauung*; it shows how he lived and the anguish he experienced while embracing himself as God. By contrast, CC holds these chapters represent Augustine's dissatisfaction with the aforementioned outlook and, through pangs of conscience, dispose the ground for his subsequent pursuit of Wisdom. These chapters disclose the beginning of Augustine's attempt to "tone down" his pear-theft *weltanschauung*. Cf. Breyfogle (38–42—cf. O'Donnell [2@150–2, 158, 160, 177 (concerning the Manicheans), 191–2]), who interprets these chapters by a triad of sins concerning the three lusts stated in 1 Jn 2:16, viz. *concupiscentia carnis*, *sacrilega curiositas*, and *ambitio saeculi* (cf. 10.30.41–41.66). These certainly show Augustine's dissatisfaction with his lifestyle and inspire him to pursue Wisdom.

97 *Conf.* 3.3.6. See O'Donnell (2@161) who remarks: "here the love of comradeship that led him into sin in the pear-theft seems to have faded a little." Cf. Wills (2011, 33).

98 Ibid., 3.3.6.

99 Ibid., 3.2.2–4.

100 Ibid., 3.3.5.

101 Ibid., 3.3.6.

102 Ibid., 3.2.4. As Breyfogle (40) states: "Augustine's love of fictional sufferings as superficial thus reveals the superfluity of all love of suffering as rooted in self-love rather than in love of another's soul." For insightful analysis of Augustine's implied view of drama, see Stock (35–7) and Vaught (2003, 70–2).

103 Ibid., 3.3.5.

104 Ibid., 3.3.6.
105 Ibid., 3.4.7.
106 Ibid., 3.1.1.
107 For discussion of Cicero's *Hortensius*, see O'Meara (1965, 57–8) and O'Donnell (2@162–3; 165–6). It seems that although the text had an extraordinary effect on Augustine, it was not an extraordinary work. All that remains of it are fragments culled from various places in Augustine's *corpus*.
108 *Conf.* 3.4.7–8.
109 Ibid., 3.4.7–8, 38–9—Chadwick.
110 What Starnes (1990, 63) writes concerning Augustine's rejection of Catholic scriptures is aptly applied to Augustine's embracing the Manichean religion as Wisdom, viz. "he confesses that he desired this knowledge only to serve his own private purposes—which is to say, to make himself a great man in the world" (Cf. Starnes [1990, 74]).
111 *Conf.* 3.4.8.
112 Ibid., 3.5.9.
113 Ibid.
114 Ibid., 3.6.10. See BeDuhn (2010, 25–36) for helpful discussion of the sophisticated aspects of then North African Manichean religion. It is beyond doubt that young, cosmopolitan Augustine would have found attractive that sophistication—especially compared with the apparently rustic character of North African Catholicism.
115 For valuable assessment of Augustine's appropriation of Manichean doctrine, see O'Meara (1965, 61–83), Starnes (1990, 64–6), O'Donnell (2@173–5), and BeDuhn (2010, 42–105).
116 *Conf.* 3.5.9. 40—Chadwick; latin/O'Donnell, 1@26.
117 See ibid., 5.10.20 for description of Augustine's Manichean view of Christ. Cf. BeDuhn (2010, 88–90).
118 Ibid., 3.6.10, 41—Chadwick.
119 Ibid., 3.6.10–11.
120 Ibid., 7.2.3.
121 Ibid. For discussion of Manichean doctrine in light of recent research, see BeDuhn (2010, 75–83).
122 See O'Meara (1965, 74) and *conf.* 8.10.22–4.
123 Ibid., 3.7.12.
124 Ibid.
125 Ibid., 3.7.12–8.15.

126 Ibid., 5.10.18.
127 Ibid., 3.7.13–8.15.
128 Ibid., 5.10.18.
129 Ibid., 3.10.18; 4.1.1.
130 Ibid., 3.10.18. See also O'Meara (1965, 76) for a brief account of Manichean dietary practice; and BeDuhn (2010, 56–60) for study of the Manichean ritual life in which Augustine participated.
131 *Conf.* 5.10.18. As Vaught (2003, 79) writes: "the Manicheans try to solve the problem of evil without placing the blame on those responsible for it."
132 See Brown, 50–1. Cf. O'Donnell's claim (2@185) this may not have been one of the principal reasons for Augustine's attraction to the Manicheans. According to BeDuhn (2010, 86), Augustine "formed a serious misunderstanding of the Manichean view of personal responsibility." For BeDuhn's account of Manichean teaching on responsibility, see 83–91. BeDuhn also thinks Augustine's view that Manicheans were determinists might have been colored by his simultaneous practice of astrology (97–8).
133 For fuller analysis of this passage, see Vaught (2003, 87–9) and Starnes (1990, 74–6).
134 *Conf.* 3.11.19–12.21.
135 Ibid., 3.11.19.
136 For helpful commentary on *conf.* 4, see Vaught (2003), 89–114; Wills (2011), 33–8; Wetzel (2003), 53–69; Starnes (1990), 89–112; O'Donnell, 2@203–80; O'Meara, (1965), 80–100; Stock, 48–53; and David (2019A), 55–66.
137 *Conf.* 4.2.2.
138 Ibid., 4.2.2.
139 Ibid., 4.2.3.
140 *Conf.* 4.3.4–6. See Vaught's erudite comparison (2003, 92) of 4.3.5–6 to Augustine's conversion, in conjunction with reading scripture, in the Milanese garden (8.12.29).
141 See Starnes's analysis (1990, 90–2) tracing most of this to Augustine's adherence to the Manichean seals of mouth, bosom, and hand. Cf. O'Meara (1965, 76–7) and BeDuhn (2010, 46–52).
142 *Conf.* 3.4.7–12.19. See O'Donnell (2@217–8) for insightful commentary about Augustine's treatment of friendship in book 4 and in *conf.* as a whole.
143 Ibid., 4.4.7.

144 I say "to some degree" since Augustine seems to have loved himself in the friend more than he loved the friend. Why? First, Augustine's persuading him to join the Manicheans shows he had been trying to mold him in his own image (see Wills [2011, 36]). Second, since Augustine is largely motivated by sense, pleasure, and utility (e.g., his friendships with his concubine and fellow Manicheans—and see 4.8.13–12.19), it is probable that this friendship, though containing a relatively greater degree of virtue, was likewise governed.

145 *Conf.* 4.4.8.

146 As Wills (2011, 36) writes: "His pride was hurt that his own views had been rejected, and he resented what the friend took to be a blessing." I believe Augustine's vain attitude toward his oratorical skills causes this.

147 See O'Meara (1965, 86).

148 *Conf.* 4.4.9, 67—Chadwick. Cf. 4.7.12 and O'Donnell's provocative commentary thereon (2@228–9) concerning Augustine's reaction to his friend's death.

149 Cf. Lewis's (110–11) comment on this passage. He accuses Augustine of cold-heartedness toward his friend (whom Lewis names "Nebridius"—perhaps from *conf.* 4.3.6). Augustine would agree the affection he then had for his friend was disordered; however, he would ascribe this, as *conf.* 4.8.13–12.19 shows, to loving that friend as if he were God.

Lewis appears to suggest that Augustine's distinction between loving someone in and loving them as God is false. By contrast, Bouton-Toubilic (138–53, 142–5) holds that Confessor Augustine intends to show precisely that the "ardor of love that should be safeguarded" in that friendship (142) is contradicted by the fact he did not love that friend in God (144).

150 *Conf.* 4.14.22, 65—Chadwick. Although it applies to his judgment on the nature of friendship with his best friend, Augustine says this while discussing his reason for dedicating his lost book, *On the Beautiful and the Fitting*, to Hierius.

151 Ibid., 4.4.9.

152 According to O'Meara (1965, 74–5), the Manicheans believed that humans had two souls—one good (since coming from God/the principle of light) the other evil (since coming from the Devil/the principle of darkness) (cf. *conf.* 8.10.22–4). Moreover, the "divine" soul was capable of liberation by imitating Christ's lifestyle.

While it is clear the Manicheans had a teaching concerning the liberation of a divine soul, it is unclear if they (or, at least, Augustine) considered this soul to be personal. In any event,

Augustine misses his friend for two complementary reasons. First, since Augustine pursues temporal goods, he is bound to miss his friend, i.e., this concrete individual, more than he would miss either the latter's divine soul or (the Manichean account of an) eternal God. (As Starnes [1990, 95] writes: "But the sensible concrete, in the form of his friend, was what Augustine had actually loved." See, in this regard, Augustine's comments about loving friends in 4.8.13.) Second, if Augustine adhered to Manichean doctrine then, for him, the friend he loved was now extinguished because either the latter had forsaken the Manichean religion on his deathbed (and therefore his divine soul had failed) or, if he had ultimately returned to that religion, only the divine soul (rather than the individual) would persist. Either way, Augustine judged his dearest friend was extinguished and, especially because of personal vanity, this caused much grief.

According to BeDuhn (2010, 91–2), Manichean religion held that only elect members could attain immortality; everyone else was subject to extinction. Hence, BeDuhn thinks Augustine's grief was, in that respect, consistent with Manichean doctrine.

153 *Conf.* 4.8.13. For discussion, see BeDuhn (2010, 92–5). He claims Augustine's consolation by Manichean community was a properly Manichean response to experiencing death since (94) "the collective experience and purpose of the community of . . . [Manichean] . . . souls . . . [provided] . . . a foretaste of their restoration to their original unity."

154 Ibid., 4.13.20–16.31.

155 See O'Donnell (2@255–9) concerning the relationship between Augustine's now lost treatise and Confessor Augustine's subsequent trinitarian considerations. BeDuhn (2010, 97–102) discusses the treatise's Manichean aspects.

156 *Conf.* 4.13.20–15.27.

157 See Chadwick (69–70), nn. 34–5. Cf. Catapano (198).

158 *Conf.* 4.16.28–31.

159 See O'Donnell (2@246–8) concerning Augustine's overall view of beauty and its connection to his composing *conf.*

160 *Conf.* 4.16.30.

161 Based on his distinctions in 10.27.38 Augustine holds that explicit relationship with God is grounded in the Catholic religion's worship of Christ. *Conf.* suggests that implicit relationship has numerous varieties, ranging from young Augustine's embracing created realities as *Summum Bonum* (10.27.38) to Job's, and likewise

David's, humble worship of God (8.1.2). Presumably, Confessor Augustine also includes the Manicheans, pagan Platonists, and Donatists among those having an implicit relationship with God since none of them worships Christ as the Catholic religion proclaims.

Therefore, although Confessor Augustine's spiritual biography distinguishes implicit relationship with God as pursuing temporal reality, his overall view of implicit relationship, as the examples of Job, David, and his own conversion show, can include everything from a wrong to an "almost complete" relationship with God. Hence, Augustine's view of implicit relationship has a wide breadth commonly overshadowed by *conf.*'s dominant account of pre-Catholic Augustine's relationship with God. That young Augustine had a hostile attitude toward God does not mean implicit relationship entails the same. (See Chapter 3, n. 3.)

162 Some, like Starnes (1990, 2–8), maintain Augustine's account of infancy has a universal scope since Augustine, having no memory of his infancy, takes his data entirely from observing other infants. Hence, Augustine claims that what is observed, especially the infant's irrational and aggressive spirit, applies to each human.

This certainly shows Confessor Augustine's universal scope, and his methodology obviously separates his account of infancy from subsequent teachings on childhood and adolescence. However, the content and methodology of Augustine's interpretation of infancy is governed by his normative account of happiness. The latter might be correct but showing that (on Augustine's terms) requires more data. Starnes is right, then, that Augustine's approach to infancy signals his focus on spiritual biography, but that approach is ultimately determined by his normative doctrine of happiness.

Chapter 2

1 For helpful commentary on *conf.* 5, see Starnes (1990), 113–43; Vaught (2003), 115–38, 172–4; Wills (2011), 39–44; Crosson (2003), 71–87; O'Donnell, 2@281–328; O'Meara (1965), 92–121; David (2019A), 67–78; and BeDuhn (2010), 135–70, 334–9.

2 *Conf.* 5.3.6.

3 Ibid., 5.3.3–4.

4 Ibid., 5.3.3; 6.10.

5 Ibid., 5.7.12.

6 Ibid., 5.6.10–11.
7 Ibid., 5.7.12–13.
8 Ibid., 5.6.11.
9 He was then a regular member, i.e., a "hearer" or "auditor," and resolved not to become an "elect." These classifications are explained by O'Meara (1965, 77–9). O'Donnell (2@304) assesses the circumstances surrounding Augustine's decision.
10 *Conf.* 5.7.13, 80—Chadwick.
11 Ibid., 5.7.12.
12 Ibid., 5.8.14, 80—Chadwick.
13 Ibid., 5.8.14.
14 Ibid., 5.8.15.
15 Note how Augustine prefers honesty in others toward accomplishing his ambitions. See also Vaught (2003, 126–30) and O'Donnell (2@307–8) for discussion of parallels between Augustine's departure from Monnica and *Aeneid* 4's depiction of Aeneas's departure from Dido.
16 *Conf.* 5.9.16–17.
17 Ibid., 5.10.19. See Vaught (2003, 133), Starnes (1990, 134–5, 147–9), and O'Donnell (2@314–15) concerning the effects of Augustine's appropriating skeptical doctrine.
18 Ibid., 5.3.4–5.
19 Ibid., 5.10.19–10.21.
20 Ibid., 5.10.19.
21 Note O'Donnell's perceptive comment (2@295): "The pervading irony of Bk. 5 is that motion in a wrong direction was the beginning of motion in the right direction."
22 See Crosson's (2003, 74) helpful remarks concerning Augustine's emphasis on the "providential hand of God." See also his comments (75–6) regarding the structure of book 5 and speculations concerning book 5's relation to *conf.* as a whole (76–87). Book 5 is viewed as a "chiasmic narrative structure" forming "the center of . . . [*conf.*'s] . . . narrative books" (83). Note, though, Crosson's qualification in his essay's conclusion, saying that his "argument does not claim exclusivity for book Five as a central book" (87) in *conf.* Cf. O'Donnell, 2@281.
23 *Conf.* 5.13.23. For discussion of Count Symmachus's role in Augustine's appointment, see Wills (2011, 42–4). For more on Symmachus, see O'Donnell, 2@320–1.

24 For discussion of Ambrose's influence on Augustine, see O'Donnell, 2@319–25.
25 *Conf.* 5.13.23.
26 Ibid., 5.14.24.
27 Ibid., 5.14.24, 89—Chadwick.
28 Ibid., 5.14.25
29 The natural philosophers presented a superior teaching than the Manicheans. That teaching, however, could not explain everything since events happen outside the patterns these philosophers study. Hence, neither party possessed complete knowledge. It is probable that on Augustine's view, some of the Catholic religion's merit was that it both did not claim a complete knowledge of Nature and was neutral concerning the natural philosopher's insights.
30 *Conf.* 5.14.25, 89—Chadwick. Some commentators (see Vaught [2003, 137–8], Starnes [1990, 131–5], and David [2019A, 76–8]) underestimate the importance Augustine's desire to cure vanity had upon his quest for Wisdom (e.g., *conf.* 3.4.7–8) and, in particular, to reenroll as a Catholic catechumen. Confessor Augustine makes it clear that young Augustine's decision was, in significant part, because he wanted to be healed of vice.
31 Ibid., 5.14.25, 89—Chadwick.
32 For helpful commentary on *conf.* 6, see Starnes (1990), 145–68; Vaught (2003), 139–54, 174–6; Wills (2011), 45–9; Plumer, 89–105; O'Donnell, 2@329–90; O'Meara (1965), 118–30; Stock, 53–64, 77–89; and David (2019A), 79–93.
33 *Conf.* 6.1.1, 90—Chadwick.
34 Ibid., 6.1.1–2.2. For commentary, see Starnes (1990, 145–7) and Plumer (92–4).
35 Ibid., 6.4.6.
36 Ibid., 6.5.7–8.
37 Cf. Starnes's (1990, 145) contrary opinion: "He could not now make any progress toward the truth but at least he was no longer going away from it." This interpretation focuses on intellectual progress rather than on *existential* or *religious* progress since, as Augustine's interaction with the drunk beggar shows (cf. Plumer [96–7, 105]), he learns something positive about his miserable lifestyle that pushes him toward Wisdom. Yet, as Starnes notices (1990, 161–2), 6.16 commences with Augustine's recognition that his experience brought him toward God.

Subjectively, catechumen Augustine did not know he was moving toward Wisdom but objectively he was. This distinction does not exclude that Augustine was motivated by misery to search for Wisdom (see O'Donnell [2@329]). Surely, his anxiety motivated him to seek the intellectual insights that, as Starnes asserts and book 7 displays, he required to find Wisdom.

38 *Conf.* 6.3.4–4.5.

39 Augustine writes: "More and more my conviction grew that all the knotty problems and clever calumnies which those deceivers of ours had devised against the divine books could be dissolved" (6.3.3, 93—Chadwick).

40 Ibid., 6.5.7–8.

41 Ibid., 6.4.6, 94—Chadwick.

42 Ibid., 6.4.6, 95—Chadwick.

43 Ibid., 6.6.9–10.

44 Ibid., 6.6.10.

45 Ibid., 6.6.9–10.

46 Ibid., 6.6.10.

47 Ibid.

48 Plumer claims *conf.* 6's accounts of Augustine, Augustine's concubine, Monnica, Alypius, Nebridius, and Ambrose (i) focus on Augustine's "understanding of divine grace and human freedom" (91), and (ii) function as "the beginning of the central part of the *Confessions*" narrating Augustine's "conversion to Christianity" (ibid.).

49 See Introduction, n. 17.

50 *Conf.* 6.7.11, 98—Chadwick.

51 Ibid., 6.7.11–12.

52 Ibid., 6.10.16, 103—Chadwick.

53 Ibid., 6.10.16.

54 As Starnes (1990, 154) writes: "But in desiring to show this virtue Alypius had already lost it since what he really sought was not virtue but the applause of the world."

55 *Conf.* 6.12.22.

56 Ibid., 6.8.13.

57 Ibid., 6.10.17.

58 Ibid., 6.7.11–12.

59 Ibid., 6.10.17.

60 Ibid., 6.13.23.

61 Ibid., 6.14.24.

62 See O'Meara (1965, 128–9) and O'Donnell (2@383–5) concerning the historical circumstances surrounding Augustine's dismissal of his longtime concubine. O'Meara (ibid., 129) claims that Augustine, though heart-stricken, was doing his "duty." Likewise, O'Donnell (ibid., 385) remarks that the "relationship should not be romanticized or thought in any way untypical of the age." (Matter [164–75] discusses Augustine's general attitude toward women.)

63 *Conf.* 6.15.25.

64 Ibid., 6.16.26.

65 Ibid., 6.12.22.

66 See Chapter 2, n. 62.

67 *Conf.* 6.11.20, 12.22, 15.25.

68 Ibid., 6.14.24. O'Donnell (2@379–81) discusses this project, including its foreshadowing Augustine's subsequent monastic community.

69 See Vaught (2003, 141–2) for erudite comparison of Ambrose and Faustus.

70 *Conf.* 6.11.18–19.

71 Ibid., 6.15.25.

72 Ibid., 6.16.26. Augustine cites certain Epicurean doctrines. Perhaps, as O'Donnell (2@388) and Catapano (203–4) suggest, Augustine and Alypius were then reading Cicero's *De Finibus Bonorum et Malorum*. Nevertheless, as O'Donnell and others remark, Augustine's preference for Epicureanism is hybrid, being subject, like his skepticism, to pursuing Wisdom. Augustine, therefore, is not an Epicurean but studies their doctrine concerning "the ultimate nature of good and evil" (6.16.26, 109—Chadwick) because he is seeking Wisdom. Confessor Augustine cites Epicureanism because part of its doctrine articulates aspects of young Augustine's mindset while pursuing Wisdom.

73 Ibid., 6.1.1–2.2.

74 Ibid., 6.4.6.

75 Ibid., 6.5.7–8. On this basis, Catapano (203) helpfully assesses Augustine's skepticism: "Academic skepticism plays, in this process [i.e., in Augustine's pursuit of Wisdom], a dual role . . . it contributes to detaching Augustine from the false wisdom of Manichaeism . . . it represents an obstacle to be overcome, insofar as it empties wisdom of every intellectual certainty and declares it unattainable on the cognitive level."

Catapano justifiably claims catechumen Augustine's skepticism keeps him from embracing Wisdom. However, as Augustine's reenrollment as a Catholic catechumen shows, skepticism is embraced not for its own sake but as a tool in pursuing Wisdom.

76 For helpful commentary on *conf.* 7, see Starnes (1990), 169–211; Vaught (2004), 25–65, 145–9; MacDonald (2006), 85–105; Wills (2011), 50–7; Cary (2020), 107–26; O'Donnell, 2@391–484; O'Meara (1965), 131–59; Stock, 65–74; and David (2019A), 95–110.

77 *Conf.* 5.10.19; 14.25. For commentary on Augustine's view of the Academics, see O'Donnell (2@314–5). It is unclear when Augustine first read their skeptical doctrine. *Conf.* suggests it was probably while he studied the liberal arts (4.16.30). In any event, Augustine tells us when he first applied these doctrines to his quest for Wisdom.

78 *Conf.* 3.4.7–8.

79 Perhaps because of *conf.* 7.7.11, Vaught (2004, 34) maintains catechumen Augustine has now taken, albeit reluctantly, the stance of "faith leads to understanding" (MacDonald [2006, 86], Cary [2020, 120], and Starnes [1990, 170] imply the same). This claim is certainly true since Augustine is a catechumen. However, Augustine's skepticism prompted him to search for indubitable knowledge of Wisdom. Augustine is not your "average" catechumen since it seems unlikely he would have become a practicing Catholic apart from attaining the knowledge of Wisdom reported in *conf.* 7. Unlike most catechumens, Augustine wanted certitude before joining the *cultus*. In this regard, Vaught and MacDonald (cf. 2006, 95) underestimate the importance of Augustine's skepticism. See Starnes (1990, 169–80) for a more complete account of Augustine's intellectual *weltanschauung* at that time.

80 *Conf.* 6.5.7 shows catechumen Augustine has moderated his opinion concerning verifying the Catholic claim *certissima ratione*.

81 Ibid., 7.7.11; cf. 6.3.4–5.8.

82 Ibid., 7.5.7.

83 Ibid.

84 Ibid.

85 Ibid., 7.3.4–5.

86 Ibid., 7.1.1: "*quod nullam patitur mutationem melius esse quam id quod mutari potest*"—latin/O'Donnell. 1@73.

87 Ibid.: "*quod corrumpi potest deterius esse quam id quod non potest*"—latin/O'Donnell, 1@73.

88 Ibid.: "*quod violari non potest incunctanter praeponebam violabi*"—latin/O'Donnell, 1@73.

89 While MacDonald (2006, 95) claims Augustine upholds these principles because of "his progress with Platonism," Starnes (1990, 170) asserts that Augustine derives them from considering the noetic character of mathematical objects. If MacDonald means this shows that Augustine assimilates Platonism from hearing Ambrose's Christian-Platonist sermons, his comment is justified.

It is evident, however, that young Augustine has not been introduced to Platonism as such. Therefore, Starnes's comment is justified concerning what we might surmise from considering Augustine's then philosophical dispositions. In a way, each comment is reasonable; perhaps, since the aforementioned principles belong both to skepticism and to Platonism, the real difference is that MacDonald looks more at Augustine's destination while Starnes considers more his origin.

90 See Starnes's perceptive comment (1990, 184–5) on this point, which also applies to Augustine's earlier understanding of natural science. Concerning the conditions Augustine puts in place regarding knowing God, Starnes writes: "It is not the case that the requirements of human thought impose any necessity on God—as if the demand that God must be thus if we are to know him compelled such a God to exist. But, on the other hand, these requirements of our thought do impose an absolute necessity on the mind which has come to understand them. They demand that it recognize the objective existence of such a God." Likewise, facility with mathematics and observation does not cause the movements of the celestial bodies. However, since mind understands those movements by these means, it is bound to know them accordingly.

91 *Conf.* 7.1.1–2.

92 Ibid., 7.5.7; 7.3.4–5.

93 Ibid., 7.6.8–10.

94 Ibid., 7.2.3.

95 Ibid., 7.7.11.

96 Ibid., 7.9.13.

97 Ibid. Confessor Augustine does not identify the specific authors, translators, and titles of the "Platonist books" he read, but research shows these include various works by Plotinus and Porphyry wherein are clarified, criticized, synthesized, and developed key doctrines of Plato, Aristotle, and their subsequent interpreters. For discussion of (i) Augustine's possible sources and (ii) the broad controversy

surrounding *both* these sources and how he integrates them, see O'Donnell, 1@ xlv–xlvi; 2@413–18, 421–4, 436–7, 454–8; O'Meara (1965), 131–59; Starnes (1990), 182–3, 202–3 nn. 63–5; Cary (2003), 112–14—though he neglects Porphyry; Vaught (2004), 36–42, 146–8, nn. 10, 22, 25–7; King (2005), 213–26; Crouse (2000), 37–50; Rist (1994) 3, 8 (n. 11); and Beatrice (1989), 248–81. As Ayres ([2000/2], 51–76, 53–5) instructs, the Platonism Augustine becomes acquainted with is highly eclectic. (Helpful comments on Augustine's approach to "Platonism" throughout his career are provided by Ayres [2012, 13–20] and Van Fleteren [651–4].)

Confessor Augustine focuses on what catechumen Augustine learned from the "Platonist books" and makes no obvious distinction between what he now thinks about that learning and what catechumen Augustine then learned. Nevertheless, as 7.9.13–15 makes evident, both view that learning as a material cause toward insight concerning the Catholic religion.

98 *Conf.* 7.9.13, 121—Chadwick; latin/O'Donnell (1@80). To whom is Augustine referring? The consensus is that Mallius Theodorus (b. *c*. 350 AD, d. *c*. 409 AD) gave catechumen Augustine the books. For discussion, see O'Donnell (2@419–20); Wills (2011, 51–4); Starnes (1990, 204, n. 66); and O'Meara (1965, 125–6, 152), who claims (125–6) that the phrase "*immanissimo typho turgidum*" refers to Porphyry (*c*. 234–305 AD), i.e., to the one who wrote the books Theodorus gave to Augustine (152).

99 Ibid., 7.9.13–14.

100 Ibid., 7.9.14–15.

101 Ibid.

102 Cf. *doc. Chr.*, 2.39.58–41.62. As Cary (2003, 112) writes: "our author wants us to know ... they taught some of the same things as Scripture, but in different words." O'Donnell (2@432–4) instructs that *conf.* 7.9.15's account of the "gold taken from Egypt" refers to Platonic philosophy because Augustine then thought this philosophy was originally developed in Egypt.

103 *Conf.* 7.9.13–14. In this instance, what exceeds pagan learning is doctrine of the "Word made flesh."

104 Ibid., 12.25.34–26.36.

105 Cary (2003, 116) maintains *conf.*'s depiction of Platonist doctrine is actually Confessor Augustine's understanding of Platonism. Cary is not suggesting Augustine is "making things up" but that young Augustine had "yet not mastered the Plotinian conceptuality that he uses so skillfully in the *Confessions*." Cary may be right about

Confessor Augustine's depiction of "Platonism" but his limiting the latter to Plotinus is arbitrary. Cf. O'Meara (1965, 131–55).

106 While some (see O'Donnell [2@394–5]) claim Augustine upholds "immutability" as God's central characteristic, MacDonald (2006, 97–8, 101) maintains it is "what truly is" (i.e., *id quod vere est*).

107 *Conf.* 7.10.16; 17.23. Helm [(2014), 135–54] claims the "Platonist books," contrary to Aristotle's *Categories*, provided young Augustine with a "grammar" to understand divine immutability (138–9, 142). While the "Platonist books" helped Augustine comprehend aspects of Nicene Christianity's philosophical theology, his application of the *Categories* to theological matters when he was twenty years old confirmed him in materialism (140–1, 144–5).

Helm is right that (i) Aristotle's text speaks of corporeal substance (Aristotle considers incorporeal substance inter alios in *Metaphysics*), (ii) young Augustine had tried to know God along those lines, and (iii) the Platonist texts (Augustine highlights) speak of God as incorporeal, immutable substance. However, *Categories* does not speak of supreme divinity—young Augustine, as part of his quest to know Wisdom, used *Categories* to know God. Moreover, *conf.* 5 implies that Augustine found in *Categories* a helpful doctrine of substance since teaching that physical realities were not, *contra* Manichean doctrine, temporary amalgams of good particles and bad particles but naturally organized units. It is likely, then, that Augustine carried into his catechumenate a doctrine of substance he applied to interpreting the "Platonist books"—even causing him to conceive Platonist philosophical theology in a different manner from what interpreters find in Plotinus' and/or Porphyry's texts (van Geest, 124–32). *Categories* could also have helped Augustine understand the Nicene Christianity theology (Helm [2014], 144–5) he was then imbibing and, 7.1.1 shows, sought to investigate; and it certainly aided his analysis of the Trinity in *trin.* 5–7 (*c.* 400–22 AD).

My point is Helm's distinction between Augustine's learning from the "Platonist books" and from Aristotle's *Categories* is too strong.

108 Ibid.
109 Ibid.
110 Ibid., 7.10.16.
111 Ibid., 7.11.17; 15.21.
112 Ibid., 7.12.18–13.19.
113 Ibid., 7.16.22.

114 Ibid., 7.10.16, 124—Chadwick. King (2014), 12, 25) says Augustine cannot attain "ecstatic" union with God (*conf.* 7.10.16 and 7.17.23—cf. O'Meara [1965] 136–42) because his negative attitude toward sexuality, caused by awareness of sexual lust, motivates him to embrace a Christian rather than pagan Platonist ascent to God. While Augustine thinks his ascent to God is the latter, he instead follows the former, learned from Bishop Ambrose, that he favors because of his aversion to sexuality. By contrast, if Augustine had followed the traditional Platonist ascent, his sexuality would have enabled him to achieve "ecstasy."

Since *catechumen* Augustine reads "the Platonic books," King is right his ascent is more Christian than pagan (King rightly places Augustine in the orbit of Ambrose's Milanese Platonism [18–25]—cf. Kenney [2005], 57–60), and this ascent's character is affected by Augustine's sexual lust. However, there appear to be three difficulties with King's analysis. First, Augustine does not pursue "ecstasy" since his principal concern, expressed in 7.10.16 and 7.17.23, pertains to achieving a stable union with God. Some of what the vision of God discloses is that divine union has a temporal duration because its subject, being mutable, dwells in a region of dissimilitude (*in regione dissimilitudinis*—O'Donnell [1@82])—and this motivates Augustine's subsequent search for mediation (e.g., 7.17.23–21.27). Hence, catechumen Augustine is not seeking "ecstasy." Second, as 7.17.23 witnesses, catechumen Augustine's sexual lust discloses his wrong relation to God. However, the principal issue, by Confessor Augustine's judgment, is not catechumen Augustine's disordered sexual inclination but ontological difference. Even if young Augustine were chaste and achieved "ecstasy," Confessor Augustine would focus on mediation. Hence, if it is right that catechumen Augustine's ascent is Christian and he is perturbed by sexual lust, the issue Confessor Augustine emphasizes applies to ascents to God, period. The problem is how selfhood, having soul and body as its proper subject, can achieve stable union with God in the here and now and complete union hereafter.

Third, it seems catechumen Augustine's ascent is influenced by Milanese-Church-Platonism more than King suggests. As *conf.* 7 shows, Augustine engages the "Platonist books" to analyze Church dogma. The latter is his formal cause. Augustine is not interested in those books for their own sake. In fact, Confessor Augustine's account of Wisdom's promise of mediation to *man* is much more like St. Paul's vision of Christ on the road to Damascus (Acts 9.1–8) *and* the newly baptized Augustine's shared vision of Wisdom with mother Monnica (*conf.* 9.19.23–6) than Plotinus' vision of the One (e.g., *Ennead* 5.1.10–12).

Hence, the ascents reported in *conf.* 7 should be viewed in the tradition of Milanese-Church-Platonism. (Cf. Byers [2020], 154–74, 173.)

115 Ibid., 7.10.16.
116 Ibid., 7.17.23.
117 Ibid., 7.19.25–20.26.
118 Ibid., 7.10.16.
119 Ibid., 7.9.14–15. Cf. 10.42.67. As *Enneads* 1.1, 10; 2.9, 2; 5.1, 10; 6.4, 14; Gerson (2020), and Armstrong suggest, the pagan Platonists Augustine is acquainted with, viz. Plotinus and Porphyry, think Wisdom's ultimate subject is not man, the soul-body composite, but either *nous* (i.e., human intelligence, considered much the same substance as supreme divinity) or soul containing *nous*. These thinkers maintain, therefore, that beatitude is achieved by *nous*' uniting itself with supreme divinity as far as possible in this life (by imitating like-minded men or spirits) and, consequently, becoming united with supreme divinity at death. Hence, Augustine eventually thinks the pagan Platonists do not have a teaching of divine mediation since it is not mutable man who seeks beatitude but a so-called divine part in man.
120 Cary (2003, 123) claims Augustine is essentially an onto-theologian supplanting the God of scripture with the God of the philosophers he finds in Platonism. (Cf. Vaught [e.g., 2004, 30, 59–60] showing Augustine's constant effort to overcome Manichean and Platonic tendencies toward philosophical dualism; and Cary [2020], 227–41.)
121 *Conf.* 7.19.25.
122 Ibid., 7.21.27.
123 Ibid., 7.21.27, 132—Chadwick.

Chapter 3

1 *Conf.*, 10.43.70, 220—Chadwick.
2 For helpful commentary on *conf.* 8, see Starnes (1990), 213–45; Vaught (2004), 67–103, 149–52; Wolterstorff (2006), 161–74; Wills (2011), 58–77; Ferrari (2003), 127–36; O'Donnell, 3@3–71; O'Meara (1965), 159–90; Stock, 89–111; and David (2019A), 111–24.
3 Augustine describes this state in *conf.* 8.1.2, 134—Chadwick: "by the witness of all creation I had found you our Creator and your

Word who is God beside you and with you is one God, by whom you created all things (John 1:1–3). There are impious people of another sort who 'knowing God, have not glorified him as God nor given thanks' (Rom. 1: 21). In this respect also I had fallen; but 'your right hand sustained me' (Ps. 17: 36). You took me thence and placed me where I could recover my strength. For you said to man 'Behold piety is wisdom', and 'Do not wish to appear wise' (Job 28: 28; Prov. 26: 50). 'Those who asserted themselves to be wise have been made foolish' (Rom. 1: 22)."

Confessor Augustine *implies* that Job and the Psalmist, unlike the pagan Platonists and pre-8.12 Augustine, exhibit a right attitude toward God. Hence, Augustine upholds as ideal the disposition of "natural" humility or natural *confessio* for those not knowing Christ. (Cf. *civ. Dei.* 18.47.) Prior to crying tears of confession, Augustine is somewhat presumptuous, when crying those tears (8.11.27–12.28) he is like David and Job; after conversion (8.12.28–9), he is like St. Paul.

Augustine *suggests* there are two (closely related) virtues of humility, viz. (i) humility, a natural virtue, and (ii) humility, the supernatural virtue. He upholds the former as the highest virtue available to man apart from Christ's grace and therefore as a middle between presumption and Christian confession (see *conf.* 8.1.2; and Starnes [1990], 196). *Conf.* teaches that (natural) humility stands toward Christian confession since the humble person recognizes God as *Summum Bonum* and therefore as having the power they need to enjoy Him. As Augustine claims throughout *conf.* 7–8, the humble person seeks out divinely promised mediation. Second, Augustine views humility as a principal Christian virtue essentially synonymous with *confessio* (see Baumann, 214-2; Vannier, 63–74, 65–7; Schlabach, 299–330; and Rist [2000], 56–8).

I use the words "implies" and "suggests" for, as post-*Simpl.* instruction on divine grace and predestination shows, Augustine's thought discloses a tension between divine grace offered generally and grace offered to Christians (or Christian grace) since he commonly annihilates the former while *distinguishing* the latter. He maintains both that certain kinds of implicit relationship with God are positive (e.g., *conf.* 8.1.2; *trin.* 14.4.21) and that all implicit relationship is negative (e.g., *civ. Dei.* 21.12). *Conf.* more often exhibits the former.

4 *Simpl.* 1.2 (O'Donnell [3@3] cites that study's importance to *conf.* 8's presentation) implies it is reasonable for someone practicing "natural" *confessio* to petition God for His gift of supernatural *confessio* since one should want *free choice of will* and therefore

the power to overcome the force of previous bad choices. In this regard, catechumen Augustine discovers he harmed himself during his previous thirty-two years and, even if he were intact, he would require God's help to have *free choice of will*. (For explanation, see *conf.* 8.8.19–11.29 and Starnes [1990, 232–5].)

5 As *conf.* 7 showed, this is, for Augustine, a key distinction, capable of holding that the human being is one substance, i.e., a soul-body composite. For while God alone is immutable the human being is mutable. As such, Augustine's key distinction likely includes Aristotle's teaching on substance's primacy (4.16.28; see also n. 107, Chapter 2).

Why do I raise this matter? Those commentators claiming that Augustine's conversion is really to "dualistic" pagan Platonist philosophy along with many of those claiming it is, instead, a conversion beyond dualisms to Christianity (e.g., Vaught, 2004, 79, 95–6) underestimate the importance of Augustine's cardinal distinction between immutable and mutable being.

6 *Simpl.* 1.2.

7 Ekenberg's analysis (28–45) overlooks a key aspect of Confessor Augustine's account of catechumen Augustine's conversion in *conf.* 8. While Ekenberg rightly notes that Augustine "does not assume or rely on a philosophical theory ... where will is distinct from, and independent of reason and emotion" (44), he also claims young Augustine's "conversion" is fundamentally involuntary (41, 44).

Ekenberg is right that catechumen Augustine cannot will Christ's grace. However, Augustine's humble realization of this inability (represented by tears of confession in 8.11.28–12.29) opens the door to receiving Him. As the earlier example of Victorinus's conversion shows, Confessor Augustine thinks God "prepares the will" for conversion and, for this reason, *conf.* 8 shows a development wherein God prepared catechumen Augustine's will. (In 8.1.1, Confessor Augustine remarks that book 8 will recount how God "broke" his chains so he became united with Him.) Therefore, it is because Augustine holds mutable substance cannot join itself to immutable substance that he explains how God joins man to Himself to prepare him for immutable union. So catechumen Augustine does not will God's grace, as that is impossible, but God's grace wills that Augustine wills Him. Since Confessor Augustine holds that God reformed young Augustine's will, analysis of Augustine's conversion also requires considering the divine role therein.

8 *Conf.* 8.1.1–2.

9 According to Wills (2011, 58), Augustine is Christian prior to the events reported in *conf*. 8 and the "garden scene is about giving up sex" (59). This claim stands contrary to what Augustine himself (8.1.1) says on these matters, viz. that he is addicted to vanity—sexual lust is the tip of the iceberg concerning what ailed him. Hence, Vaught (2004, 68) asserts: "when he [i.e. Augustine] responds to the voice of God in the garden, he not only relinquishes sexuality and renounces ambition at the surface of life, but also abandons the willfulness at the center of his being."

10 *Conf*. 8.1.1, 133—Chadwick.

11 E.g., ibid., 6.12.22–15.25 and 7.17.23.

12 E.g., ibid., 8.1.2, 7.17, 11.26–7.

13 Ibid., 8.1.2, 133–4—Chadwick.

14 Ibid., 8.2.3, 135—Chadwick.

15 Ibid., 8.2.3–4.9. Since Victorinus, like Augustine, was a famous orator and shared similar apprehensions toward the Catholic religion, Simplicianus's account of Victorinus's conversion is shrewd. For discussion of Victorinus's life and scholarship, see O'Donnell, 3@13–15, 20–2.

16 Ibid., 8.5.10.

17 Ibid., 8.5.12, 141—Chadwick. See O'Donnell (3@30–1) for discussion of Augustine's concept of will (*voluntas*) in 8.5.10, including recognition that Augustine's doctrine "marks a distinct philosophical advance and an important differentiation from neo-Platonism" (ibid., 31). (Cf. Introduction, n. 31.)

18 Ibid., 8.6.13–15.

19 Ibid., 8.7.17.

20 Ibid., 8.7.18–8.20.

21 Ibid., 8.8.20, 147—Chadwick.

22 For helpful commentary on Augustine's argument in 8.10.22–4 against the Manichean notion that man has two minds and therefore two wills, one good the other evil, see David (2019A), 117–19, and O'Donnell, 3@48–51.

23 *Conf*. 8.11.25–26, 151—Chadwick.

24 As Vaught (2004, 90–1) writes: "Augustine finally abandons his willfulness and opens himself to a source of power . . . beyond him. This does not mean Augustine renounces either his will or his friends, but . . . is willing to stand alone before God. In this moment of solitude, he finally exercises the will of absolute receptivity rather

than the willfulness of self-accentuation." I italicize "imitates" since imitation admits of degrees. I do not claim Augustine explicitly imitates Christ's supernatural humility (e.g., 8.12.29–30), but he imitates Christ's humility by "natural" humility. Since Augustine is yet unconverted to Christ, I understand that Vaught (2004, 91) means the same by "the will of absolute receptivity."

25 Ferrari (2003, 129) claims "*irrefutable proof* of the fictional nature of the description of Augustine's famous conversion scene . . . of 386 in the garden of Milan." (For discussion of precedents, in the scholarship, disputing the factual basis of *conf.*'s account of Augustine's conversion, see O'Meara [1965, 182–90] and O'Donnell [3@9–61, esp. 60 for a more balanced view of the matter]).

26 *Conf.* 8.11.27.

27 Ibid., 8.12.28.

28 Ibid., 8.12.29, 153—Chadwick.

29 See Starnes (1990, 232–6) and O'Donnell (3@55–69) for helpful discussion of Augustine's account of his conversion in 8.12.28–9.

30 *Conf.* 8.12.29, 153—Chadwick.

31 Ibid., 8.12.30, 153—Chadwick.

32 Ibid., 8.12.30, 153–4—Chadwick.

33 Starnes completes his analysis of *conf.* 8 (1990, 236) with the claim that books 1–9, viewed as a whole, have a trinitarian structure (to which Vaught [2004, 106—citing Starnes] agrees). (See also Starnes [1987], 95–103, 95–6, 103, 95, nn. 1–2; 102, n. 10; 103, n. 12.)

34 For helpful commentary on *conf.* 9, see Starnes (1990), 247–76; Vaught (2004), 105–38, 152–4; Helm (2006), 147–60; Wills (2011), 78–97; Paffenroth (2003), 137–54; O'Donnell, 3@72–149; O'Meara (1965), 191–209; Stock, 112–21; Kenney (2005), 73–86, 110–28; and David (2019A), 125–41.

35 *Conf.* 9.1.1, 155—Chadwick.

36 Ibid.

37 As Paffenroth (2003, 147) says concerning Augustine's love of persons: "Book 9 is . . . the beginning of a new, more healthy, and more sanctifying conception of earthly attachments." This results from Augustine's transition from a secular to incarnational mindset. Based on *conf.* 13.5–6–11.12, this is because young Augustine (*pace* Starnes [1990, 236]) is now guided by the Holy Spirit.

38 Paffenroth (2003, 143–4), looking ahead in *conf.*, helpfully notes how book 9's emphasis on "a universal story of humankind" (143) prepares the reader for Augustine's ecclesial focus in books 10–13.

39 *Conf.* 9.2.2–4.
40 Ibid., 9.3.5–6; 8.17.
41 Ibid., 9.4.7.
42 Ibid., 9.4.8–11; 6.14.
43 Ibid., 9.4.12.
44 Ibid., 9.6.14–7.16.
45 Ibid., 9.8.17–11.28.
46 Ibid., 9.12.29–13.37.
47 Ibid., 9.2.4.
48 E.g., ibid., 9.8.17.
49 Ibid.
50 Ibid., 9.3.5.
51 Ibid., 9.3.6, 158–9—Chadwick.
52 Ibid., 9.4.7. For discussion of Cassiciacum's Italian location, see O'Donnell, 3@81–2.
53 Ibid., 9.4.7, 159—Chadwick.
54 Ibid., 160—Chadwick.
55 Ibid., 159–60—Chadwick. For commentary on the character of these dialogues (viz. *Against the Academics*, *On the Happy Life*, *On Order*, and *The Soliloquies*)—are they Christian or pagan Platonist?—see O'Donnell (3@84–91); Starnes (1992, 251–3); Vaught (2004, 112–14); and O'Meara (1965, 193–9). For recent study, see Foley (2019, 2020).
56 For helpful commentary concerning why Augustine feels compassion toward the Manicheans and how this shows his maturing emotions, see Starnes (1990, 253), Paffenroth (2003, 150–2), and Vaught (2004, 114–5).
57 *Conf.* 9.4.8–11.
58 Ibid., 9.4.12.
59 Ibid., 9.6.14, 164—Chadwick.
60 Ibid., 9.6.14.
61 Ibid., 9.8.17.
62 Ibid., 166—Chadwick.
63 Thus, Augustine remarks (in a manner reflecting *conf.* 4's analysis of young Augustine's dearest friend), how Monnica's death devastated him because their lives had become one. He writes (9.12.30, 174–5—Chadwick): "Now that I had lost the immense support that she gave

me, my soul was wounded, and my life as it were torn to pieces, since my life and hers had become a single thing."

64 Ibid., 9.9.19–22.

65 Ibid., 9.10.23–6.

66 Ibid., 9.11.27.

67 Ibid., 9.13.36–7.

68 Ibid., 9.10.23, 171—Chadwick.

69 Ibid.

70 This vision of Wisdom, as its formal object shows, is Christian rather than pagan Platonist. For analysis, see Kenney (2005, 73–86, 110–28); Starnes (1990, 259–63); Vaught (2004, 127–33); O'Donnell (3@122–37); O'Meara (1965, 201–3); Drever (75–91, 86–90); and Byers (2020, 154–74).

71 *Conf.* 9.12.29.

72 Ibid., 4.4.7–10.13.

73 See Helm (2006, 147–51) for comparison of Augustine's earlier grief at the death of his teenage friend (c*onf.* 4) to his grief at Monnica's death (*conf.* 9). For Helm, Confessor Augustine, *contra* the Stoic view of grief and Wolterstorff's opinion (2006), countenances grief when the latter is "soundly based" (158).

74 *Conf.* 9.12.33.

75 Ibid., 9.13.34–5.

76 See Paffenroth's (2003, 149–50) insightful comments concerning Augustine's incarnational loves for his parents, Patricius and Monnica, expressed at *conf.* 9's conclusion. Wills (2011, 89) probably means Augustine cites Patricius by name "for the first time" in 9.9.19.

77 Cf. *conf.* 7.17.23 and 8.1.1.

78 For helpful commentary on *conf.* 10, see Starnes (1987), 95–103; Vaught (2005), 27–99, 230–42; Wills (2006), 195–208, *idem.*, (2011), 98–111; Bright, 137–54; O'Donnell, 3@150–249; Stock, 207–32; Kenney (2005), 89–109; Wolterstorff (2014), 46–70; and David (2019A), 143–60.

79 For discussion of *conf.* 10's liturgical aspect, see O'Donnell, 3@245–6; Wills (2011), 99–100; and Foley (2019), 425–52; *idem.*, (2006), 191, n. 16, 192, n. 26, 212, n. 95, 229, nn. 221–2, 327, 329–30; and *idem.* (2005), 30–64. It is easily agreed that Bishop Augustine considers liturgical matters while writing *conf.*

80 Since it contradicts Augustine's comments at book 10's outset and in his *retr.*, I am puzzled by Vaught's remark (2005, 28) that beginning with book 10 Augustine no longer intends "to stir up the heart toward God, or to delight the ones who have been converted, but to express the struggle of a convert as he joins other Christians in moving from conversion to fulfillment at both the experiential and reflective levels." CC agrees that book 10 represents a shift in context but this should not be exaggerated since Augustine, now a Christian for about thirteen years, continues to encourage *confessio* (see n. 82).

81 As O'Donnell (3@162) writes: "*Even* the best readers of this text will end by *believing* but not *knowing* what Augustine says of himself is true."

82 This is an important point, but some commentators (e.g., Vaught [2005, 27–36] and Starnes [1987, 97–9]) exaggerate its importance. First, *retr.* informs that Augustine includes book 10 within *conf.*'s first major confession detailing God's schooling him to practice *confessio*. Second, there is not a huge difference between what Augustine asked of his reader in books 1–9 and what he now asks, viz. belief. Third, Augustine now provides his reader with an objective standard to measure his inward dispositions. These include his account of soul in 10.6.8–26.37; reliance on the biblical standard of 1 Jn 2:16 to consider his relation to the temptations of the flesh, world, and devil; and book 10's conclusion (10.43.67–70) concerning Christ's mediation.

83 Certainly, the Christian relationship with God is unique. But Augustine's principal audience from *conf.*'s outset is Christian. So that is not unique. Moreover, Augustine has always confessed his experience for universal purposes. The difference (as n. 82 implies) is that whereas, earlier, particularities were linked to specific temporal events viewed by others, now they are psychological/inward realities that only Augustine can view. In this sense, the latter are unique.

84 Cf. Starnes's claim (1987, 99) that 10.6.8–25.36 contains "knowledge which was unique to himself [i.e. to Augustine]."

85 O'Donnell (3@150–4) defends book 10's unity and its integral role in *conf.* However, while he claims book 10 centers the ascent toward God constituting *conf.* (viewing books 1–9 in terms of *memory*, 10 concerning *present awareness*, and 11–13 regarding *present expectation* [153]), CC maintains the entirety belongs to Augustine's book-long *confessio*. This does not deny O'Donnell's claim that *conf.* represents an ascent toward God but intends to set that ascent within a larger framework. For explanation, see ahead CC's "Conclusion."

86 *Conf.* 10.6.9, 184—Chadwick. With O'Donnell (3@168) we note how Augustine's ascent begins, as always, with corporeal reality (cf. 7.17.23) and often while emphasizing beauty.
87 See Vaught's (2005, 45) discussion of Augustine's use of *anima* and *animus* from 10.6.9 onward.
88 *Conf.* 10.7.11, 185—Chadwick; latin/O'Donnell, 1@123.
89 Ibid., 10.8.13–15.
90 See O'Donnell (3@174–8, 184), Vaught (2005, 46–7), Cipriani (553–5), and Rist (1994, 73–85) for helpful discussion of the provenance and meaning of Augustine's notion of memory (*memoria*). In *trin.* 14.3.13 Augustine identifies memory with mind.
91 *Conf.* 10.8.12–15.
92 Ibid., 10.9.16, 187—Chadwick.
93 Ibid., 10.10.17–13.20.
94 Ibid., 10.14.22, 191—Chadwick.
95 Ibid., 10.15.23.
96 Ibid., 10.16.24–5, 193—Chadwick.
97 Ibid., 10.17.26. In other words, Augustine has recognized that God must transcend mind—yet he knows God. How, then, does this occur?
98 Ibid., 10.17.26, 195—Chadwick.
99 Ibid., 10.18.27–19.28.
100 Vaught (2005, 78–9) attributes Augustine's knowing God to "divine illumination." This requires qualification for Augustine has several teachings on illumination. First, there is natural illumination, which his teaching that each pursues "happiness in truth" upholds; second, there is illumination Augustine speaks of in 10.22.32 whereby mind identifies truth with God and rejoices in Him. While the first sort pertains to God's natural presence, the second refers to explicit presence through Christ.
101 *Conf.* 10.20.29, 196—Chadwick; latin/O'Donnell, 1@130.
102 Ibid., 10.22.32, 199—Chadwick.
103 Ibid., 10.22.32. Cf. Menn (90–1), who also considers Augustine's account of God as Truth in *conf.* 7.
104 Ibid., 10.22.32–23.34.
105 Ibid., 10.25.36–27.38. O'Donnell (3@196) writes that Augustine's argument here is "the complete bald-faced flipflop, that rescues him from the solipsism to which his reasoning has led him. All his

argument from 10.6.8 has shown that God is only found in the self. Now he brusquely asserts the reverse as the only tenable position: by implication, all his argument is put in a new perspective."

This claim overlooks both the significance of Augustine's earlier arguments concerning God (e.g., 7.10.16 and 7.17.23) and Augustine's focus, from *conf.*'s beginning, regarding divine presence and, related to that, on encouraging *confessio*. First, Augustine has not said "God is only found in the self," at least if that means He is part of the self. Rather, from 10.6.8 onward, Augustine tries to distinguish "what he loves when he loves God," and he initially shows the conditions whereby God *cannot be* present to soul to disclose the conditions whereby He can be present. In agreement with *conf.*'s earlier philosophical theology, Augustine maintains God cannot be a body, a part of the soul, or the soul itself. Rather, in the argument running from 10.6.8–10, he considers God, from the beginning, as "the life of the soul." Therefore, what Augustine claims in 10.25.36 about the divine nature (that it is immutable) and divine presence (that it is permanent) is not a "flipflop." Rather, it belongs to the argument commenced in 10.6.8 and is consistent with *conf.*'s earlier arguments.

However, O'Donnell reasonably implies Augustine introduces rather quickly his conclusion concerning divine immutability and account of divine presence's conditions. Augustine would have helped his cause by introducing premises leading to his conclusion. He did this, for instance, in supporting divine immutability in 7.17.23 by explaining why degrees of mutability depend on immutability. Here, then, he might have explained that if God is "the life of the soul" and soul is mutable (but structured by permanent orientation toward happiness in truth/God), then soul's ultimate source must be something immutable, a.k.a. God. So, Augustine's claim about immutability and the nature of His presence could be supported from various sources in *conf*.

106 Stock (226) writes: "But in what sense is God 'there'? Not as an image, a mental state, a metacognitive awareness, or even as mind itself. . . . God is not a place in the mind; he exists in the mental activity by which a mind desires to know him (10.26.6–10)." Stock's helpful view leaves out mentioning two important factors. First, mind's quest for happiness is both that through which it knows God's presence and the latter itself. Second, it follows that God's presence is spiritual both regarding structuring mind and, consequently, concerning reflection on happiness. Augustine's point, of course, is that none of this is God but that soul's omnipresent activity of pursuing happiness depends on His permanent spiritual presence to soul.

107 *Conf.* 10.27.38. CC's "Conclusion" considers this passage's importance to Augustine's doctrine of *confessio*.
108 Ibid., 10.27.38, 201—Chadwick.
109 The certain or indubitable character of Augustine's distinction is overlooked because his focus on *confessio* and, in that respect, his ground-level anti-skeptical orientation are widely ignored.
110 Ibid., 10.23.33–4.
111 Ibid., 10.29.39, 202—Chadwick: "When I shall have adhered (Ps. 72: 28) to you with the whole of myself, I shall never have 'pain and toil (Ps. 89: 10)', and my entire life will be full or you. You lift up the person whom you fill."
112 Ibid.: "But for the present, because I am not full of you, I am a burden to myself."
113 Ibid., 10.43.70.
114 Ibid., 10.30.41; 41.66. For helpful commentary on Augustine's use of this distinction in *conf.* 10 and in *conf.* as a whole, see O'Donnell, 3@203–8.
115 Ibid., 10.29.40–34.53.
116 Ibid., 10.35.54–36.58.
117 Ibid., 10.36.59–39.64.
118 Although Augustine does not mention the Donatists by name in 10.28.39–39.64, criticism of their teaching on clerical perfection is everywhere implied. See O'Donnell, 3@208, 218, 235–6.
119 *Conf.* 10.30.41–2.
120 Ibid., 10.26.59. See O'Donnell (3@229–31) for helpful commentary concerning Augustine's "perplexity and fear" (229) regarding his role as bishop. Together with other bishops, Augustine was worried about temptations arising from exercising power.
121 Ibid., 10.26.59, 214—Chadwick.
122 Ibid., 10.28.39, 202—Chadwick. Augustine is disappointed he does not love God in all things. As Wolterstorff (2014, 65) writes, "What Augustine desires is that there be nothing in his life that is not an expression of his love of God."
123 Ibid., 10.29.40, 202—Chadwick; latin/O'Donnell, 1@134. Cf. 10.30.45 and 10.37.60. Starnes (1987, 101) rightly notes this is "Augustine's prayer throughout the second half of the book." For commentary, see O'Donnell, 3@200–1.
124 Ibid., 10.40.65, 218—Chadwick. O'Donnell (3@238) perspicuously relates this to Augustine's earlier ascent at Ostia.

125 Wolterstorff (2014, 65–70) suggests (65) Augustine recognizes a fourth sort of temptation, viz. "to tolerate fragments in his life that have not been incorporated into the love of God" and this imperfection helped him recognize (68) "that those who love God are to be united in an empathetic solidarity of grieving and rejoicing." They should grieve each other's miseries while rejoicing at God's presence. Hence, Wolterstorff recognizes how Augustine sees, from personal misery and the similar misery suffered by Christian brothers, that the present life which (70) "leads to true joy and peace in the life to come is a path of sorrow and misery."

Confessor Augustine implies, however, that charity entails recognizing the problem of "slow growth." He agrees one should love God in all things—hence the phenomenon of "slow growth" should not be an excuse for despair, sloth, or laziness. Nevertheless, as 10.45.60 shows, Augustine also thinks "slow growth" is a permanent fixture, which properly encourages charity, under the forms of humility, gratitude, and patience. Augustine's considering this phenomenon prior to mentioning his becoming a priest suggests he views "slow growth" as a divinely ordained encouragement for *confessio*.

126 *Conf.* 10.43.68–9.

127 Ibid., 10.43.70.

128 See Starnes (1987, 102–3) concerning the importance of Augustine's consideration of Antony and its relation to *conf.* 11–13's exegesis. Starnes connects the latter with 10.43.70's statement regarding meditating on God's law. However, Starnes does not connect Augustine's citing of Antony with his becoming a priest—though that is also mentioned toward the end of 10.43.70, 200—Chadwick, viz. "I think upon the price of my redemption, and I eat it and drink it and distribute it." If Augustine intends *conf.* 11–13's exegesis to benefit fellow bishops (Brown, 161–2), his priesthood is obviously an important corollary to meditating on God's law.

That said, CC maintains Augustine's transition from *conf.* 1–10 to 11–13 is centered in confessing Christ's infinite goodness. Augustine's confession of Christ as God-man mediator in 11.2.4 is decisive since "in Him is found all the treasures of wisdom and knowledge." Augustine, therefore, pledges to continue presenting Christ as the goal and way to beatitude (cf. 10.42.67–43.70) but adds to this an understanding of eternal and temporal things belonging to pursuing beatitude. Augustine views scripture as a specially created reality directly participating in Christ (like the Church, priests and bishops, the gift of faith, the sacraments, and

Catholic friends [like Monnica]), so that exegesis leads the exegete toward immutable participation in Christ. Hence, what ultimately links Augustine's earlier major confession (books 1–10) to his later one (books 11–13) is confessing Christ. (Cf. Wills [2011], 99, 111, and Bright [157–9, 165–6].)

Chapter 4

1 Why does Augustine feature scripture in books 11–13 after citing a multitude of verses in books 1–10? Confessing Christ via scripture provides evidence for the Catholic religion's claim that Wisdom's way is Christ (e.g., 6.3.4–5.8; 7.9.13; 7.21.27) and, since Augustine understands scripture as a mutable reality specially participating in Christ (i.e. as "the Word made flesh" by a mode of analogy), exegesis can bring greater participation in Christ by sharing in His "knowledge and wisdom" (11.2.4).

2 Chadwick's footnotes (1992), showing parallels between Augustine's and Plotinus'/Porphyry's philosophical theologies and anthropologies, imply a masterful account of what Augustine's Christian teaching holds in common with pagan Platonist teaching. Of course, Chadwick is not claiming Confessor Augustine has read each of these texts; nor is Chadwick claiming Augustine's doctrine is essentially the same as theirs. Those matters belong to study. See Hankey (2010), 127–44, for interpretation of *conf.* in light of considering Chadwick's footnotes; and *idem.*, (2017), 63–100, 65–95, for development of the thesis the aforementioned article expresses.

3 For helpful commentary, see Vaught (2005), 101–49; O'Donnell 3@250–99; David (2019A), 161–80; Sorabji, 209–35; Kennedy, 167–83; Stock, 232–40; McMahon (1989), 117–41; Wills (2011), 112–20; Jordan, 255–79; Hochschild, 155–68; and Helm (2014), 135–54.

4 *Conf.* 11.1.1, 221—Chadwick: "Your vision of . . . may be complete." Cf. *conf.* 1.1.1 in league with O'Donnell's (3@254) and Foley's comments ([2006], 233 n. 1) showing the parallel between 1.1.1 and 11.1.1.

5 I say "collective" or "general" since this confession is especially for those with whom Augustine shares (i) the disposition that Christ is Wisdom and (ii) ponder His scripture to learn key aspects of His providence. It is for "everyman" because by the logic of Augustine's argument from *conf.*'s outset, each should embrace Christ as

Wisdom (and scripture as authoritative). The veracity of Augustine's confession in books 11–13 depends on whether his account of happiness is true—if so, his confession is universal or objective. Secondarily (and subjectively), it depends on whether those belonging to Augustine's subaltern audience agree with him.

6 *Conf.* 11.2.2.

7 Ibid., 11.2.2, 221—Chadwick: "But when shall . . . to your people?" Foley (2006, 233, n. 7) notes that since it was North African custom that only bishops could preach, Augustine's reference to "word" and "sacrament" in 11.2.2 is the first time in *conf.* he "refers to his bishopric." That this introduces Augustine's meditation on the scriptures supports Brown's claim (161–2) that 11–13's exegesis intends to encourage fellow North African bishops, like Alypius, to devote themselves, as Ambrose had done, to scripture study.

8 *Conf.* 11.2.3, 221—Chadwick.

9 I say "in principle" since Augustine explains that God creates all mutable things. However, Augustine formally signals God's creating His church in 13.12.13.

10 Augustine's purpose in *conf.* 11–13 is governed by his desire to achieve beatitude through Christ. This is why he focuses on discovering Christ's "wisdom and knowledge."

11 *Conf.* 11.2.4, 223—Chadwick.

12 Ibid., 11.3.5, 223—Chadwick.

13 Ibid., 11.4.6.

14 Ibid., 11.5.7. See David (2019A, 167–9) for analysis of Augustine's argument in 11.4.6 and its relationship with 11.5.7. As Vaught notes (2005, 111–12), Augustine thinks his insight in 11.4.6 derives from "divine illumination" (see n. 100, Chapter 3).

15 Ibid., 11.9.11, 227—Chadwick.

16 I say this because, in 7.9.13–16.22, Augustine has claimed that pagan Platonist philosophy knows (i) God has created all things good (7.12.18) and (ii) that divine creating, regarding the Godhead, is grounded in the relationship between the Father and His consubstantial Word (7.9.13). (See O'Donnell's opinion (3@264) concerning Augustine's handling of Platonism within his exegesis, viz. "that he has clearly made a conscious decision not to invoke the Platonists as authorities.") Likewise, Vaught (2005, 109) and van Geest (123–37, 128) maintain Augustine's account of divine creating transcends Plotinus' view of divinity's relationship with non-divine reality by "working from an entirely new trinitarian view of creation."

17 *Conf.* 11.10.12, 228—Chadwick. For commentary on this question's provenance, see Kennedy (2003, 175); Karfíková, (175–90, 182); and O'Donnell (3@272–4). This question, or some version thereof, was asked by Manicheans, Epicureans (particularly against the Stoics), Gnostics, and certain Platonists. O'Donnell supports the claim that Augustine's response might not only be toward the Manicheans but also, as van Geest argues (127–8), against Plotinian Platonism's claim that creation is coeternal with God and the product of "near-automatic emanation from the generosity of the One alone" (128). According to van Geest, Augustine holds that (i) "the Word of Christ was able to create out of nothing what has not existed before," (ii) "God's act of creation was based on a plan, in which the creature was created on behalf of the creature" and (iii) "God the Creator is a Triune God" (ibid.). Augustine's teaching, then, belongs to his notion of Nicene Christianity.

18 See Vaught (2005, 119) for helpful analysis of this question as a *trilemma*.

19 For assessment of the originality of Augustine's answer, see Sorabji (225–30).

20 *Conf.* 11.12.14, 229—Chadwick.

21 Ibid., 11.13.15, 230—Chadwick.

22 Ibid., 11.11.13, 229—Chadwick. See Jordan (257), Kennedy (176), Karfíková (183–4), and Helm (2006, 136–7, 153–4) for recognition of Augustine's primary confessional concern. As Jordan writes (257), Augustine's reason for considering time is "a moral-religious one."

23 For discussion of the provenance of Augustine's notion of time and brief analysis of scholarly views thereof, see O'Donnell (3@278). Based on what is stated earlier (n. 22), O'Donnell justifiably questions interpretations separating the discussion of time from Augustine's scriptural preoccupations.

24 *Conf.* 11.26.30. O'Donnell (3@289) highlights Augustine's spiritual use of this term: "It is a colourful and highly novel metaphor, to be translated not so much by the term 'extension' as by 'tension' or 'distraction causing anxiety.'"

25 Ibid., 11.26.33–28.38.

26 Ibid., 11.29.39–30.40.

27 Ibid., 11.14.17–20.26. See O'Donnell (3@283–5) for discussion of the (i) importance of the triad *memoria, contuitus, expectatio*, to interpretations of *conf.*'s general structure and (ii) provenance, including Porphyrean, of Augustine's triad.

28 Ibid., 11.21.27–24.31.
29 Ibid., 11.25.32–26.33.
30 Ibid., 11.27.34–28.38.
31 Ibid., 11.28.36, 242—Chadwick. For analysis of Augustine's claim concerning time's nature, see Vaught (2005, 123–44), Sorabji (212–20), Jordan (256–74), and Helm (2006, 135–54).
32 *Conf.* 11.27.37–8. In this respect, Augustine makes the familiar point that although nothing is closer to mind than itself, its power over itself is limited (cf. 8.9.21 and 10.8.15).
33 Presumably, Augustine thinks his close friend during adolescence (bk. 4), Monnica, Vercundus, Nebridius, Patricius, and Adeodatus are enjoying this. Looking ahead to *conf.* 12 (e.g., 12.13.16), this "place" of participation in divine immutability, what some (e.g., Jordan, 266) call *aeveternity*, is the obvious meaning of "the heaven of heavens."

For a somewhat different interpretation of "the heaven of heavens," see Teske (2008), 259–74, 272, who claims Augustine's notion includes key features from Plotinus' notion of "World-Soul" (see n. 57 for discussion).
34 *Conf.* 11.29.39.
35 As Jordan writes: "Augustine . . . carries his reader breathlessly to the true goal of his endeavors, sweeping away times and changes and pressing on to the eternal [261]. . . . for Augustine, time is an invitation to participate in eternity [275]." See also Kennedy (182) and (again) O'Donnell (3@289) for discussion of various meanings of "distension" Augustine employs in 11.29.39.
36 *Conf.* 11.29.39, 244—Chadwick.
37 While certain commentators consider the philosophical merits of Augustine's doctrine of time, CC emphasizes how his doctrine encourages *confessio*.
38 *Conf.* 11.31.41, 245—Chadwick.
39 Ibid.—latin/O'Donnell, 3@164.
40 For helpful commentary, see Vaught (2005), 151–90; O'Donnell, 3@300–42; David (2019A), 181–95; Sorabji 209–35; Martin; Stock, 240–1; McMahon (1989), 130–3; Wills (2011), 120–4; Kenney (2005), 102–3, 113–22; and *idem.*, (2010), 145–65; Teske (2008), 259–74; Jordan, 255–79; Hochschild, 169–82; and Tornau, 181–218.
41 As O'Donnell maintains (3@302–3), Augustine bases his exegesis of Gen. 1:1's "heaven" on Ps. 113:16 (12.2.2). While surveying scholarly opinions concerning the meaning of *caelum caeli*,

O'Donnell claims Augustine derives his notion from scripture but interprets it "in a context in which the Plotinian categories were available" (303). Hence, Augustine's notion of *caelum caeli* changes the aforementioned categories (ibid.).

42 See *conf.* 12.11.12, 251—Chadwick: "Its [i.e., the heaven of heaven's] delight is . . . the successiveness of time."

43 According to Chadwick (12.3.3, 247) and O'Donnell (3@305), Augustine's interpretation of "formless matter" takes direction from Wisdom 11:18. See O'Donnell (3@305–6) for discussion of Augustine's doctrine of "formless matter" in his *corpus*.

44 Since Augustine understands each creature, being composed of matter and form, is mutable, he implies that mind's mutability grounds its analysis of time. As Hochschild (172) writes: "the significance of formless matter . . . is the idea that there is an intrinsic instability at the heart of created things, understood as mutability, or an ontological non-necessity. This is the tendency to non-being that Augustine experiences as an embodied creature in the eleventh book."

45 *Conf.* 12.2.2.

46 Ibid., 12.3.3.

47 For commentary on the Plotinian and biblical background to Augustine's notion of "formless matter" (*informis materia*), including its distinction from Aristotle's account thereof, see Teske (2008, 266–7), Hochschild (172–4), and Tornau (184–94).

48 *Conf.* 12.4.4–7.7.

49 What follows supersedes the account of formless matter in David (2019A, 184–8) since it (i) refers to mutable, i.e., created, substance as such rather than only to bodies, (ii) considers the role Augustine thinks "form" plays in mutability, and (iii) analyzes more of Augustine's spiritual purpose for studying formless matter. In large part, David's earlier analysis relied on Aristotle's instead of Plotinus' account of formless matter.

50 *Conf.* 12.29.40, 270—Chadwick.

51 Ibid., 12.5.5–7.7.

52 Ibid., 12.29.40, 268–9—Chadwick; latin/O'Donnell (1@181). Foley [(2003), 607–22] considers the provenance of Augustine's distinctions in this matter, tracing them (621) to 11b15–15b32 in Aristotle's *Categories*. Augustine obviously read more of the *Categories* than reported in *conf.* 4.16.28 and was willing to apply his learning from the *Categories* to help toward understanding other matters. (See also n. 108, Chapter 2.)

53 Ibid., 12.7.7. Vaught (2005, 157) maintains Augustine's teaching on formless matter exceeds Plotinus' doctrine since "he avoids the embarrassment that the existence of matter as the source of evil causes Plotinus in some of his writings." Augustine, unlike Plotinus, holds that "matter" is good, thereby implying a robust account of God's goodness—supporting scripture's claim that God has made all things good (cf. 7.12.18).

Note, however, O'Donnell's comment (3@308) concerning Augustine's anti-Manichean treatment of "heaven and earth" in Gen. 1:1—though he also asserts Augustine's teaching rules out "Gnostic/Priscillianist emanation" (ibid.). Contrary to Manichean teaching, Augustine's exegesis upholds that God is immutable and incorruptible (cf. Kenny [2010, 150–1]). O'Donnell (see also his first remark concerning 12.8.8, 310), like Vaught, notices that Augustine's teaching has anti-Plotinian overtones but, like Kenny (2010) and Martin, 188–91, O'Donnell claims Augustine's obvious target is the Manicheans.

Since certain elements common to pagan Platonist philosophy (e.g., 7.10.16–16.22) are required for accurate scriptural interpretation, it is easier to recognize Augustine's criticism of the Manicheans and, for that matter, of ill-formed Catholics (cf. Martin, 193–5) than of pagan Platonists.

54 Ibid., 12.7.7.

55 For commentary on *conf.* 12.8.8, where Augustine considers the fittingness of God's initial creating of "formless matter" and "the heaven of heavens," see O'Donnell (3@310–11). He distinguishes the "un-Plotinian" (310) aspect of Augustine's doctrine of creation *de nihilo* since Augustine emphasizes creation is about "ascent" while Plotinus views "coming to be" by the mode of "descent."

Among other things, this shows the importance of recognizing Augustine's concern with knowing scripture and that his exegesis commonly handles pagan Platonist sources as a preeminent *material* cause. (Cf. Tornau [194–201] who agrees that Augustine's teaching takes its guidance from scripture but considers the relationship between Plotinian metaphysics and Christian scripture to be closer than O'Donnell maintains.)

56 *Conf.* 12.7.7; 11.11.

57 Ibid., 12.9.9; 12.10.12–12.15. Kenney (2005, 119) distinguishes non-Plotinian features of Augustine's doctrine of the "heaven of heavens"/*caelum caeli*, including that the latter is a created reality which "is the future home for the fallen soul." Therefore, while Plotinus (e.g., *Ennead 1.6*) holds the embodied soul's proper object is immutable divinity, Augustine claims that *man*'s enjoyment of

God can be permanent since God has created a place where that occurs. So, Augustine's views of man and *caelum caeli* differ from those of Plotinus; and they differ, as well, from Porphyry (at least as Augustine understands him—*civ. Dei.* 22.26).

Augustine's concept of *caelum caeli* is widely interpreted. While some (e.g., Vaught [2005, 162–3], Kenny [2010, 150–5], and Tornau [181–218]) view his meaning simply as "heaven," i.e., the ultimate abode of the blessed, others (e.g., Karfíková [188] and Teske [2008, 267–73]) view it as something akin to the Plotinian notion of World-Soul. According to Teske, "heaven of heaven" means both the abode of the blessed and "the fatherland from which some angels fell and from which human souls fell, from which we souls are presently on pilgrimage, and to which we are returning" (272).

This prompts two related observations. First, if the first party is correct, Augustine's transformation of his Platonic inheritance, and therefore reliance on Nicene Christianity, is more profound than Teske and Karfíková suggest. Second, while it may be difficult to know how Augustine engages pagan Platonist philosophy in *conf.* 12, he obviously transforms that inheritance to show scripture's intelligibility.

58 E.g., *conf.* 12.11.11–13.
59 Ibid., 12.11.11–12.15.
60 Ibid., 12.13.16, 253—Chadwick; latin/O'Donnell, 1@ 169.
61 Ibid., 12.15.18–22. See Kenney's analysis (2010, 155–60) of Augustine's response to those *contradictores* denying his spiritual reading of the Old Testament and, therefore, his bedrock doctrine of divine transcendence. O'Donnell (3@316–7) claims that after 12.14.17 one cannot be sure Augustine has the Manicheans in mind; rather (318), Augustine's enumeration of possible interpretations of Gen. 1:1 (12.15.19) results from "thinking out loud" (Cf. 325, 329).
62 Ibid., 12.14.17.
63 Ibid., 12.17.24–2.
64 Ibid., 12.18.27–22.31.
65 For insightful consideration of how Augustine's exegesis responds to pagans, Manicheans, Donatists, and "ignorant" or ill-educated Catholics, see Martin (188–95) who claims Augustine intends not only to grow in holiness but also, in conjunction with his fellow Catholic bishops, "to reinvigorate the Catholic community in Roman Africa" (196). Teske (2008, 264–74) comments on Augustine's exegesis' (implied) response to Plotinian teaching mediated through the concerns of "conservative Catholics."

The commentators maintain that Augustine's primary concern is to display the nature and object of biblical exegesis to his fellow Catholics. However, that entails showing them how scripture contains insights that both answer and transcend what rival Christian parties hold. In this respect, aspects of pagan Platonist philosophy (as 11.4.6–5.7 shows) represent a kind of "line in the sand."

As n. 16 mentioned, Augustine's transformation of pagan Platonist philosophy is mysterious. Since he encourages his principal audience to embrace Church teaching, because he never speaks of the relationship between pagan Platonism and Christian wisdom in books 11–13, and because of our ignorance concerning what he thinks pagan Platonism shares with Christian wisdom, we speculate (like Vaught, Teske, O'Donnell, Kenney, and Tornau) regarding Augustine's transformation of pagan Platonist teaching. Augustine's direction is clear, but his content is not.

66 *Conf.* 12.23.32, 263—Chadwick.
67 Ibid.
68 Ibid.
69 Ibid., 12.24.33, 264—Chadwick.
70 Ibid.,12.25.35; 30.41. Dutton (155–80) claims Augustine's method is more interested in "truth rather than correctness" (156) and, in league with certain interpreters, names his approach "the Doctrine of the Privacy of the Mind." The advantage of Dutton's analysis is that it shows something of the reasonableness of Augustine's approach; the disadvantage, however, is that reasonableness is truncated by downplaying the *confessio* nature of Augustine's teaching (178–9).
71 Ibid., 12.25.34.
72 Ibid., 12.30.41–31.42.
73 Ibid., 12.26.36–28.38.
74 Concerning 12.27.37, O'Donnell (3@336) comments there is irony beneath Augustine's willingness to accept anthropomorphic conceptions of God since he earlier indicts Manichean anthropomorphisms (e.g., *conf.* 3.7.12).
75 *Conf.* 12.30.41–32.43.
76 Ibid., 12.32.43.
77 For helpful discussion concerning Augustine's approach, in this context, to scripture, see Hochschild, 181–2.
78 For commentary, see Vaught (2005), 190–226, 249–55; O'Donnell, 3@343–421; David (2019A), 197–252—note, however, that his

p. 229 requires correction: "metaphysical" and "physical" should read "immutable" and "mutable." See also McMahon (2003), 207–23, *idem.*, (1989), 142–55; Stock, 240–2; Wills (2011), 125–32; Kenney (2005), 120–8; and Hochschild, 182–5.

79 CC agrees with McMahon (2003, 212–13), following Solignac (23–6), that *conf.* exhibits a "return to Origin," *exitus-reditus*, structure. But, by linking that claim to Augustine's confessing, it qualifies McMahon's assertion that the aforesaid structure's principal sign consists in the Church's eternal enjoyment of God.

McMahon (2003, 213) maintains the Church is the "sacrament or sign of this universal and historical return to the Origin," and therefore (214) it is appropriate that *conf.* ends when Augustine speaks of the Church in divine eternity. McMahon implies the Church signifies the *exitus-reditus* structure of God in Himself—as Father, incarnate Word, and Spirit (e.g., *conf.* 13.5.6, 31.11.12–12.13)—that Augustine identifies in book 13.

By contrast, *CC* focuses on the relationship Augustine strongly implies between God's activity in creating, broadly conceived, and his own activity as confessor. As *CC*'s "Conclusion" explains, *conf.* is centered not only in God but also in Augustine's confessing God. It is true Augustine understands his confessing and, therefore, God's creating His church to participate in the Godhead. But Augustine presents his activity of confessing, and therefore his participating in God's church, to show he is "being created right before his reader's eyes." Augustine does this so others, by confessing, can be likewise created. The *exitus-reditus* dimension of Augustine's confessing, therefore, is what, by God's grace Augustine maintains, motivates his confessing the *exitus-reditus* characters of God in Himself, divine goodness, and through that (*pace* McMahon) the Church. Hence, Augustine's confessing discloses many forms of *exitus-reditus*.

It is fitting, then, that Augustine names his book *Confessiones* rather than, for example, *divina Bonitas*, *Ecclesia*, *de Trinitate*, *Memoria*, *Exitus-Reditus*. Augustine certainly thinks the Church signifies "the universal and historical return to Origin" that permeates *conf.*, but this is through the *exitus-reditus* structure of confessing.

Perhaps the ultimate difference between McMahon's perspective and mine is that he focuses more on the order of being, whereas I focus more on discovery. Again, McMahon is right that Augustine finishes *conf.* by confessing the Church in the Sabbath rest and this is a sign of "the universal return to Origin." But that last passage in *conf.* is even more fundamentally *Augustine's* confessing the Sabbath rest.

80 Augustine concluded 11.1.1 by citing the first line from Psalm 117, viz. "For 'you are good (*bonus*), for your mercy is for ever'" (Ps. 117:1)"—Chadwick (221); latin/O'Donnell (1@148). It is fitting, therefore, that Augustine completes his confession by focusing on divine goodness.

81 My point is Augustine thinks God creates rational creatures to share in His eternal bliss. Hence, the *exitus-reditus* process is ordered to that end. While *exitus* designates creatures' coming into existence (i.e., being created *de nihilo*), *reditus* designates creatures' conformity to their divinely established *telos*. If *reditus* refers to the process of return (rather than to its goal of enjoying timeless eternity [e.g., 12.13.16]) then *telos* determines the *exitus-reditus*. *Reditus*, however, can also refer both to the process of return and to the latter's goal of participated eternity. I am using *reditus* in the latter sense, meaning both the return to and enjoyment of Origin, i.e., to and of God.

82 McMahon's thesis concerning *conf.*'s unity ignores this matter by dividing *conf.* into books 1–9 and books 10–13. In *retr.* 2.6.1, however, Augustine, divides *conf.* into books 1–10 and 11–13. I discuss this matter's importance in n. 107.

83 *Conf.* 13.1.1. Cf. 10.27.38.

84 O'Connell (159) notices an anti-Manichean (see also A. Kotzé [2004], 233), and perhaps anti-pagan Platonist, element in Augustine's argument for soul's created nature. According to O'Connell, Augustine thinks the Manicheans and certain pagan Platonists view soul's substance as identical to supreme divinity—yet Plotinus, O'Connell states, thinks (*Ennead* 6.9) the One "stands utterly 'without need' of the beings emanating from It." However, O'Connell later (178, 184–5) claims Augustine collapses his own distinction between Creator and creature so that Augustine ultimately holds to the pantheistic doctrine he elsewhere denies and thereby betrays his determination to follow scripture.

By contrast, Kenney (2005, 123–4), focusing on 13.31.46, argues that Augustine follows scripture by employing and transcending Plotinian insight. Augustine, he thinks, is more successful in articulating Christian contemplation than O'Connell suggests.

85 *Conf.* 13.1.1, 273—Chadwick.

86 Ibid., 13.2.2.3, 274—Chadwick. As Vannier (63–71) writes (71): "In *conf.* 13.2.2–3.3, Augustine pointed out that creation, conversion, and *formatio* were the expression of the overabundance of God's love.... Everything was grace." See O'Donnell's claim (3@347–8) that Augustine's account of *conversio* in 13.2.3 represents books 11–13's continued "adaptation of Platonism."

87 Ibid., 13.3.4.
88 Ibid., 13.4.5, 275—Chadwick.
89 Ibid.
90 Drever (80) rightly points out Augustine's focus on the Spirit in book 13 and His significant relation to divine creating.
91 Concerning Augustine's account of the Spirit's responsibility for right behavior, see, inter alios, Drever (81), Vannier (71), Tornau (213), and van Geest (129).
92 *Conf.* 13.4.5.
93 Ibid., 13.9.10. For helpful discussion of the (i) trinitarian and Platonic aspects and (ii) provenance and subsequent history of Augustine's famous claim that "my weight is my love" (*pondus meum amor meus*), see O'Donnell, 3@356–9.
94 Ibid., 13.7.8–10.11.
95 Ibid., 13.5.6, 276—Chadwick. For commentary on this passage's importance to Augustine's overall argument in *conf.*, see Crouse (1987). It also shows Augustine's reliance on Church authority.
96 For general discussion of the provenance and uniqueness of Augustine's claim, see O'Donnell (3@360–2) and Ayres (2010, 133–41). From their analysis, it is obvious that Augustine offers here a uniquely Christian account of mind, taking its impetus from Christian doctrine and employing in its service various theological and philosophical sources.

Augustine's account of trinitarian mind begins from a Christian doctrine of God (disclosed in the Church's Creeds—see *conf.* 13.5.6), rather than from mind itself. As 13.11.12 shows, Augustine guards against anthropomorphism. Cf. Hankey's claim (2017), 65–6 and 97 (stating "the Augustinian tradition projects the finite into the infinite"). Yet, see 63.
97 *Conf.* 13.11.12—latin/O'Donnell, 1@188.
98 Ibid., 13.11.12, 279—Chadwick.
99 Ibid.
100 Ibid.—latin/O'Donnell, 1@188.
101 Ibid., 13.11.12, 280—Chadwick.
102 Ibid.
103 Ibid., 13.12.13. Like his account of the Trinity in 13.5.6, this underscores how Augustine's exegesis takes its impetus from Church and scripture rather than from pagan Platonist philosophy. For commentary, see O'Donnell, 3@362–4.

104 E.g., *conf.* 10.27.38; 13.1.1.
105 While claiming that Augustine's summary begins in 13.31.46, O'Donnell (3@410) emphasizes the anti-Manichean aspect of Augustine's exegesis. See also (ibid.), 413 and 419.
106 O'Donnell (3@344–5) presents a hypothetical reconstruction of the Gen. 1:1–2:2 text Augustine was viewing.
107 This is another reason why CC departs from McMahon's interpretation. McMahon (2003, 207–8) cites nine distinctions within Augustine's account of divine creating in book 13 corresponding with Augustine's specific confessions in *conf.* 1–9, and claims book 13's allegory of the Church has a "return to Origin" pattern governing *conf.* 10–13. Instead, CC follows more closely Augustine's obvious distinctions and interprets *conf.* accordingly. First, Augustine (*retr.* 2.6.1) divides *conf.* into books 1–10 and 11–13. Second, Augustine's principal distinctions in *conf.* 13's exegesis of the Church pertain to the seven days of creation. Accordingly, CC cites Augustine's seven days of creation and maintains these correspond with the principal stages in his relationship with God as distinguished in 10.27.38. Most important CC, following Augustine, holds these distinctions also apply to the Church's origin, development, and ultimate destiny. Therefore, God's creating the Church can be simplified from seven into three distinctions. CC's interpretation, therefore, has the relative advantage of textual integrity and simplicity. It not only follows Augustine's distinctions (i) between the seven days of creation and (ii) concerning three principal stages in created persons' relationship with God but also uses one primary and one secondary structure by which to interpret Augustine's accounts of personal and Church development.

Finally, CC holds, like McMahon, that *conf.* has an *exitus-reditus* structure, and the latter governs particular portions of *conf.* But, in accord with Augustine's division of *conf.* into books 1–10 and 11–13, it identifies instances of *exitus-reditus* within that division. CC distinguishes Confessor Augustine's accounts, first, of young Augustine's departure from and return to *confessio* (books 1–10) and, second, of God's creating and His creation's return to Him in His Sabbath rest (books 11–13). This does not deny the "fittingness" of McMahon's interpretation. Rather, it suggests it is plausible by the doctrine of charity Augustine ascribes to scriptural exegesis in *conf.* 12.
108 Augustine takes guidance from the Catholic religion—commonly referred to as Nicene Christianity. Augustine's reliance on Catholic doctrine is visible at many moments in his exegesis not only as he

discovers and/or implies that scripture contains "high" philosophy (e.g., 11.7.9–9.11) but also as he finds and/or claims scripture is rightly interpreted in light of doctrinal matters like the Trinity (e.g., 13.5.6). For brief discussion of Augustine's reliance on Nicene Christianity, see n. 39, Chapter 5.

109 *Conf.* 11.2.4.
110 Ibid., 11.2.4, 223—Chadwick.
111 McMahon (2003), 218–23.
112 I say "belong to" because, as Augustine claimed at *conf.*'s outset (1.1.1–5.6), God is spiritually present to lead man to Himself. God's goodness is not partially but totally exhibited.

Chapter 5

1 E.g., Crouse (1976); Starnes (1983), 105–11, *idem.* (1987), *idem.* (1990); McMahon (1989), *idem.* (2003); Stephany (1989), 129–42; Crosson (1989), *idem.* (2003); Wills (2011); David (2003), 1–29, *idem.* (2019), *idem.* (2020), 45–76; Teske (2000); Hankey, (2010); and Conybeare (2016).
2 E.g., Marrou, 75; and O'Meara (1965), 13.
3 E.g., O'Donnell (1@xxiii) writes: "But for a text as multi-layered and subtle as the *Confessions*, any attempt to find a single key is pointless. Augustine says himself that he meant to stir our souls, not test our ingenuity as lock-picks" (cf. ibid., i–ii). Likewise, Vaught (2005, 23) states: "no single principle is an adequate way of binding Augustine's text together" (Cf. Kotzé [2020, 34]). Looked at another way, each implies *conf.* has a formal unity (hence the first commentator speaks of Augustine's intention "to stir our souls") but the "single principle" interpretations (they have studied) are reductive.
4 Hence, Kotzé (2020, 33) writes: "Thus while it is true that scholarship has not yet come up with one satisfactory explanation that adequately expresses the essence of the *Confessions* (and probably never will), the many different ways of explaining its unity all reinforce the other." Therefore, she (Kotzé [2004], 21, n. 38) agrees with Starnes's (1990) claim that *conf.* has a trinitarian structure, but views this as "only one of the grids holding together the structure of the *Confessions*."
5 For discussion, see David (2020), 46, 63–4.
6 If Augustine's notion of a triune God is correct then, since every effect is like its cause, this interpretation is objective. For Augustine,

divine Trinity is first cause of creatures (e.g., 13.5.6) and, therefore, of divine incarnation and *confessio*. Accordingly, each person *implicitly* enjoys the Trinity, but right relation to God means each should confess Him as Trinity (e.g., 13.11.12–12.13). Hence, *conf.* suggests a trinitarian structure. CC argues, however, that Augustine's *explicit* message of *confessio* relates more to his notion of divine incarnation than to divine Trinity. Augustine implies that *conf.* is trinitarian but emphasizes that *conf.* is incarnational since Christ, by disclosing the nature of God's goodness toward man, properly leads to the Trinity. So, man's right disposition toward God consists in *confessio*, but that is established, first and foremost, by embracing Christ, and finds fulfilment in God the Trinity since Christ's love for man, as God the Son/Word having taken to Himself a human nature, is grounded in His love for God the Father and God the Spirit. Hence, the human person loving God and neighbor, represented by Augustine's *confessio*, imitates Christ's human nature—thereby loving God and neighbor first through the divine Word but ultimately (since Christ is a divine Person) by God the Trinity. For some discussion, see this chapter's *conclusion*.

7 David (2020).
8 *Conf.* 12.30.41, 270—Chadwick.
9 In this regard, I generally follow my account (David, 2020, 46–7, 63–5) of the strengths and weaknesses in ascribing to *conf.* an *exitus-reditus* pattern governed by (i) affective mimesis, (ii) the parable of the Prodigal Son, or (iii) a divine Trinity. While the common strength is setting together God with man (where the trinitarian interpretation is superior), the shared weakness is failure to recognize that *confessio* underlies both the biography in books 1–10 and the exegesis (including trinitarian considerations) in 11–13.
10 Cf. O'Meara (1965), 69–79; and BeDuhn (2010), 42–105; (2013), 331–6.
11 See Ayres (2010), 13–20.
12 See, for example, Armstrong 3–37, 4–9; and Gerson (2019), 191–208, 200–8.
13 I say "pregnant" because it can be claimed that Augustine's account of God's power, wisdom, and goodness refers respectively to God the Father, Word, and Holy Spirit. That Augustine does not confess God as Trinity at *conf.*'s outset gives evidence his primary doctrine in *conf.* is divine incarnation. (For further explanation, see this chapter's *conclusion*.)
14 The phrase "almost certainly" refers to catechumen Augustine's standard of certitude. As Augustine presents the matter in *conf.* 7,

while some aspects of Wisdom can be known with certitude, others, viz. matters disclosed through temporal realities, are known by probability grounded in certitude.

15 For commentary, see CC Chapter 4, and David (2020), 53–8.

16 Cf. Crosson (1989), 92. Crosson claims that classifying Augustine's *itineraria* by the mode of "*ab exterioribus ad interioria, ab inferioribus ad superiora*" is "inadequate, if not misleading" because of what it means to "encounter . . . the God of Jesus" (concerning the significance given to temporal realities). While Crosson reasonably claims that Augustine's principal *itineraria*, and therefore *conf.*'s ultimate message, differs from the Plotinian ascent to God, CC maintains that *conf.*'s *itineraria* contain both Christ and the mutable realities He includes through His church. Augustine not only recognizes that the Plotinian ascent to supreme divinity is incomplete but furnishes a new, specifically Christian, mode of ascent using aspects of the Plotinian ascent (and perhaps also aspects of St. Paul's vision of Christ reported in Acts 9:1-8) as part of its material cause (cf. King [2014], 6–27). In fact, Augustine's ascent structures *conf.* itself, viz. "*ab superioribus ad exteriora, ab exterioribus ad interiora, ab inferioribus ad superiora*." Hence, *conf.* exhibits an *exitus-reditus* structure beginning, developing, and ending with an account of the proper relationship man should have with God, i.e., of *confessio*.

17 *Conf.* 1.5.5 begins in a manner designating Christ, the "Word made flesh," since Augustine understands Him as the corridor toward perfect divine union. Hence, in a manner evoking 1.1.1's account of Christ, Augustine writes (1.5.5, 5—Chadwick): "Who will enable me to find rest in you? Who will grant me that you come to my heart and intoxicate it, so that I forget my evils and embrace my one and only good, yourself?"

18 *Conf.* 1.5.6 speaks of God but, based on Augustine's implicit signification of God's Spirit in 1.1.1 and explicit account of Spirit as love in books 12–13, it seems reasonable to maintain Augustine has in mind God's Spirit. He writes (1.5.6, 6—Chadwick): "The house of my soul is too small for you to come to it. May it be enlarged by you. It is in ruins: restore it."

19 This certainly suggests the *exitus-reditus* aspect of Augustine's *confessio* exhibits a structure akin both to God in Himself and to the scriptures. *Conf.* shows a pattern similar to the Godhead wherein, according to Creeds Augustine knows, the Father "eternally begets" the Word (11.13.16) and the eternal Spirit (13.5.6) designates L/ love. (Augustine's statements concerning divine Trinity in 11.13.16,

13.5.6, 13.11.12–12.13, and 13.16.19 show he interprets scripture in general and Genesis in particular according to the theology given in the Church's Creeds. Augustine probably relies on some combination of the Nicene [*c.* 325 AD] and Romano-Milanese [*c.* 380 AD] Creeds that his book *De fide et symbolo* [*f. et symb.*] [*On Faith and the Creed*], written in 393 AD, likely engaged. For discussion of Augustine's acquaintance with Church Creeds prior to his baptism and immediately thereafter, see Lienhard, 254–5, and Clancy, 360–1.) Likewise, *conf.* shows a pattern similar to the scriptures, which begin with Genesis, finish with the book of Revelation, and progress in between from human particularity to universality, i.e., from individuals to families to tribes to a nation to the Church and, through that, to humanity as such.

Hence, the "departure from and return to origin" pattern found in *conf.* is similar to more significant structures Augustine knows. (However, this chapter's *conclusion* argues these structures are grounded in the doctrine of divine incarnation.)

20 E.g., *conf.* 11.1.1, 221—Chadwick: "Lord, eternity is yours . . . for love of your love."
21 A. Kotzé, (2004), 250.
22 Ibid., 249. Agreeing with Kotzé (2004, 250), BeDuhn emphasizes *conf.*'s *protreptic-paraenetic* structure and maintains the text is aimed toward Manicheans. However, he also mentions that Augustine responds to Platonist intellectuals and Donatists (2020, 46–8).
23 E.g., Martin (187–97).
24 See Chapter 4, n. 96, for discussion of Augustine's philosophical method therein.
25 Ibid., 7.17.23, 127—Chadwick: "I asked myself . . . my mutable mind."
26 Ibid.: "And so step by step I ascended from bodies to the soul which perceives through the body, and from there to its inward force, to which the bodily senses report external sensations, this being as high as the beasts go."
27 Ibid.: "From there again I ascended to the power of reasoning (*ad ratiocinantem potentiam*) to which is to be attributed the power of judging the deliverances of the bodily senses"—latin/O'Donnell (1@84).
28 Ibid.: "This power, which in myself I found to be mutable, raised itself to the level of its own intelligence (*erexit se ad intelligentiam suam*), and led my thinking out of the ruts of habit"—latin/O'Donnell (1@84).

29 Ibid.: "It [i.e., the power of reason] withdrew itself from the contradictory swarms of imaginative fantasies, so as to discover the light [i.e., the power of intelligence but, more so, the source of intelligence, viz. God] by which it [i.e., the power of intelligence] was flooded."

30 Ibid.: "At that point it [viz. reason, upon recognizing mind's power of intelligence] had no hesitation in declaring that the unchangeable (*incommutabile*) is preferable to the changeable (*mutabili*), and that on this ground [i.e. on the basis of reason's considering the power of intelligence] it can know the unchangeable [i.e. it can know God] since, unless it could somehow know this [i.e. know that God is the source of intelligence and, therefore, of its immutable principles], there would be no certainty [i.e. no sure ground] in preferring it [i.e. the immutable] to the mutable"—latin/O'Donnell (1@84).

31 Ibid.—latin/O'Donnell, 1@84.

32 As Augustine sees no difference between immutable and God, he sees no difference between goodness and God. Of course, Augustine maintains God's creatures participate in His immutability and goodness.

33 *Conf.* 11.4.6, 224—Chadwick.

34 Ibid.—latin/O'Donnell, 1@150.

35 Ibid., 13.11.12—latin/O'Donnell, 1@188.

36 Hence, Augustine maintains the Trinity's mode far exceeds mind's mode since it seems likely that the activity *esse-nosse-velle* constituting mind somehow belongs to each divine Person and what we mean by *esse* and *nosse* and *velle* is somehow affiliated respectively with Father, Word, and Spirit. Augustine writes: "When, however, through . . . simplicity and multiplicity" (13.11.12, 279–80—Chadwick).

37 The aforementioned differences Augustine cites between the Trinity and trinitarian mind do not deny likeness but show it is wide and ultimately beyond human comprehension.

38 Ibid., 8.12.30, 154—Chadwick.

39 Together with considering Augustine's many statements about the Trinity in books 11–13 (e.g., 13.5.6) and his exposure to and assimilation of various Church Creeds both before and immediately after his baptism, helpful analysis of Augustine's debt to Latin Nicene Christianity is made by Kenney (2019), 12–14, 110–11, 118–21; BeDuhn (2013, ix–25), and Ayres (2010), 13–71. As Ayres argues, catechumen Augustine's "Platonist books" probably included treatises written by Latin Christians, like Marius Victorinus, and, as Augustine shows in *conf.* 7, study of pagan Platonism was conducted through the prism of Latin Christianity mediated through the Milanese

church (5.14.25) in general and by Bishop Ambrose in particular. In this respect, Ayres (like Kenney [2019, 118–19]) displays agreement with Cochrane's (441) remark that "his [i.e., Augustine's] spiritual affiliations were with Athanasius and Ambrose rather than with Plotinus or Porphyry."

40 My accounts of divine incarnation and Trinity rely on Augustine's *f. et symb.*

41 See the helpful article by Fitzgerald (2014), 108–21. While mentioning *conf.* (109–11) Fitzgerald traces Christ's centrality to Augustine's thought over the course of his career, claiming that Augustine's "Christology" is a unifying principle in his theology, underlying his intimately related approaches to theology both as *confession* and as spiritual method. CC generally agrees with Fitzgerald's analysis but concentrates on Augustine's doctrine of Christ in *conf.*

42 I judge Augustine refers here to his formal union with Wisdom beginning with his profound vision of Wisdom (7.10.16) but culminating in conversion (8.12.29–9.1.1). Augustine thinks the latter event marked his transition from an implicit to explicit relationship with God.

43 *Conf.* 10.27.38, 20—Chadwick.

44 As n. 3 in Chapter 3 mentioned, Augustine *implies* that apart from embracing divine incarnation, man (like the ancient Hebrews and Job) can know his *telos* is God.

45 It is noteworthy that 7.9.13–15 does not mention the Holy Spirit, i.e., the divine Person leading persons to immutable divine union (13.9.10—cf. *civ. Dei.* 10.23). This shows, first, Augustine's preference for the incarnation and, second, his view that the incarnation leads to the Trinity since the divine union the incarnation promises is effected through the Spirit's work. For Augustine, adherence to *the order of human discovery within the order of being* mandates that learning about, imitating, and enjoying divine incarnation properly precedes the same concerning the Trinity. (Cf. *trin.* 13.19.24: "Our knowledge (*scientia*), therefore . . . wisdom and knowledge [Col. 2:3]." See CC's epigraph for the entire text.)

46 This is obvious in *conf.* 7.10.16, and Augustine reiterates the matter in 7.17.21 when voicing disappointment concerning inability to rest with God: "I was astonished to find that already I loved you. . . . But I was not stable in the enjoyment of my God" (7.17.21, 127—Chadwick).

47 Ibid., 7.21.27, 131–2—Chadwick.

48 Ibid., 7.18.24, 128—Chadwick.

BIBLIOGRAPHY

Primary Texts and Translations

Confessions in Latin

"Confessionum Libri XIII." In *Corpus Christianorum, Series Latina*, edited by L. Verheijen, vol. 27. Turnhout: Brepols Publishers, 1981.

O'Donnell, J. J. *Augustine: Confessions, Volume 1, Introduction and Text*. Oxford: Clarendon Press, 1992, 3–205; Augustini, Aureli. *Confessionum: Libri Tredecim*.

Confessions in Translation

The Confessions: Saint Augustine of Hippo, translated by M. Boulding, with an introduction and contemporary criticism, edited by D. V. Meconi, *Ignatius Critical Editions*. San Francisco: Ignatius Press, 2012.

Chadwick, H. *Saint Augustine: Confessions*. New York: Oxford University Press, 1992.

Les Confessions, Livres I–VII: Texte de l'édition de M. Skutella; introduction, traduction, et notes par A. Solignac, traduction de E. Tréhorel et G. Bouissou. Bibliothèque Augustinienne: *Oeuvres de saint Augustin*, Paris, 1962, 1992, 1998, Vol. 13.

Clark, G. (ed.). *Augustine: Confessions Books I–IV*, Cambridge Greek and Latin Classics. Cambridge, UK: Cambridge University Press, 1995.

Sheed, F. J. *Augustine: Confessions*, 2nd ed., introduction by P. Brown, edited and notes by M. P. Foley. Indianapolis, IN: Hackett Publishing Co., 2006.

Williams, T. *Augustine: Confessions*, translated, with introduction and notes by T. Williams. Indianapolis and Cambridge: Hackett Publishing Company Inc., 2019.

Assorted Primary Texts

Against the Academics: St. Augustine's Cassiciacum Dialogues, Vol. I, translation, annotation, and commentary by M. P. Foley. New Haven and London: Yale University Press, 2019.

City of God, translated by H. Bettenson with an introduction by
J. O'Meara. New York: Penguin Books, 1972, 1984.

De civitate Dei, Libri XI–XXII, edited by B. Dombart, A. Kalb, in *Corpus Christianorum, Series Latina*, vol. 48. Turnhout: Brepols Publishers, 1955.

De libero arbitrio, Libri Tres, edited by W. M. Green, in *Corpus Christianorum, Series Latina*, vol. 29. Turhout: Brepols Publishers, 1970, 205–321.

Les révisions: Texte de l'edition Benedictine, introduction, traduction, et notes par G. Bardy, Vol. 13. Bibliothèque Augustinienne: Oeuvres de saint Augustin: Paris, 1950.

Letters to Simplician, Augustine: Earlier Writings, translated with introductions by J. H. S. Burleigh. Philadelphia: The Westminster Press, 1953, 385–405.

On *Faith and the Creed*, translated by D. F. Salmond, from *Nicene and Post-Nicene Fathers, First Series*, vol. 3, edited by P. Schaff. Buffalo, NY: Christian Literature Publishing Co., 1887. Revised and edited for *New Advent* by K. Knight. http://www.newadvent.org/fathers/1304.htm.

On *Free Choice of the Will*, Saint Augustine, translated by A. S. Benjamin and L. H. Hackstaff, introduction by L. H. Hackstaff. New York, NY: Macmillan/Library of Liberal Arts, 1964.

On *Order: St. Augustine's Cassiciacum Dialogues, Vol. III*, translation, annotation, and commentary by M. P. Foley. New Haven and London: Yale University Press, 2020.

On *the Happy Life: St. Augustine's Cassiciacum Dialogues, Vol. II*, translation, annotation, and commentary by M. P. Foley. New Haven and London: Yale University Press, 2019.

Plotinus: The Enneads, translated by S. MacKenna, introduction and notes by J. Dillon. New York, NY: Penguin Books, 1991.

Soliloquies: St. Augustine's Cassiciacum Dialogues, Vol. IV, translation, annotation, and commentary by M. P. Foley. New Haven and London: Yale University Press, 2020.

The Trinity, The Works of Saint Augustine: A Translation for the 21st Century, translated by E. Hill. Brooklyn, NY: New City Press, 1991, Part I, Vol. 5.

The Retractations, The Fathers of the Church: A New Translation, translated by Sister M. I. Bogan. Washington, DC: The Catholic University of America Press, 1968, Vol. 60.

General Studies

Ayres, L. *Augustine and the Trinity*. New York: Cambridge University Press, 2010.

BeDuhn, J. D. *Augustine's Manichean Dilemma, 1: Conversion and Apostasy, 373–388 C.E.* Philadelphia: University of Pennsylvania Press, 2010.

BeDuhn, J. D. *Augustine's Manichean Dilemma, 2: Making a "Catholic" Self, 388–401 C.E.* Philadelphia: University of Pennsylvania Press, 2013.

Bonner, G. *St. Augustine of Hippo: Life and Controversies*, 2nd ed. Norwich, UK: Canterbury Press, 1986.

Bonner, G. *Freedom and Necessity: St. Augustine's Teaching on Divine Power and Human Freedom.* Washington, DC: Catholic University of America Press, 2007.

Brown, P. *Augustine of Hippo: A Biography.* Boston: Faber and Faber, 1967.

Cary, P. *Augustine's Invention of the Inner Self.* Oxford: Oxford University Press, 2000.

Cary, P. *Inner Grace: Augustine in the Traditions of Plato and Paul.* New York: Oxford University Press, 2008.

Cochrane, C. N. *Christianity and Classical Culture: A Study of Thought and Action from Augustus to Augustine.* Oxford: Oxford University Press, 1940, reprinted by USA: Liberty Fund Inc., 2003.

Fitzgerald, A. D. *Augustine through the Ages: An Encyclopedia*, gen. ed. Grand Rapids, MI: Wm. B. Erdmans, 1999.

Fredricksen, P. *Augustine and the Jews: A Christian Defense of Jews and Judaism.* New York, NY: Doubleday, 2008.

Hochschild, P. E. *Memory in Augustine's Theological Anthropology.* Oxford: Oxford University Press, 2012.

Hollingworth, M. *Saint Augustine of Hippo: An Intellectual Biography.* New York: Oxford University Press, 2013.

Kenny, J. P. *Contemplation and Classical Christianity.* New York: Oxford University Press, 2013.

Kenny, J. P. *On God, the Soul, and the Rise of Christianity.* New York: Bloomsbury Academic, 2019.

Kirwan, C. *Augustine.* London and New York: Routledge, 1989.

Levering, M. *The Theology of Augustine: An Introductory Guide to His Most Important Works.* Grand Rapids, MI: Baker Academic, 2013.

Lewis, C. S. *The Four Loves.* Glasgow, Great Britain: Collins Fount Paperbacks, 1960.

Marrou, H. I., *Saint Augustin et la fin de la culture antique.* Paris: Boccard, 1938, 1965.

O'Meara, J. J. *The Young Augustine: The Growth of St. Augustine's Mind up to His Conversion.* London: Longmans, Green, 1965.

O'Meara, J. J. *Porphyry's Philosophy from Oracles in Augustine.* Paris: Études Augustiniennes, 1959.

Rist, J. M. *Augustine: Ancient Thought Baptized.* Cambridge: Cambridge University Press, 1994.

Rist, J. M. *On Inoculating Moral Philosophy against God.* USA: Marquette University Press, 2000.

Stock, B. *Augustine the Reader: Meditation, Self-knowledge, and the Ethics of Interpretation.* Cambridge, MA and London, England: The Belknap Press of Harvard University Press, 1996.

TeSelle, E. *Augustine the Theologian.* New York: Herder and Herder, 1970.

Wetzel, J. *Augustine and the Limits of Virtue.* Cambridge: Cambridge University Press, 1992.

Wills, G. *Saint Augustine.* London: Phoenix, 1999.

Collections of Essays

Cary, P., Doody, J., and Paffenroth, K. (ed.) *Augustine and Philosophy.* Lanham, MD: Lexington Books, 2010.

Dodaro, R. and Lawless, G. (ed.) *Augustine and His Critics.* London and New York: Routledge, 2000/2002.

Markus, R. A. *Augustine: A Collection of Critical Essays.* Garden City, NY: Doubleday & Company Inc., 1972.

Stump, E. and Kretzmann, N. (ed.) *The Cambridge Companion to Augustine.* Cambridge and New York: Cambridge University Press, 2001.

Stump E. and Meconi, D. (ed.) *The Cambridge Companion to Augustine*, 2nd ed. Cambridge and New York: Cambridge University Press, 2014.

Teske, R. J. *To Know God and the Soul: Essays on the Thought of St. Augustine.* Washington, DC: The Catholic University of America Press, 2008.

Books

Conybeare, C. *The Routledge Guidebook to Augustine's Confessions.* New York, NY: Routledge, 2016.

David, B. *Pursuing and Praising God: Augustine's "Confessions."* Hobe Sound, FL: Lectio Press, 2019.

Kenney, J. P. *The Mysticism of Saint Augustine: Rereading the Confessions.* London: Routledge, 2005.

Kotzé, A. *Augustine's Confessions: Communicative Purpose and Audience.* Leiden and Boston: Brill, 2004.

Mann, W. E. (ed.) *Augustine's Confessions: Critical Essays*. New York: Rowan & Littlefield Publishers, Inc., 2006.
Mann, W. E. *Augustine's Confessions: Philosophy in Autobiography*, ed. W. E. Mann. New York: Oxford University Press, 2014.
Marion, J-L. *In the Self's Place: The Approach of Saint Augustine*, trans. J. L. Kosky. Stanford, CA: Stanford University Press, 2008, 2012.
McMahon, R. *Augustine's Prayerful Ascent: An Essay on the Literary Form of the Confessions*. Athens, Georgia: University of Georgia Press, 1989.
Miles, M. *Desire and Delight; A New Reading of Augustine's "Confessions."* New York, NY: The Crossroad Publishing Company, 1991.
O'Connell, R. J. *St. Augustine's Confessions: The Odyssey of Soul*. Cambridge, MA: The Belknap Press, 1969.
O'Donnell, J. J. *Augustine: Confessions, Volume 2, Commentary, Books 1–7; and Volume 3, Commentary, Books 8–13*. Oxford: Clarendon Press, 1992.
Paffenroth, K. and Kennedy, R. P. (ed.) *A Reader's Companion to Augustine's Confessions*. Louisville, KY: Westminster John Knox Press, 2003.
Rigby, P. *The Theology of Augustine's Confessions*. Cambridge: Cambridge University Press, 2015.
Starnes, C. J. *Augustine's Conversion: A Guide to the Argument of Confessions I–IX*. Waterloo, ON and Canada: Wilfred Laurier University Press, 1990.
Toom, T. (ed.) *The Cambridge Companion to Augustine's "Confessions."* New York: Cambridge University Press, 2020.
Vaught, C. G. *The Journey toward God in Augustine's Confessions: Books I–VI*. Albany, NY: State University of New York Press, 2003.
Vaught, C. G. *Encounters with God in Augustine's Confessions: Books VII–IX*. Albany, NY: State University of New York Press, 2004.
Vaught, C. G. *Access to God in Augustine's Confessions: Books X–XIII*. Albany, NY: State University of New York Press, 2005.
Wills, G. *Saint Augustine's Childhood*. New York: Viking Penguin, 2001.
Wills, G. *Saint Augustine's Memory*. New York: Viking Penguin, 2002.
Wills, G. *Saint Augustine's Sin*. New York: Viking Penguin, 2003.
Wills, G. *Saint Augustine's Conversion*. New York: Viking Penguin, 2004.
Wills, G. *Augustine's Confessions: A Biography*. Princeton and Oxford: Princeton University Press, 2011.

Short Studies

Armstrong, A. H. "St. Augustine and Christian Platonism." *Augustine: A Collection of Critical Essays* (*op. cit.*), 3–37.

Ayres, L. "The Fundamental Grammar of Augustine's Trinitarian Theology." *Augustine and His Critics* (op. cit.), 51–76.
Babcock, W. S. "Augustine's Interpretation of Romans (AD 394–396)." *Augustinian Studies* 10 (1979), 55–74.
Baumann, N. "Pride and Humility." *The Cambridge Companion to Augustine's "Confessions"* (op. cit.), 208–26.
Beatrice, P. F. "Quosdam Platonicorum Libros: The Platonic Readings of Augustine in Milan." *Vigiliae Christianae* 43 (1989), 248–81.
BeDuhn, J. D. "Anticipated Readers." *The Cambridge Companion to Augustine's "Confessions"* (op. cit.), 46–59.
Bloom, P. "Word Learning and Theory of Mind." *Augustine's Confessions: Critical Essays* (op. cit.), 17–29.
Breyfogle, T. "Book Three: No Changing Nor Shadow." *A Reader's Companion to Augustine's Confessions* (op. cit.), 35–52.
Bright, P. "Book Ten: The Self Seeking the God Who Creates and Heals." *A Reader's Companion to Augustine's Confessions* (op. cit.), 155–66.
Bouton-Toubilic, A. I. "Happiness and Friendship." *The Cambridge Companion to Augustine's "Confessions"* (op. cit.), 138–53.
Burns, J. P. *The Development of Augustine's Doctrine of Operative Grace.* Paris: Études Augustiniennes, 1980.
Byers, S. C. "The Meaning of *Voluntas* in Augustine." *Augustinian Studies* 37 (2006), 171–89.
Byers, S. C. "Love, Will, and Intellectual Ascents." *The Cambridge Companion to Augustine's "Confessions"* (op. cit.), 154–74.
Cameron, M. "Enneratones in Psalmos." *Augustine through the Ages: An Encyclopedia* (op. cit.), 290–6.
Cary, P. "Book Seven: Inner Vision as the Goal of Augustine's Life." *A Reader's Companion to Augustine's Confessions* (op. cit.), 107–26.
Cary, P. "Soul, Self, and Interiority." *The Cambridge Companion to Augustine's "Confessions"* (op. cit.), 227–41.
Catapano, G. "Philosophy." *The Cambridge Companion to Augustine's "Confessions"* (op. cit.), 191–217.
Cavidini, J. C. "Book Two: Augustine's Book of Shadows." *A Reader's Companion to Augustine's Confessions* (op. cit.), 25–34.
Cipriani, N. "Memory." *Augustine through the Ages: An Encyclopedia* (op. cit.), 553–5.
Clark, M. T. "Augustine the Christian Thinker." *From Augustine to Eriugena: Essays on Neoplatonism and Christianity in Honor of John O'Meara* (op. cit.), 56–65.
Clancy, F. G. "*Fide et symbolo*, De." *Augustine through the Ages: An Encyclopedia* (op. cit.), 360–1.
Crosby, J. "How Is It Possible Knowingly to Do Wrong?" *American Catholic Philosophical Association Proceedings* 74 (2001), 325–33.

Crosson, F. J. "Structure and Meaning in St. Augustine's *Confessions*." In *The Augustinian Tradition*, edited by G. B. Matthews, 27–38. Berkeley, London: University of California Press, 1999, reprinted from *Proceedings of the American Catholic Philosophical Association* 63 (1989), 84–97.

Crosson, F. J. "Book Five: The Disclosure of Hidden Providence." *A Reader's Companion to Augustine's Confessions* (*op. cit.*), 71–87.

Crouse, R. D. "Recurrens in te unum: The Pattern of St. Augustine's *Confessions*." *Studia Patristica*, 14 (1976), 389–92.

Crouse, R. D. "'In Aenigmate Trinitas' (*Confessions*, XIII, 5,6)." *Dionysius* 11 (1987), 53–62.

Crouse, R. D. "'*Paucis mutabis verbis*': St. Augustine's Platonism." *Augustine and His Critics* (*op. cit.*), 37–50.

David, B. A. "The Philosophical Unity of *Confessions*: It Is Christ, the Incarnate Word." *Fides Quaerens Intellectum* III, no. 1 (2003), 1–29.

David, B. A. "Divine Providence in Augustine's *City of God*: A Doctrine of *Confessio*." *International Journal of Philosophy and Theology* 5, no. 2 (2017), 1–16.

David, B. A. "Augustine's Analysis of His Theft of Pears—the Medium Represents the Message." *Humanities Bulletin* 1, no. 2 (2018), 8–32.

David, B. A. "Evaluating Augustine's 'Proof for God' in *De Civitate Dei* 8.6." In *Passionate Mind: Essays in Honor of John M. Rist*, edited by B. David, 233–61. Baden-Baden, Germany: Academia Verlag, 2019b.

David, B. A. "Towards Articulating the Unity of Augustine's Confessiones." *Humanities Bulletin* 3, no. 2 (2020), 45–76.

Drecoll, V. H. "Grace." *The Cambridge Companion to Augustine's "Confessions"* (*op. cit.*), 107–220.

Drever, M. "Creation and Recreation." *The Cambridge Companion to Augustine's "Confessions"* (*op. cit.*), 75–91.

Dillon, J. "Logos and Trinity: Patterns of Platonist Influence on Early Christianity." *The Philosophy in Christianity*, edited by G. Vessey, 1–13. Cambridge, NY and Melbourne: Cambridge University Press, 1989.

Djuth, M. "Will." *Augustine through the Ages: An Encyclopedia* (*op. cit.*), 881–5.

Dutton, B. D. "The Privacy of the Mind and the Fully Approvable Reading of Scripture: Augustine on Genesis 1:1." *Augustine's Confessions: Philosophy in Autobiography* (*op. cit.*), 155–80.

Edwards, M. J. "Porphyry and the Intelligible Triad." *Journal of Hellenic Studies* 110 (1990), 14–25.

Ekenberg, T. "Practical Rationality and the Wills of *Confessions* 8." *Augustine's Confessions: Philosophy in Autobiography* (*op. cit.*), 28–45.

Eodice, A. R. "Keeping Time in Mind: Saint Augustine's Proposed Solution to a Perplexing Problem." *Augustine and Philosophy* (*op. cit.*), 61–78.

Ettenhuber, K. "Reception in the Period of Reformations: The *Confessions*, 1500–1650." *The Cambridge Companion to Augustine's "Confessions"* (*op. cit.*), 277–94.

Ferrari, L. "The Pear-Theft in Augustine's *Confessions*." *Revue des Études Augustiniennes* 16 (1970), 233–41.

Ferrari, L. "The Theme of the Prodigal Son in Augustine's *Confessions*." *Recherches Augustiniennes* 12 (1977), 105–18.

Ferrari, L. "Ecce audio vocem de vicina domo, (Conf. 8.12.29)." *Augustiniana* 33 (1983), 232–45.

Ferrari, L. "Augustine's Conversion Scene: The End of a Modern Debate?" *Studia Patristica* 22 (1989), 235–50.

Ferrari, L. "Book Eight: Science and the Fictional Conversion Scene." *A Reader's Companion to Augustine's Confessions* (*op. cit.*), 127–36.

Fitzgerald, A. "Confession, Prayer, Transformation." *The Confessions: Saint Augustine of Hippo* (*op. cit.*), 491–503.

Fitzgerald, A. "Jesus Christ, the Knowledge and Wisdom of God." *The Cambridge Companion to Augustine*, 2014 (*op. cit.*), 108–21.

Foley, M. P. "Augustine, Aristotle, and *The Confessions*." *The Thomist* 67 (2003), 607–22.

Foley, M. P. "The Sacramental Topography of the *Confessions*." *Antiphon* 9, no. 1 (2005), 30–64.

Foley, M. P. "The Fruit of Confessing Lips: Sacrifice and the Genre of Augustine's *Confessions*." *Augustinianum* 59, no. 2 (December 2019), 425–52.

Gerson, L. P. "Plotinus and the Rejection of Aristotelian Metaphysics." *Aristotle in Late Antiquity*, edited by L. P. Shrenk, 3–21, Washington, DC: The Catholic University of America Press, 1994.

Gerson, L. P. "Virtue with and without Philosophy in Plato and Plotinus." *Passionate Mind: Essays in Honor of John M. Rist* (*op. cit.*), 191–208.

Hammond, C. "Title, Time, and Circumstances of Composition; The Genesis of the *Confessions*." *The Cambridge Companion to Augustine's "Confessions"* (*op. cit.*), 11–27.

Hankey, W. J. "'Knowing as We Are Known' in Confessions 10 and Other Philosophical, Augustinian and Christian Obedience to the Delphic Gnothi Seauton from Socrates to Modernity." *Augustinian Studies* 34, no. 1 (2003), 23–48.

Hankey, W. J. "Recurrens in te unum: Neoplatonic Form and Content in Augustine's Confessions." *Augustine and Philosophy* (*op. cit.*), 127–44.

Hankey, W. J. "Augustine's Trinitarian Cosmos." *Dionysius* XXXV (December 2017), 63–100.

Harrison, S. "Do We Have a Will? Augustine's Way into the Will." *The Augustinian Tradition* (*op. cit.*), 195–205.

Helm, P. "Augustine's Griefs." *Augustine's Confessions: Critical Essays* (*op. cit.*), 147–60.

Helm, P. "Thinking Eternally." *Augustine's Confessions: Philosophy in Autobiography* (*op. cit.*), 135–54.

Jordan, R. "Time and Contingency in Augustine." *Augustine: A Collection of Critical Essays* (*op. cit.*), 255–79.

Karfíková, L. "Memory, Eternity, and Time." *The Cambridge Companion to Augustine's "Confessions"* (*op. cit.*), 175–90.

Kennedy, R. P. "Book Eleven: The *Confessions* as Eschatological Narrative." *A Reader's Companion to Augustine's Confessions* (*op. cit.*), 167–83.

Kenney, J. P. "The *Contradictores* of Confessions XII." *Augustine and Philosophy* (*op. cit.*), 145–65.

King, P. "Augustine's Encounter with Neoplatonism." *The Modern Schoolman* 82, no. 3 (2005), 213–26.

King, P. "Augustine's Anti-Platonist Ascents." *Augustine's Confessions: Philosophy in Autobiography* (*op. cit.*), 6–27.

Kotzé, A. "Structure and Genre of the *Confessions*." *The Cambridge Companion to Augustine's "Confessions"* (*op. cit.*), 28–45.

Lienhard, J. T. "Creed, *Symbolorum*." *Augustine through the Ages: An Encyclopedia* (*op. cit.*), 254–5.

Lilla, S. R. C. "The NeoPlatonic Hypostases and the Christian Trinity." In *Studies in Plato and the Platonic Tradition, Essays Presented to J. Whitattaker*, edited by M. Joyal, 127–89. Brookfield, VT: Ashgate Publishing Co., 1997.

MacDonald, S. "Petit Larceny, The Beginning of All Sin: Augustine's Theft of the Pears." *Faith and Philosophy* 20, no. 4 (2003), 393–414.

MacDonald, S. "The Divine Nature." *Augustine's Confessions: Critical Essays* (*op. cit.*), 85–105.

Mann, W. E. "The Theft of Pears." *Apeiron* 12 (1978), 51–9.

Mann, W. E. "Inner-Life Ethics." *The Augustinian Tradition* (*op. cit.*), 140–65.

Mann, W. E. "The Philosopher in the Crib." *Augustine's Confessions: Critical Essays* (*op. cit.*), 1–16.

Martin, T. F. "Book Twelve: Exegesis and Confessio." *A Reader's Companion to Augustine's Confessions* (*op. cit.*), 185–206.

Mathewes, C. T. "Book One: The Presumptuousness of Autobiography and the Paradoxes of Beginning." *A Reader's Companion to Augustine's Confessions* (*op. cit.*), 7–23.

Mathews, G. B. "Augustine on the Teacher Within." *Augustine's Confessions: Critical Essays* (*op. cit.*), 31–43.
Matter, E. A. "Christ, God and Woman in the Thought of St. Augustine." *Augustine and His Critics* (*op. cit.*), 164–75.
McMahon, R. "Book Thirteen: The Creation of the Church as the Paradigm for the *Confessions*." *A Reader's Companion to Augustine's Confessions* (*op. cit.*), 207–23.
McQueen, D. J. "Augustine on Free Will and Predestination: A Critique of J. M. Rist." *Museum: West Africa Journal of Theology* (1974), 17–28.
Menn, S. "The Desire for God and the Aporetic Method in Augustine's *Confessions*." *Augustine's Confessions: Philosophy in Autobiography* (*op. cit.*), 71–107.
O'Donnell, J. J. "Augustine, *Confessions* 10.1.1–10.4.6." *Augustiniania* 29 (1979), 280–303.
Ortiz, J. "Creation in the *Confessions*." *The Confessions: Saint Augustine of Hippo* (*op. cit.*), 475–90.
Paffenroth, K. "Tears of Grief and Joy: Chronological Sequence and the Structure of *Confessions*, Book 9." *Augustinian Studies* 28 (1997), 141–54.
Paffenroth, K. "Book Nine: The Emotional Heart of the *Confessions*." *A Reader's Companion to Augustine's Confessions* (*op. cit.*), 137–54.
Partoens, G. "Manuscript Transmission, Critical Editions, and English Translations." *The Cambridge Companion to Augustine's "Confessions"* (*op. cit.*), 245–62.
Peters, E. "What Was God Doing before He Created the Heavens and the Earth." *Augustiniana* 34 (1984), 53–74.
Plumer, E. "Book Six: Major Characters and Memorable Incidents." *A Reader's Companion to Augustine's Confessions* (*op. cit.*), 89–105.
Ratzinger, J. "Originalität und Überlieferung in Augustins Begriff der Confessio." *Revue des Ètudes Augustiniennes* 3 (1957), 375–92.
Riley, P. "Reception during the Enlightenment: A for Anti-Augustine." *The Cambridge Companion to Augustine's "Confessions"* (*op. cit.*), 295–316.
Rist, J. M. "Augustine on Free Will and Predestination." *Journal of Theological Studies* 20 (1969), 420–47.
Rist, J. M. "Faith and Reason." *The Cambridge Companion to Augustine*, 2001 (*op. cit.*), 26–39.
Rist, J. M. "Could Augustine Have Produced a More Edifying Account of Predestination?" *Augustiniana* 60, no. 1 (2020), 67–89.
Saak, E. L. "Reception in the Middle Ages." *The Cambridge Companion to Augustine's "Confessions"* (*op. cit.*), 263–76.
Schlabach, G. W. "Augustine's Hermeneutic of Humility: An Alternative to Moral Imperialism and Moral Relativism." *Journal of Religious Ethics* 22, no. 2 (1994), 299–330.

Sorabji, R. "Time, Mysticism, and Creation." *Augustine's Confessions: Critical Essays* (*op. cit.*), 209–35.
Starnes, C. J. "The Unity of the *Confessions*." *Studia Patristica* 18, no. 4 (1983), 105–11.
Starnes, C. J. "The Place and Purpose of the Tenth Book of the *Confessions*." *Studia Ephemeridis Augustinianum* 25 (1987), 95–103.
Starnes, C. J. "Augustine's Conversion and the Ninth Book of the *Confessions*." *Augustine: From Rhetor to Theologian*, edited by J. McWilliam, 51–65. Waterloo, ON: Wilfred Laurier University Press, 1992.
Steinhauser, K. B. "The Literary Unity of the *Confessions*." *Augustine: From Rhetor to Theologian*, (*op. cit.*), 15–30.
Stephany, W. A. "Thematic Structure in Augustine's *Confessions*." *Augustinian Studies* 20 (1989), 129–42.
Stump, E. "Augustine on Free Will." *The Cambridge Companion to Augustine*, 2001 (*op. cit.*), 124–47.
TeSelle, E. "Pelagius, Pelagianism." *Augustine through the Ages: An Encyclopedia* (*op. cit.*), 633–40.
Teske, R. J. "The World-Soul and Time in St. Augustine." *Augustinian Studies* 14 (1983), 75–92.
Teske, R. J. "The Heaven of Heaven and the Unity of St. Augustine's *Confessions*." *American Catholic Philosophical Quarterly* 74 (2000): 29–45; reprinted in *To Know God and the Soul: Essays on the Thought of Saint Augustine* (*op. cit.*), 259–74.
Tornau, C. "Intelligible Matter and the Genesis of Intellect: The Metamorphosis of a Plotinian Theme in *Confessions* 12–13." *Augustine's Confessions: Philosophy in Autobiography* (*op. cit.*), 181–218.
Van Fleteren, F. "Augustine's Ascent of the Soul in Book VII of the *Confessions*: A Reconsideration." *Augustinian Studies* 5 (1974), 29–71.
Van Fleteren, F. "*Confessiones*" and "Porphyry" and "Plato, Platonism." *Augustine through the Ages: An Encyclopedia* (*op. cit.*), 227–32, 661–3, and 651–4.
Van Geest, P. "God." *The Cambridge Companion to Augustine's "Confessions"* (*op. cit.*), 123–37.
Vannier, M.-A. "Aversion and Conversion." *The Cambridge Companion to Augustine's "Confessions"* (*op. cit.*), 63–74.
Vessey, M. "Reading (in) Augustine's *Confessions*." *The Cambridge Companion to Augustine's "Confessions"* (*op. cit.*), 317–34.
Wetzel, J. "Snares of Truth: Augustine on Free Will and Predestination." *Augustine and His Critics* (*op. cit.*), 124–41.

Wetzel, J. "Predestination, Pelagianism, and Foreknowledge." *The Cambridge Companion to Augustine*, 2001 (*op. cit.*), 49–58.
Wetzel, J. "Book Four: The Trappings of Woe and *Confession* of Grief." *A Reader's Companion to Augustine's Confessions* (*op. cit.*), 53–70.
Wetzel, J. "Augustine on the Will." in *Companion to Augustine*, edited by M. Vessey, 339–52. West Sussex, UK: John Wiley & Sons, 2015.
Wills, G. "The Book of Memory." *Augustine's Confessions: Critical Essays* (*op. cit.*), 195–208.
Wolterstorff, N. "God's Speaking and Augustine's Conversion." *Augustine's Confessions: Critical Essays* (*op. cit.*), 161–74.
Wolterstorff, N. "Happiness in Augustine's *Confessions*." *Augustine's Confessions: Philosophy in Autobiography* (*op. cit.*), 46–70.

INDEX

Academic, the   43, 45–6, 52, 57, 61, 161 n.75. *See also* philosophy, Academic
Adam   13, 36
Adeodatus   50, 70, 148 n.42, 182 n.33
affective   61, 63, 79, 81, 83, 120, 124, 136
   mimesis   116, 192 n.9
afterlife   1, 9, 19, 33, 35, 78, 107, 118–19
Alypius of Thagaste, Bishop   3, 5, 49–51, 65, 67, 69–70, 81, 142 n.18, 160 n.48, 160 n.54, 161 n.72, 180 n.7
Ambrose, Bishop   4, 43, 46, 48, 50, 57–8, 61, 66, 70, 73, 78, 80, 140 n.11, 141 n.14, 147 n.14, 160 n.48, 163 n.89, 166 n.114, 180 n.7, 196 n.39
Aristotle   32, 34, 37, 163 n.97, 165 n.107, 169 n.5, 183 n.47, 183 n.49, 183 n.52
ascend   74
   from   123, 194 n.26
   to   123, 194 n.27
astrology   32, 37, 53, 131, 154 n.132
astronomy   61

baptism   5, 22, 25–6, 33, 63, 69–70, 80–1, 83, 149 n.62, 194 n.19, 195 n.39

baptized   3, 63, 69–71, 73, 80, 83–4, 140 n.11, 149 n.62, 166 n.114
beatitude   15, 25, 55, 76, 79, 103, 108, 110, 141 n.14, 167 n.119, 178 n.128, 180 n.10
being (*esse*)   24, 53, 63, 88, 90, 93, 99, 103–6, 110, 128–30, 195 n.36, 140 n.14, 146 n.6
   created   91
   divine   6, 52–3, 60, 105
   human   12, 15, 25, 30, 128, 169 n.5
   immutable   129, 169 n.5
   mutable   67, 129, 169 n.5
   non-,   183 n.44
   non-divine   30
   order of   133–7, 187 n.79, 196 n.45
Bible   30, 48, 69
biblical   5, 15, 136–7, 143 n.44, 146 n.5, 150 n.83, 174 n.82, 186 n.65
bishop   3–4, 46, 57, 72–3, 78–80, 82, 89, 107, 120, 140 n.8, 177 n.120, 178 n.128, 180 n.7, 185 n.65
body   17–18, 28, 30, 44, 46, 58, 61, 66, 71, 74, 89, 92, 94, 103, 124, 127–8, 163 n.90, 166 n.114, 176 n.105, 183 n.49, 194 n.26. *See also* soul-body composite
bodily   92, 119
bodily senses   74, 194 n.26–7

cause 68, 87, 98, 133, 191 n.6
exemplar 115
first 15, 22–3, 133, 192 n.6
final 68
formal 6, 166 n.114
intellectual 4
material 5–7, 53–4, 164 n.97, 184 n.55, 193 n.16
primary 22, 61
principal 29
proximate 115, 134
remote 134
secondary 15
celibate 66–7, 69, 80
celibacy 66, 78, 130–1
certitude 43, 48–9, 51–4, 56, 59–60, 74–6, 83, 93, 95, 97, 100–1, 105–6, 120, 122, 162 n.79, 192–3 n.14
next to 60, 83
charity 59, 63, 71, 73, 76–7, 81, 100–1, 115, 121, 136–8, 178 n.125, 190 n.107
chastity 27, 50
childhood 22, 25–6, 32, 35, 37–9, 41, 149 n.62, 157 n.162
Church 4, 14–15, 19–20, 25, 27, 36, 47, 53, 59–60, 66, 80–1, 87–9, 96–7, 100, 102–3, 106–12, 117, 119, 121, 123, 125, 127, 129, 131, 133–4, 142 n.21, 149 n.62, 150 n.72, 166–7 n.114, 178 n.128, 180 n.9, 186 n.65, 187 n.79, 189 n.95, 189 n.103, 190 n.107, 193 n.16, 194 n.19, 195–6 n.39
Cicero 11, 29–30, 37, 39, 48, 117, 161 n.72
cogent 51–3, 56, 62, 64, 76, 80–1, 104, 106, 120
cognitive 11, 43, 48–9, 56, 60–1, 76, 78–9, 83, 120, 124, 127, 131, 161 n.75

cognitively 49, 63, 79, 81, 124, 136
common good 32–3
community 15, 23–5, 67–70, 81, 101, 156 n.153, 161 n.68, 185 n.65
composite 31, 33–4, 98–9, 118. See also soul-body composite
concubine 32, 37, 50, 57, 130, 155 n.144, 160 n.48, 161 n.62
concupiscence 111, 125
conscience 28–9, 31, 34, 39, 47, 152 n.96
examination of 73, 76–7, 82, 130
conversion 3, 28, 64–8, 72, 75, 82–3, 103, 107, 112, 117, 130, 134, 143 n.35, 154 n.140, 157 n.161, 160 n.48, 168 n.3, 169 n.5, 169 n.7, 170 n.15, 171 n.25, 171 n.29, 174 n.80, 188 n.86, 196 n.42
corporeal 17–21, 30–1, 34, 53, 103, 109, 122–3, 165 n.107, 175 n.86. See also incorporeal
non-corporeal 17–18
cosmology 44–5, 53, 57–8
creaturely 103, 129

death 33–4, 44, 71, 119, 156 n.153, 167 n.119
Christian response to 69
death of Augustine's friend 32–3, 35, 37, 39, 41, 44, 71, 155 n.148, 173 n.73
death of Monnica 63, 69, 71–2, 80–1, 84, 172 n.63, 173 n.73
desire 2, 5, 12, 23–9, 32, 34–5, 38, 45–7, 49–51, 53, 55, 60,

65–6, 68, 70, 83, 107, 119, 136, 151 n.89, 153 n.110, 159 n.30, 176 n.106, 177 n.122, 180 n.10
disorder   24, 26, 33, 155 n.149, 166 n.114. *See also* order
divine nature   15, 18, 129, 132, 176 n.106
divinity   14, 26, 29–31, 37, 64, 87, 109, 119, 122, 124–5, 127–8, 130, 135, 137, 140 n.14, 165 n.107, 167 n.119, 180 n.16, 184 n.57, 188 n.84, 193 n.16
Donatist   4, 140 n.8, 142 n.21, 145 n.64, 157 n.161, 177 n.118, 185 n.65, 194 n.22

education   23–5, 27
effect   15, 61, 68, 130, 149 n.62, 191 n.6
end   1, 70, 72, 96, 118, 124, 136, 152 n.93
  eternal   68
  finite   27
eternity   54, 70, 90–1, 94, 98, 100, 110, 121, 126, 131, 182 n.35, 187 n.79, 188 n.81, 194 n.20
eucharist   72
evil   4, 7, 11, 18, 28, 30–1, 34, 44–6, 53–4, 59, 80, 142 n.26, 142 n.32, 154 n.131, 155 n.152, 161 n.72, 170 n.22, 184 n.53, 193 n.17
  moral   5, 55
  is a privation   54, 59
Evodius   70
examination of conscience. *See* conscience
exegesis   19, 87–9, 95–7, 100–4, 106–10, 112, 116, 121, 124, 130–1, 133, 136–7, 140 n.9, 179 n.128, 179 n.1, 180 n.7, 180 n.16, 182 n.41, 184 n.53, 184 n.55, 185–6 n.65, 189 n.103, 190 n.105, 190 nn.107–8, 192 n.9
exemplar   8, 10, 55, 132. *See also* cause, exemplar
exist   16, 65, 129, 163 n.90
  existing   18, 55, 88, 98–9, 103–4, 106, 129
existence   16, 52, 76, 83, 88, 93, 98, 103, 134, 163 n.90, 184 n.53, 188 n.81
existential   61, 63, 76, 78, 81, 91, 108, 124, 130–1, 159 n.37
existentially   63, 67, 79, 108, 120
exitus-reditus   6, 8, 10, 21, 35, 38, 40, 61, 83, 87–90, 96–7, 100, 102–3, 110–11, 116–17, 119–21, 123–4, 126, 187 n.79, 188 n.81, 190 n.107, 192 n.9, 193 n.16, 193 n.19
exteriora-interiora-superiora   74, 82, 123, 127, 193 n.16

faith   3, 5, 14–15, 19, 48, 51, 59–60, 67, 78, 82, 118, 122, 147 n.13, 162 n.79, 178 n.128
Father, God the   13, 15, 22, 64, 79, 87–8, 90–1, 93, 95, 97, 99, 101–2, 104, 106, 109, 116, 121, 133, 140–1 n.14, 146 n.7, 147 n.12, 180 n.16, 187 n.79, 192 n.6, 192 n.13, 193 n.19, 195 n.36
Faustus, Bishop   44–5, 57
fitting   6, 15, 34, 52, 56, 84, 88–9, 103, 107, 112, 138, 147 n.13, 184 n.55, 187 n.79, 188 n.80

form 13, 98–9, 104, 128,
    183 n.44, 183 n.49
free choice of will. *See* will
friend 3, 22–3, 25, 32–3, 35,
    37, 39, 45, 49–50, 57,
    69–71, 81, 134, 151 n.93,
    155 n.144, 155 n.146, 155
    nn.149–50, 156 n.152, 170
    n.24, 172 n.63, 173 n.73,
    179 n.128, 182 n.33. *See
    also* death, of Augustine's
    friend
friendship 33, 49–50, 61, 67, 71,
    155 n.144, 155 nn.149–50

good 1–2, 4–5, 7, 9, 11, 18,
    21, 28, 30, 33–4, 36, 44,
    50, 53–4, 59, 77, 80, 124,
    129–30, 142 n.26, 155
    n.152, 161 n.72, 165 n.107,
    170 n.22, 180 n.16, 184
    n.53, 188 n.80, 193 n.17.
    See also common good;
    material, good; matter, good
    and evil
goodness 125, 129
    God's 1, 6–9, 12–14, 18–22,
        36–8, 40, 52, 57, 60–1, 64,
        68, 79–81, 83, 87, 97, 99,
        102–4, 106–10, 112, 115,
        117, 119, 121–2, 124–7,
        129–36, 141 n.14, 144 n.58,
        144 n.62, 145 n.64, 146
        n.7, 147 n.13, 178 n.128,
        184 n.53, 187 n.79, 188
        n.80, 191 n.112, 192 n.13,
        195 n.32
grace 4–5, 9, 12–14, 56, 63, 65,
    67–8, 90, 96, 120, 125–6,
    134, 160 n.48, 168 n.3, 169
    n.7, 187 n.79, 188 n.86

happiness 2, 19, 21, 35, 37–8,
    40, 57, 64, 74–6, 80, 82, 93,
    95, 101, 105–6, 109, 122,
    133, 139 n.5, 157 n.162,
    175 n.100, 176 nn.105–6,
    180 n.5
happy 40, 54, 82
happy life 2, 38, 75–6, 82, 84,
    95, 102, 120
heart is restless until it rests in
    God, the 2, 12, 76, 126
    restless heart 3, 121, 138
heaven 69, 71–2, 95, 97,
    99–101, 109, 111, 134, 145
    n.64, 182 n.41, 185 n.57
    and earth 7, 15–17, 36,
        89–91, 94, 96–7, 99, 101,
        111–12, 129, 137, 184 n.53
    heavenly 135
    heavenly city 89
    heavenly Jerusalem 81, 112
    of heavens 96–7,
        99–102, 109–10, 121,
        182 n.33, 184 n.55,
        184 n.57, 185 n.57
Hierius 34–5, 37
Holy Spirit 13, 22, 64, 79, 88,
    101, 103–4, 112, 133,
    141, 146 n.7, 171 n.37,
    192 n.13, 196 n.45
hope 48, 51, 59, 64
human nature 8, 14–15, 25,
    37, 52, 56, 60, 106, 132–3,
    147 n.13, 192 n.6
humility 14, 22, 26, 32, 36,
    39–40, 45, 47–8, 54, 63–4,
    66–8, 70, 81, 83, 120, 125,
    132, 151 n.93, 168 n.3,
    171 n.24, 178 n.125

imagination 31, 39, 47, 58, 128
imago Dei 5
imago trinitatis 108, 131
immutable 1, 8–9, 14, 18–19,
    21, 30–1, 34, 36, 39,
    52–57, 59–60, 64–5, 67–8,

74–6, 79, 87, 90–6, 99–100, 104–6, 109–11, 118–19, 121–9, 134–5, 140–1 n.14, 144 n.62, 146 n.7, 148 n.32, 165 nn.106–7, 169 n.5, 169 n.7, 176 n.105, 182 n.33, 184 n.53, 184 n.57, 187 n.78, 195 n.30, 195 n.32. *See also* immutable-mutable
participation 1, 8, 15, 18–20, 22, 36–7, 96, 99, 109, 118–19, 122, 124, 146 n.7, 179 n.128
union 1, 8, 36, 99, 123, 132, 135, 145 n.64, 169 n.7, 196 n.45
immutable-mutable 8, 19–20, 68, 125
incarnate 1–3, 8–10, 14–15, 19, 22, 38, 53, 56, 61, 64, 79, 88, 108, 111, 115, 123, 132–3, 146 n.7, 147 n.12, 187 n.79
incarnation 5, 8, 13–15, 19–22, 52, 115, 118–19, 125, 132–7, 141 n.14, 144 n.63, 145 n.64, 146 n.7, 147 n.13, 192 n.6, 192 n.13, 194 n.19, 196 n.40, 196 nn.44–5
incarnational 3, 9, 19, 22–3, 35–6, 72, 115, 122, 125–6, 145 n.64, 171 n.37, 173 n.76, 192 n.6
incorporeal 19–21, 31, 54, 59, 118–19, 122, 128, 165 n.107. *See also* corporeal
infancy 11, 22–3, 25–6, 30, 32, 35, 37–9, 41, 157 n.162
infant 23–5, 37, 148 n.44, 149 n.47, 157 n.162
intellect 65, 68–9, 81, 106, 120, 123, 140 n.14

joy 67, 178 n.125
in God 2, 40, 75
in the truth 2, 64, 75, 80, 139 n.5
judgment 30, 32–3, 47, 58, 70, 122, 127, 155 n.150, 166 n.114
value 127–8

knowledge 10, 23, 29, 34, 39, 46, 48, 53–5, 58, 65, 74–6, 78–9, 82, 89–90, 93–7, 99, 106, 108–11, 122, 133, 135–6, 153 n.110, 159 n.29, 162 n.79, 174 n.84, 178 n.128, 179 n.1, 180 n.10, 196 n.45
indubitable 43, 48–9, 53–4, 59, 73, 75, 78, 81, 94–5, 99, 101, 132, 162 n.79
philosophical 60
positive 51
self-, 74, 93
speculative 81

liberal arts 32, 34, 37, 43, 45, 47, 57–8, 61, 74, 162 n.77
love (the virtue) 48, 51, 68, 70, 106, 108
Christ's 71, 111, 192 n.6
of God 9, 12, 50, 54, 63, 70, 73–4, 77, 80, 82, 84, 97, 100–2, 104, 108, 116, 121, 131, 135–8, 176 n.105, 177 n.122, 178 n.125, 192 n.6, 196 n.46
God's 87, 93, 97, 101, 132, 137, 188 n.86
Late have I loved you, beauty so old and so new 134
of neighbor 77, 101, 116, 152 n.102, 155 n.144, 155 n.149, 156 n.152

self-, 70, 77, 152 n.102,
  155 n.144
lust   29, 150 n.69, 152 n.96
  for power   77, 131
  sexual   26–8, 37, 41, 50,
    60, 80, 130, 150 n.69,
    152 n.93, 166 n.114,
    170 n.9
  spiritual   26, 150 n.69

Manichean   3, 5, 9, 11, 15,
  17, 20–1, 28, 30–5, 37,
  39–41, 43–7, 53, 57–8,
  61, 70, 73, 117–18, 120,
  122, 126–7, 140 nn.8–9,
  141 n.14, 145 n.64,
  146 n.1, 146 n.3, 148 n.39,
  153 n.110, 153 n.114,
  154 nn.131–2, 154 n.141,
  155 n.144, 155–6 nn.152–3,
  157 n.161, 159 n.29,
  165 n.107, 167 n.120,
  170 n.22, 172 n.56,
  181 n.17, 184 n.53, 185 n.61,
  185 n.65, 186 n.74, 188 n.84,
  194 n.22
marriage   27, 31, 48, 50, 59, 66
material   72, 98, 115–16, 119.
  See also cause
  evil material   30–1, 44
  good material   31, 44
matter   98–9, 183 n.44,
  184 n.53
  formless   96, 98–100,
    103–4, 109, 112, 121,
    183 n.44, 183 n.49,
    184 n.53, 184 n.55
  good and evil   31
means   1, 12, 15, 19, 21–2, 34,
  37, 44, 49, 51–2, 55–6,
  58–60, 68–70, 72, 118–19,
  121, 134, 136, 151 n.92,
  163 n.90

mediate   25, 55, 78, 82, 119,
  185 n.65, 195 n.39
mediation   14, 20, 24, 52,
  55–6, 59–60, 64, 73, 76,
  96, 108–9, 118–19, 123–4,
  166 n.114, 167 n.119,
  168 n.3, 174 n.82
mediator   55–6, 73, 82, 90, 101,
  106, 110, 178 n.128
mind   6, 13, 30, 34, 39, 47,
  74, 81, 83, 88, 91–5,
  99–101, 105–7, 122–3,
  126–30, 148 n.32,
  163 n.90, 175 n.90, 175 n.97,
  175 n.100, 176 n.106,
  182 n.32, 189 n.96,
  193 n.18, 195 n.36
  trinitarian   109–10, 121, 129,
    189 n.96, 195 n.37
monastery   69–70, 80
monastic   68, 70, 81, 161 n.68
monasticism   66, 80, 83
Monnica   3, 5, 22, 25–7, 31,
  43, 48, 51, 59, 63, 67,
  69–72, 79–81, 84, 99,
  101, 120, 122, 131,
  142 n.18, 149 n.62,
  160 n.48, 166 n.114,
  173 n.76, 179 n.128,
  182 n.33. *See also* death, of
  Monnica
moral   11, 56, 60, 81, 142 n.31,
  181 n.22. *See also* evil,
  moral
  law   25
  progress   35, 48, 96, 102
mutable   1, 8, 14–15, 17–21,
  23, 30, 34, 36–7, 39, 52–7,
  65, 67–8, 74, 76, 87, 90–3,
  98–9, 101–2, 105, 110–11,
  118–19, 121–5, 127–9,
  134, 166 n.114, 167 n.119,
  169 n.5, 169 n.7, 176 n.105,

179 n.1, 180 n.9, 183 n.44, 183 n.49, 187 n.78, 193 n.16, 194 n.28, 195 n.30. *See also* immutable-mutable

nature   5, 9, 12–15, 19, 22, 31, 34, 36–7, 44, 46–7, 57–8, 75, 79, 82, 87, 89, 93, 95–7, 100, 102, 109, 112, 117, 119–22, 128, 132–6, 150 nn.69–70, 155 n.150, 159 n.29, 161 n.72, 171 n.25, 176 n.106, 182 n.31, 186 n.65, 186 n.70, 188 n.84, 192 n.6. *See also* divine nature; human nature
Nebridius   50–1, 69–70, 155 n.149, 160 n.48, 182 n.33
Nicene   20, 40, 132, 140 n.13, 148 n.39, 165 n.107, 181 n.17, 185 n.57, 190–1 n.108, 194 n.19, 195 n.39
nous   119, 167 n.119

omnipotence   18, 70, 151 n.85, 151 n.89
order   23–4, 32, 93, 136, 152 n.93. *See also* disorder
counterfeit   39
created   16, 22, 88–90, 102–3
divine   24–5, 27–9
higher   23
human   25–9, 38–9
objective   48
of being   133–7, 187 n.79
of discovery   134, 136
of discovery within the order of being   133–4, 136–7, 196 n.45
origin   6, 9, 21, 53–4, 68, 88, 98–9, 102, 107, 109–10, 119, 121, 125–6, 163 n.89, 187 n.79, 188 n.81, 190 n.107, 194 n.19
Original sin. *See* sin

pagan   5, 15, 18, 20–1, 37, 40, 43, 52–5, 57, 60, 62, 75, 88, 90, 95, 140 nn.8–12, 140 n.14, 145 n.64, 157 n.161, 164 n.103, 166 n.114, 167 n.119, 168 n.3, 169 n.5, 172 n.55, 173 n.70, 179 n.2, 180 n.16, 184 n.53, 184 n.55, 185 n.57, 185–6 n.65, 188 n.84, 189 n.103, 195 n.39
participating   28, 108, 111, 121
in divine eternity   121, 182 n.35
in divine goodness   125, 129, 134, 195 n.32
in divine immutability   93, 100, 122–3
in God   1, 8, 18–19, 37, 55, 80, 96, 99, 109, 111, 124, 127, 146 n.7, 178 n.128, 179 n.1, 187 n.79
participation   36, 55, 109, 125, 130, 132, 179 n.1, 182 n.33. *See also* immutable, participation
past, present, and future   65, 73, 75, 92, 95–6, 125, 133
Patricius   23, 25, 27, 71, 150 n.74, 173 n.76, 182 n.33
Paulinus   3, 141 n.17
pear-theft   11, 22–3, 26–8, 32, 37–9, 41, 145–6 n.1, 151 n.88, 152 nn.96–7
Pelagius   4, 143 n.34

personal sin. *See* sin
philosophers
  natural   43–4, 46–7, 57–8,
    159 n.29
  Platonist   55, 75
philosophical   5, 20, 30, 43,
    58, 60, 69, 76, 88, 98–
    100, 106, 119–20, 127,
    130, 135–6, 143 n.44,
    145 n.65, 147 n.13, 163 n.89,
    165 n.107, 167 n.119,
    169 n.7, 170 n.17, 176 n.105,
    179 n.2, 182 n.37, 189 n.96,
    194 n.24
philosophy   29, 69, 191 n.108
  Academic   57
  Platonist   3, 9, 43, 52, 54–5,
    57, 60, 62, 88, 90, 95, 101,
    120, 164 n.102, 169 n.5,
    180 n.16, 184 n.53, 185 n.57,
    186 n.65, 189 n.103
Platonism   3, 5, 53,
    140 n.13, 141 n.14,
    163 n.89, 164 n.97, 164–5
    n.105, 166–7 n.114,
    167 n.120, 170 n.17,
    180 n.16, 181 n.17, 186 n.65,
    188 n.86, 195 n.39
Platonist   3, 5, 9, 15, 18,
    20–1, 40, 54–5, 57, 59–60,
    118–19, 122, 127, 135,
    140 n.8, 140 nn.9–12, 140–
    1 n.14, 145 n.64, 146 n.3,
    157 n.161, 163 n.89, 163–4
    n.97, 164 n.105, 165 n.107,
    166 n.114, 167 n.119,
    168 n.3, 173 n.70,
    179 n.2, 180 n.16, 181 n.17,
    184 n.53, 184 n.55,
    186 n.65, 188 n.84,
    194 n.22, 195 n.39.
  See also philosophers;
    philosophy

pleasure   2, 7, 12, 27–8, 49, 66,
    155 n.144
  sensual   27, 32, 76
  sexual   26–7, 37, 43, 130
  transient   51, 59
Plotinus   55, 118, 140–1 n.14,
    163 n.97, 165 n.105,
    165 n.107, 166 n.114,
    167 n.119, 179 n.2,
    180 n.16, 182 n.33,
    183 n.49, 184 n.53,
    184 n.55, 184–5 n.57,
    188 n.84, 196 n.39
Ponticianus   65–6, 80, 83
Porphyry   34, 118, 140–1 n.14,
    163–4 n.97–8, 165 n.107,
    167 n.119, 179 n.2,
    185 n.57, 196 n.39
prayer   5, 70, 77, 177 n.123
presence
  divine   6, 8–9, 12, 15–16, 20–
    2, 36, 75, 82, 87–9, 95, 101,
    105–6, 109, 111–12, 121–3,
    133, 146 n.3, 176 n.105
  explicit   20, 36, 175 n.100
  implicit   20, 36
presumption   14, 24, 26, 29, 32,
    63, 65, 68, 81, 83, 168
pride   5, 30, 54, 70, 132,
    150 n.69, 151 n.83,
    155 n.146
priest   3–6, 14, 63, 72–3,
    76–80, 82, 84, 89, 107,
    120, 140 n.9, 178 n.125,
    178 n.128
priesthood   5, 20, 79, 178 n.128
privation. *See* evil, is a privation
Prodigal Son parable   116,
    150 n.83, 192 n.9
progressive   6, 8–11, 13, 35,
    38–40, 56–7, 60–1, 65,
    79–80, 83, 87–90, 106,
    108–10, 116, 121–4

providence   64, 69, 71, 89,
    179 n.5
Psalms, David's   5–6, 69–70, 81

rational   25, 44, 58, 67, 97,
    102–3, 119–20, 150 n.70,
    152 n.93, 188 n.81
  power   26, 128
reason   128, 142 n.31, 152 n.93,
    169 n.7, 195 n.29–30
relationship with God   6,
    12–13, 15, 37–8, 63,
    72–3, 75–6, 79–80, 82, 89,
    93, 106–7, 125, 130–1,
    136–7, 157 n.161, 174 n.83,
    190 n.107
  explicit   12, 14–15, 35, 57,
    137, 156–7 n.161, 196 n.42
  implicit   12, 57, 157 n.162,
    168 n.3
rest   111. *See also* the heart is
    restless until it rests in God;
    Sabbath rest
  divine   19
  eternal   107
  in God   18, 119, 126, 135,
    193 n.17, 196 n.46
restless heart. *See* heart is
    restless until it rests in God,
    the
rhetor   3, 46, 50, 57, 69, 80, 83
rhetoric   25–6, 29, 32–3

Sabbath rest   7, 20, 36, 68,
    87–9, 96, 102, 107, 109–12,
    116, 121, 124, 126, 131,
    187 n.79, 190 n.107
sacrament   14, 25, 36, 107,
    134, 149 n.62, 178 n.128,
    180 n.7, 187 n.79
science   45–7, 163 n.90
scripture   5–7, 25, 30, 54–6,
    67, 81, 88–91, 95–7,
    99–103, 105–9, 117, 121,
    123, 125, 134, 153 n.110,
    154 n.140, 164 n.102,
    167 n.120, 178 n.128,
    179 n.1, 179–80 n.5,
    180 n.7, 183 n.41, 184 n.53,
    184 n.55, 185 n.57, 186 n.65,
    188 n.84, 189 n.103,
    191 n.108, 193–4 n.19
sense   33, 39, 44, 47, 49, 74,
    76, 94, 122–3, 128, 135,
    147 n.13, 155 n.144,
    194 nn.26–7
  sensation   127–8, 194 n.26
sexual lust. *See* lust
sexual pleasure. *See* pleasure
share   110
Simplicianus   4, 65–6, 80, 83,
    170 n.15
sin   4, 12–13, 27, 53, 59, 77,
    130, 149 n.62, 152 nn.96–7
  Original   148 n.47
  Original and personal   13, 20
  personal   6, 22, 71
skeptical   43, 45–6, 48, 52,
    57–8, 60–1, 120, 158 n.17,
    162 n.77, 177 n.109
soul (*anima*)   8, 13, 19–20,
    30–1, 37, 47, 54, 63–4,
    66, 70, 72–5, 77, 79–82,
    89, 91, 93–5, 101–2,
    119, 122, 124–5, 127–8,
    138, 142 n.31, 146 n.2,
    147 n.12, 152 n.102, 155–6
    n.152, 156 n.153,
    166 n.114, 167 n.119,
    173 n.63, 174 n.82,
    176 n.105–6, 184–5
    n.57, 188 n.84, 191 n.3,
    193 n.18, 194 n.26
soul-body composite   33,
    118–19, 167 n.119, 169 n.5
spiritual lust. *See* lust

substance   17, 19–20, 30, 34,
    44, 54–5, 59, 93–4, 98–9,
    124, 127–8, 132, 144 n.62,
    165 n.107, 167 n.119,
    169 n.5, 169 n.7, 183 n.49,
    188 n.84
Summum Bonum   27, 32, 43,
    122–3, 156 n.161, 168 n.3
Symmachus, Count   46

teleological   8, 115, 126
telos   9, 13, 21, 53, 55, 63, 88,
    90, 96–7, 102, 104, 107,
    110, 118, 121, 125–6, 133,
    135–7, 188 n.81, 196 n.44
temporal   32, 34, 64, 68,
    70–2, 81, 94, 99, 156 n.152,
    157 n.161, 166 n.114,
    174 n.83, 178 n.128,
    193 n.14, 193 n.16
temporality   92–5, 110–11
temptation   73, 76–7, 82,
    111, 125, 130, 174 n.82,
    177 n.120, 178 n.125
theology   5, 17, 20, 43, 58,
    88, 103, 119–20, 122,
    130, 141 n.14, 145 n.64,
    147 n.13, 165 n.107,
    176 n.105, 179 n.2,
    194 n.19, 196 n.41
toothache   69–70, 80
Trinity   5, 13, 20, 22, 64, 79,
    104–6, 110, 115–16, 121,
    125–7, 132–8, 144 n.63,
    146 nn.5–6, 165 n.107,
    189 n.103, 191 n.108,
    192 n.6, 192 n.9, 192 n.13,
    193 n.19, 195 n.37, 195 n.39,
    196 n.40, 196 n.45
    trinitarian   13, 22, 88–9,
        97, 105–6, 109–11, 121,
        129–30, 133, 141 n.14,
        144 n.63, 146 n.7, 149 n.65,
    156 n.155, 171 n.33,
    180 n.16, 189 n.93, 189 n.96,
    191 n.4, 192 n.6, 192 n.9,
    195 n.37
    triune   89, 105–6, 122–3, 127,
        129–30, 132, 181 n.17,
        191 n.6
    triunity   122
truth   2, 4, 10–11, 22–3, 25,
    27, 31, 34, 37, 47–50,
    52–2, 55, 59–60, 71, 75,
    80, 90, 93, 95, 97, 100–1,
    116, 136–8, 139 n.5,
    146 n.1, 148 n.39, 152 n.93,
    159 n.37, 175 n.100,
    176 n.105, 186 n.70. *See
    also* joy, in the truth

union   8, 13, 18–22, 24, 36,
    44, 60, 64, 73, 77–8, 89,
    96, 103, 115, 118–19,
    121, 123, 125–6, 132–5,
    151 n.92, 166 n.114,
    169 n.7, 193 n.17, 196 n.42,
    196 n.45
unity   9, 20, 77–8, 105, 115–17,
    119, 123, 125–7, 132–4,
    145 n.64, 156 n.153,
    174 n.84, 188 n.82,
    191 nn.3–4
universal   2, 6, 8, 10–11,
    13, 23, 35–7, 39–40,
    52, 56, 60–1, 73, 76,
    79–80, 83, 87–90, 103,
    106–9, 139 n.5, 147 n.14,
    157 n.162, 171 n.38,
    174 n.83, 180 n.5,
    187 n.79, 194 n.19

vain   29, 31, 34, 39, 44–5, 47,
    49, 51–2, 58–9, 65–6, 76,
    130, 135, 155 n.146
value judgment. *See* judgment

vanity 29, 34–5, 39, 44–7,
    49–51, 55, 58–59, 66,
    72, 82, 116, 156 n.152,
    159 n.30, 170 n.9
Verecundus 69–70
vice 27, 144 n.58, 151 n.92,
    159 n.30
virtue 28, 50, 115, 151 n.92,
    155 n.144, 160 n.54,
    168 n.3

will 4, 39, 47, 65–6, 68–9, 81,
    83, 101, 106, 120, 123,
    142 n.31, 142 n.32, 169 n.7,
    170 n.17, 170–1 n.24
  choice of will 4, 55, 59, 67,
    151–2 n.93

free choice of 4–5, 53, 67,
    151 n.93, 168–9 n.4
  God's 69, 72, 90, 137
  willing (*velle*) 105, 110, 129,
    195 n.36
Wisdom
  vision of Wisdom 70–2,
    80–1, 84, 101, 147 n.13,
    166 n.114, 173 n.70,
    196 n.42
Word made flesh, the 8, 19–20,
    30, 44, 52, 55–6, 59, 72,
    76, 83, 120, 123–4, 132,
    135, 141 n.14, 164 n.103,
    179 n.1, 193 n.17
worship 29, 36, 55–6, 70, 103,
    108, 121, 125, 156–7 n.161

www.ingramcontent.com/pod-product-compliance
Ingram Content Group UK Ltd.
Pitfield, Milton Keynes, MK11 3LW, UK
UKHW020820240326
469204UK00019B/105